D0245978

# Working with Sources

## Case Studies in Twentieth-Century History

W.O. Simpson

TELEPEN

014086

Stanley Thornes (Publishers) Ltd

Text © W.O. Simpson 1988
Original line artwork © Stanley Thornes (Publishers) Ltd 1988

All rights reserved. No part of this publication may be reproduced, stored in a retrieval system or transmitted in any form or by any means, electronic, mechanical, photocopying, recording or otherwise, without the prior written consent of the copyright holders. Applications for such permission should be addressed to the publishers: Stanley Thornes (Publishers) Ltd, Old Station Drive, Leckhampton, CHELTENHAM GL53 0DN, England.

First published in 1988 by:
Stanley Thornes (Publishers) Ltd
Old Station Drive
Leckhampton
CHELTENHAM GL53 0DN
England


British Library Cataloguing in Publication Data

Simpson, W.O.
    Working with sources: case studies in
    Twentieth century history.
    1. Historiography
    I. Title
    907 D13

    ISBN   0–85950–690–8

Cover illustration: Photograph of *Tyneside 1936* is reproduced by kind permission of Humphrey Spender.

Typeset by Tech-Set, Gateshead, Tyne & Wear in 11/12½ Garamond.
Printed and bound in Great Britain at The Bath Press, Avon.

# CONTENTS

# ACKNOWLEDGEMENTS

The author and publishers are grateful to the following for permission to reproduce text extracts:

Philip Allan Publishers Ltd for extracts from *The British Economy between the Wars* by D.H. Aldcroft, 1983 (pp. 189–91)

Associated Book Publishers (UK) Ltd for extracts from *Irish Historical Documents* edited by E. Curtis and R.B. MacDowell, Methuen, 1943 (pp. 99, 101, 111–12, 122–5); and *The Private Papers of Douglas Haig, 1914–19* edited by R. Blake, Eyre & Spottiswoode, 1953 (pp. 54, 55, 61–2, 73, 74–5)

B.T. Batsford Ltd for extracts translated from German from *July 1914* by I. Geiss, 1967 (pp. 24–8); and tables from *The Inter-War Economy: Britain 1914–19* by D.H. Aldcroft, 1970 (pp. 192, 193, 203)

The British Library for an extract from the Long Papers, 19 July, 1914 (p. 104)

John Burnett for tables from *A Short History of the Cost of Living,* Penguin Books Ltd, 1969 (p. 204)

Cambridge University Press for extracts from *Abstract of British Historical Statistics* by B.R. Mitchell and P. Deane, 1962 (pp. 191–2); and *Men Without Work,* the Pilgrim Trust, 1938 (pp. 209–10)

Jonathan Cape Ltd for extracts from *The Slump* by J. Stevenson and C. Cook, 1977 (pp. 201, 218)

The Controller of Her Majesty's Stationery Office for Crown copyright material (pp. 206, 218–20)

Curtis Brown Group Ltd on behalf of C. & T. Publications Ltd for extracts from *Winston S. Churchill,* Companion Volume II, Part 3: 1911–14 by Randolph S. Churchill; copyright © 1969 C. & T. Publications (pp. 17–18, 32)

Grafton Books for extracts from *The Easter Rising, 1916* edited by Owen D. Edwards and Fergus Pyle, MacGibbon & Kee, 1968 (pp. 110, 116–17)

A.M. Heath & Co. Ltd, on behalf of the Estate of the late Sonia Brownell Orwell, and Secker & Warburg Ltd, for extracts from *The Road to Wigan Pier* by George Orwell, 1959 (pp. 206, 211–12)

William Heinemann Ltd for extracts from *English Journey* by J.B. Priestley, 1984 (pp. 213–14)

*Irish Historical Studies* for extracts from 'Eoin MacNeill and the 1916 Uprising' by F.K. Martin, *Irish Historical Studies,* XII (p. 110); and 'Conservative Opinion, the Ulster Question and the Partition of Ireland' by D.G. Boyce, *Irish Historical Studies,* 1970–1 (p. 120)

Michael Joseph Ltd for extracts from *They Called It Passchendaele* by Lynn MacDonald, 1978 (pp. 71–2, 76)

Labour Research Department for extracts from *The General Strike, May 1926: Its Origin and History* by R. Page Arnot, 1926 (pp. 141–3, 145–8, 149, 154–5, 160–1, 168–9, 172, 176)

Macmillan Publishers Ltd for extracts from *The General Theory of Employment Interest and Money* by J.M. Keynes, 1936 (pp. 224–5); and *The Middle Way* by Harold Macmillan, 1938 (pp. 225–7)

Oxford University Press for extracts from *Whitehall Diary* by Thomas Jones, edited by K. Middlemas, vol. II, 1969 (pp. 150–2, 177–8); and *A Survey of the Social Structure of England and Wales* by A.M. Carr-Saunders and D. Caradog Jones, 2nd edition, 1937 (pp. 202–3)

A.D. Peters & Co. Ltd on behalf of the author for extracts from *Politicians and the Slump* by R. Skidelsky, Penguin Books Ltd, 1970 (pp. 217–18, 222)

Joseph Rowntree Memorial Trust for extracts from *Poverty and Progress* by B. Seebohm Rowntree, Longman, 1941 (pp. 197–200)

*Spectator* for extracts from their 3 January, 1958 issue (pp. 77–8)

The Trustees of the National Library of Scotland and Earl Haig for extracts from the Haig Collection (pp. 57, 68)

Unwin Hyman Ltd for extracts from *The Miners, Years of Struggle* by R. Page Arnot, Allen & Unwin, 1953 (pp. 139–40, 140–1, 143–4, 162–3, 170–1)

Yale Law Journal Company and Fred B. Rothman & Company for extracts from 'The Legality of the General Strike in England' by A.L. Goodhart, the *Yale Law Journal*, Feb. 1927 (p. 174)

We also with to thank the following for supplying and giving permission to reproduce prints and artwork:

BBC Hulton Picture Library (pp. 164, 215)
Constable & Co. Ltd (p. 66)
The Controller of Her Majesty's Stationery Office; Crown copyright (p. 48)
Faber & Faber Ltd (p. 125)
Heinemann Publishers (NZ) Ltd (p. 91)
Ivor Nicholson & Watson Ltd (p. 65)
*Punch* (pp. 39, 42, 43, 99)
Scottish Labour History Society (p. 165)
Solo Syndications (p. 166)
Topham Picture Library (p. 215)

Every attempt has been made to contact copyright holders, but we apologise if any have been overlooked.

# INTRODUCTION

It has long been a declared principle that the study of History, both at school and university level, should be based on the study of primary sources. More honoured in the breach than the observance, this principle is now closer to being realised. The Schools Council History Project, launched in 1976, took as its starting point the nature of evidence. In 1983 a working party on which all A level examining boards were represented listed among the objectives to be tested 'the ability to evaluate and interpret source material and to show facility in its use'. Most recently, the National Criteria for the General Certificate of Secondary Education, published in 1985, require History candidates 'to show the skills necessary to study a wide variety of historical evidence which should include both primary and secondary sources . . .'. Thus examination requirements have been called on to ensure that History students should be made aware of the foundations of their subject and of the way in which it is written. If this laudable objective is to be achieved, it is necessary first to be clear about what is meant by sources, and secondly to establish the criteria by which they may be evaluated. This book has been written with these considerations in mind.

# THE NATURE OF SOURCE MATERIAL

In 1940 the eminent French medieval historian Marc Bloch was serving in the French Resistance. Meditating on the nature of his chosen profession, he sought to justify his life's work. Tragically, Bloch was executed in 1944 before he could complete his task. But he left behind him a number of observations which were collected and published by his surviving colleagues in a book entitled *The Historian's Craft.* In it Bloch thus defined the characteristics of historical knowledge: 'Its primary characteristic is the fact that knowledge of all human activities in the past, as well as of the greatest part of those in the present, is, as François Simian aptly phrased it, a "knowledge of their tracks".'[1] Sources are simply the tracks left by our predecessors, and they are the raw materials out of which historians construct their accounts of the past. Without such tracks there can be no History.

It has become conventional to distinguish between different kinds of source, arranging them in a hierarchy of authenticity and reliability. The most obvious distinction is that beween primary and secondary sources. In broad terms, a primary source is contemporary with the event or the society to which it relates. Haig's despatches from the Western Front, or the mortality figures compiled by the Registrar-General for a particular year would both fit into this category. Another distinction to be made is that between evidence written 'for the intentional record',

Cabinet minutes for example, and 'unwitting testimony',[2] such as the private correspondence of a politician. Asquith's letters to his young confidante, Venetia Stanley, for
instance, provide an invaluable insight into his premiership. Other written primary
sources include many government records, which now occupy several miles of shelving
in the Public Record Office; *Hansard* (the daily account of parliamentary debates);
newspapers and diaries.

Primary sources do not need to be written. The landscape is a primary source for the
history of farming, old mine workings for the history of technology. The architecture,
painting and music of an era are as important a guide to the cultural and intellectual
climate as its literature. Oral history, too, can make a valuable contribution, especially
in the field of social history.

The difference between a primary and a secondary source is a matter of degree rather
than of kind, and depends on the immediacy of the written record to the event it
describes. Thus an eyewitness account of the murder of the Archduke Franz Ferdinand
at Sarajevo in 1914 is a primary source. *The Times*'s version of the same event, gleaned
from the continental press, is strictly speaking a secondary source. But its editorial,
commenting on the event, could be regarded as a primary source for the purpose of
assessing British reaction to the assassination. A more significant difference lies in the
respective purposes of primary and secondary sources. Most secondary sources are
attempts to give some coherence to the inchoate mass of evidence deposited, either by
accident or design, by previous generations. At one end of the spectrum we have the
scholarly article, largely based on primary sources, and narrowly focused on a particular
issue. A good recent example is G.C. Peden's article 'A Matter of Timing: The Economic
Background to British Foreign Policy, 1937–39', which examines the influence of the
Treasury on British foreign policy during these critical years.[3] At a slightly greater
remove from the primary sources, though still to some extent reliant upon them, is the
book aimed at a larger problem, such as A.J.P. Taylor's *The Origins of the Second World
War*.[4] Furthest from the primary sources are likely to be those works of synthesis
designed for the coffee table or the television series which, while they may still use
artefacts for illustration, are bound to rely on secondary authorities for their information. This does not necessarily make them unreliable. A book such as *The Triumph of
the West* by John Roberts, which seeks to trace the influence of Western civilisation
on the rest of the world from *c.* 500 BC to the present day, is still in its way a work of
scholarship.[5] But inevitably such a task entails a ruthless process of selection and a high
degree of generalisation which renders its conclusions more open to question.

The relationship between primary and secondary sources is a symbiotic one. Each
depends on the other. Philip Guedalla's gibe that 'History does not repeat itself; it is
historians who repeat one another'[6] is a standing reproach to the historian whose work
is based exclusively on the work of others. But the facts may be reassembled in
different patterns and with new emphases. Familiar material may yield new insights
when looked at in a different light. If the frontiers of knowledge are to be significantly
extended, however, new evidence must be brought under scrutiny. The truth about
the Suez Crisis of 1956 is still emerging. For these reasons every research student is
urged to go to the primary sources. But no historians begin there. Without a reconnais-
sance of the field they will not even know where to look. Nor can they assess the

significance of what they find without a knowledge of the context into which the evidence they have unturned fits. It follows that historians must approach their fields of study by reading the relevant secondary authorities. Only then will they be able to make sense of their investigations. In the same way History students need to be introduced to primary sources through textbooks and monographs, for until they have acquired some background knowledge they will be in no position to submit such sources to critical evaluation.

# THE EVALUATION AND INTERPRETATION OF SOURCES

## Evaluation

### I. Origin

Sources survive for a variety of reasons: in some cases, Cabinet minutes for example, because deliberate decisions were taken to record them. Cabinet minutes date from Lloyd George's assumption of the premiership in 1916, unemployment statistics from 1920 when for the first time unemployment insurance was extended to the bulk of the working population. In other cases, as with Asquith's correspondence with Venetia Stanley, survival is largely accidental. As a general rule the 'unwitting testimony' is a more reliable guide than the 'deliberate record', precisely because it was never intended for publication. The correspondence of ordinary soldiers writing from the Western Front may actually be a better guide to the sentiments of the frontline soldier than the more articulate views expressed by poets such as Wilfred Owen or Siegfried Sassoon. One of the first questions to be asked, therefore, about any source is the purpose for which it has been written.

### 2. Selection

The problem of selection is an intractable one. Every primary source will have gone through a winnowing process before it sees the light of day. Under the rule adopted in 1967 Cabinet records are technically open to inspection after a lapse of thirty years. When they are finally made available, references to matters of national security will have been 'weeded out'. The minutes of Cabinet meetings do not record what was actually said, and are notoriously prone to conceal the disagreements that afflict any Cabinet. Despite these restrictions, politicians have long made it their practice to use copies of Cabinet papers when writing their own memoirs. Both Lloyd George and Churchill did this in their accounts of the First World War, as Churchill also did in his account of the Second.[7] More recently, Richard Crossman and Barbara Castle in their published diaries have included extensive but carefully selected accounts of Cabinet meetings they attended.[8]

Historians also need to be aware of the fact that they may only be seeing what they are intended to see. In their efforts to assign responsibility for the First World War all the major European powers published volumes of selected documents. The German

Foreign Office, in particular, exercised tight editorial control over the German collection in its anxiety to refute the War Guilt Clause in the Treaty of Versailles.[9] In a similar context E.H. Carr cites the example of the papers of Gustav Stresemann, German Foreign Secretary from 1925 to 1929. The first printed collection of Stresemann's papers, which filled 300 boxes, was made by his secretary, Bernhard, who was anxious to stress Stresemann's constructive Western policies: the Dawes Plan, the Treaties of Locarno and German entry into the League of Nations. He omitted much of the material relating to Stresemann's policies towards the Soviet Union. A British translation of Bernhard's selection reduced yet further the documents dealing with the Soviet Union. It was only the accidental discovery of the full Stresemann archive in 1945 that revealed how important relations with the Soviet Union had been to him.[10]

### 3. Motive

Allied to the problem of selection is that of motive. Any politician or general seeks to have a favourable construction placed upon his career. Mistakes are likely to be glossed over, successes highlighted. No one would go to Winston Churchill's account of the First World War, *The World Crisis,* for a dispassionate view of the Gallipolli Campaign for which he bore the main responsibility. Nor would one expect a wholly reliable account of the battle of El Alamein from the pen of the victor, Field Marshal Montgomery. There may even be deliberate suppression of the evidence. In Eden's second volume of memoirs, *Full Circle,* he gives his own account of the Suez Crisis of 1956, but fails to mention a critical meeting at Chequers on 14 October, 1956, between himself and two French officials, at which the use of force against Egypt was discussed.[11]

### 4. Bias

Motive may lead to the deliberate slanting or suppression of evidence. Bias is largely unconscious. It may take many forms: political, religious, national, racial, sexist – to mention only the most obvious categories. Every witness to an event sees it within his or her own frame of reference. John Reed's account of the Bolshevik Revolution of November 1917, *Ten Days that Shook the World,* was based on his own experiences in Petrograd, but valuable as his testimony is, his left-wing sympathies also coloured his view of the Bolsheviks.[12] The Easter Rising in Dublin in 1916 looks very different when seen through the eyes of the *Catholic Bulletin* rather than the *Irish Times.* The era of reconstruction after the American Civil War, when Blacks for the first time enjoyed a measure of political influence, has been portrayed as an orgy of misgovernment in Southern states by White supremacists, and as a period of enlightened experimentation by Black historians and their White sympathisers. The activities of the militant suffragettes in the decade up to 1914 have been condemned or admired, depending on the commentator's attitude to feminism.

There are, of course, many degrees of bias, and where value judgments are *not* involved the reliability of the evidence need not be affected by the point of view of the observer. There are no two opinions about the date of the battle of Waterloo. But wherever the reporter of an event has a vested interest in the outcome, because of either personal involvement or identification with one side or another, the historian needs to be on guard.

## Interpretation

Once the reliability of the sources has been evaluated, there is the question of the inferences that may properly be drawn from them. Two problems in particular call for comment:

### 1. Relating the 'particular' to the 'general'

Historians deal in particular events, out of which they try to construct valid generalisations. How typical, they must always be asking themselves, is this event or experience of the total situation or process? Were the football matches played between police and strikers in 1926 more characteristic of the general mood of the country during the General Strike than the derailing of the *Flying Scotsman* or the angry demonstrations that greeted the food convoys coming from the London docks? How common were the experiences of working-class families encountered by George Orwell on his visit to the north of England in 1936, subsequently recorded in *The Road to Wigan Pier*?[13] Such questions depend for their answers on a huge body of local research, and may, in the present state of the evidence, be strictly unanswerable. But they point to the dangers of drawing unwarranted conclusions from too narrow a range of examples.

### 2. Hindsight

Is the historian justified in using the benefit of hindsight? S.R. Gardiner, when writing his great history of the Early Stuarts, resolutely refused to consider any evidence in advance of the year about which he was currently writing, so that he should see events through the eyes of contemporaries. When Wilhelm II saw the Serbian reply to the Austrian ultimatum to Serbia in July 1914 (see Case Study 1) he commented: 'A great moral success for Vienna, but with it all reason for war disappears.'[14] In assessing Wilhelm's responsibility for causing the First World War, does this piece of evidence need to be read in the light of Germany's subsequent aggressive war aims?

To these questions there are no easy answers. Historical knowledge is a matter of probabilities, not certainties. But there is one safe rule. The more closely historians stick to the 'tracks', the less likely they are to be misled. Conversely, the better they know the terrain, the more surely will they be able to follow the tracks.

# PLAN OF THE BOOK

This book has been designed with these considerations in mind. The five case studies that follow have been chosen to illustrate the different kinds of source material on which historians have to rely: official documents; politicians' memoirs; correspondence; newspaper articles; statistics; photographs and cartoons; personal reminiscence. Each case study is focused on a particular issue which has given rise to controversy, and each raises the specific problems that arise in different kinds of historical writing. Thus the first case study, on British entry into the First World War, brings up the conduct of diplomacy and the making of high policy. The second, on the battle of

Passchendaele, raises the problems of military strategy as they are seen by the high command and by the ordinary soldier. The third, on Anglo-Irish relations between 1912 and 1922, examines the influence of national sentiment both in the decision-making process and in the way events are described. The fourth case study, on the General Strike, examines an industrial dispute and the extent to which it became a constitutional and a class conflict, and was portrayed as such. Finally, the fifth case study, on the inter-war depression in Britain, focuses on the behaviour of the British economy between 1929 and 1939, and the plight of the unemployed; it also provides an exercise in the interpretation of statistics and social observation. The case studies have all been drawn from recent British history, and have been chosen for their intrinsic importance, as well as for the light they can shed on the use of source materials.

There is a brief historical introduction to each case study, explaining why it has been chosen, and giving an account of the context to which the sources relate and the issues which they raise. This is followed by a short list of relevant and readily available secondary authorities which can be used for further background information. Within each case study, the sources are grouped into different sections. Each source or group of sources is prefaced by a note on its origins or originator. At the end of each section there is a series of questions. These have been designed to test particular skills:

*Comprehension* (the analysis and interpretation of a particular document);

*Evaluation* (the assessment of the reliability of different pieces of evidence, and the inferences that may properly be drawn from them);

*Synthesis* (the comparison of different sources and the ability to locate sources in their historical context, and to draw conclusions from them).

These skills are indicated by (C), (E) and (S) respectively at the end of each question, though in some cases they will be seen to overlap. Finally, at the end of each case study there is a summary of all the printed sources that have been used.

# NOTES

1  Marc Bloch, *The Historian's Craft* (Manchester University Press, 1954) pp. 54–5

2  See A. Marwick, *The Nature of History* (Macmillan, 1970) pp. 136–7

3  G.C. Peden, 'A Matter of Timing: The Economic Background to British Foreign Policy, 1937–39' (*History*, Feb. 1984)

4  A.J.P. Taylor, *The Origins of the Second World War* (Hamish Hamilton, 1961)

5  J.M. Roberts, *The Triumph of the West* (BBC, 1984)

6  Cited by S.T. Bindoff in H.O.R. Finberg (ed.), *Approaches to History* (Routledge & Kegan Paul, 1956) p. 4

7  See Winston S. Churchill, *The World Crisis* (Thornton Butterworth, 1922); D. Lloyd George, *War Memoirs* (Ivor Nicholson & Watson, 1933–6); Winston S. Churchill, *The Second World War* (Cassell, 1948–54)

8 See R.H.S. Crossman, *The Crossman Diaries* (Hamish Hamilton, 1979)

9 See I. Geiss, *July 1914* (Batsford, 1967) p. 10

10 E.H. Carr, *What is History* (Macmillan, 1961) pp. 10–13

11 Sir Anthony Eden, *Full Circle* (Cassell, 1960) pp. 507–14

12 John Reed, *Ten Days that Shook the World* (Boni & Liveright, New York, 1919)

13 George Orwell, *The Road to Wigan Pier* (Gollancz, 1937)

14 L.C.F. Turner, *The Origins of the First World War* (Arnold, 1970) p. 103

# Case Study 1

# BRITAIN'S DECISION TO GO TO WAR IN 1914

## INTRODUCTION

By 1914 Europe was divided into two power blocs. In 1879 Germany became formally linked to Austria-Hungary under the terms of the Dual Alliance. This was extended to include Italy in 1882, when it became the Triple Alliance. Each signatory was bound to come to the others' assistance in the event of an attack upon any one of them. In the face of this grouping France and Russia joined forces. Military conversations began in 1892 and culminated in a formal alliance in 1894. Each power was similarly bound to come to the other's aid in the event of an attack by a member of the Triple Alliance.

The two power blocs were speedily transformed into two armed camps. Conscription was introduced in all five countries. By 1914 Germany and France each had 700 000 men under arms with a further 5 million reservists on call. Russia had an army of 1.5 million with a further 3 million trained reserves. Each country also prepared for the contingency of war by drawing up a war plan. Of these the most significant was the Schlieffen Plan, designed specifically to deal with the threat to Germany posed by the Franco-Russian Alliance and the attendant danger of a war on two fronts.

The Schlieffen Plan committed the bulk of the German army to a massive offensive against France on the outbreak of war. This was to be launched through Belgium, enabling Paris to be encircled and France brought to her knees within six weeks. German armies would then be shifted East to meet the Russian armies, which, it was hoped, would take longer to mobilise.

## 1. BRITAIN'S OBLIGATIONS UNDER THE ANGLO-FRENCH CONVERSATIONS, 1905–12

Britain refused to commit herself to either side. Anglo-German negotiations in 1898 and 1901 proved abortive and all subsequent initiatives were thwarted because of the

Anglo-German naval race, which had begun with the passage of the first German Navy Law in 1898. In the face of a growing threat from Germany Britain turned first towards France, then towards Russia. In 1904 an understanding (*entente*) was reached with France, covering the main points of dispute between the two countries. In December 1905 this led to military and naval conversations which were continued at various intervals until the outbreak of war. Though no formal obligations were entered into, these talks undoubtedly strengthened the *entente* and had an important bearing on British policy in 1914.

In 1907 Britain also signed an *entente* with Russia, covering matters of dispute in Afghanistan, Persia and Tibet. Secret naval talks took place in May 1914. The understanding with Russia was viewed with much greater suspicion than that with France, especially by Liberals such as John Morley who disliked associating with a country under autocratic rule.

Just how firm Britain's commitments to France and Russia were as a consequence of these agreements remains a matter of dispute, as can be seen in Sources 1–8. When the Archduke Franz Ferdinand and his wife were assassinated on 28 June, 1914, the strength of the *ententes* was put to the test. The Archduke was the nephew of and heir to the Emperor of Austria, Franz Joseph. His assassin, Gabriel Princip, was a Serb. There can be little doubt that the Austrian government determined to use the assassination as an excuse to crush Serbia. Having ascertained that German support would be forthcoming, on 5 July preparations for the invasion of Serbia went ahead. On Thursday, 23 July the Austrian government delivered to the Serbian government a 48-hour ultimatum whose terms had been framed so harshly as to be virtually unacceptable.

On 28 July, not content with the conciliatory Serbian reply, Austria declared war on Serbia. This was followed on Thursday, 30 July by the Russian decision to mobilise in Serbia's defence. This move in turn prompted German mobilisation on 31 July, and when Russia refused to stop her military preparations, the German General Staff decided that the Schlieffen Plan must now be put into effect.

On 1 August Germany declared war on Russia. For a brief moment the Kaiser, Wilhelm II, hoping that France and Britain would stay neutral, urged that German armies should be deployed in the East rather than the West. Moltke, Chief of the German General Staff, convinced him that this was quite impracticable, and on 2 August an ultimatum was delivered to Belgium demanding unimpeded passage for German armies. The invasion of Belgium had to be justified by a supposed threat from France, and on 3 August such a threat was fabricated. The French were accused of frontier violations and of dropping bombs on German cities. In fact all French troops had been instructed to withdraw 10 kilometres from the frontier with Germany. It made no difference. Germany duly declared war on France, and German troops entered Luxemburg on 3 August. Meanwhile the Belgian government rejected the German ultimatum, and when German troops entered Belgian territory in the early hours of 4 August, they met with fierce resistance. Only twelve days after the Austrian ultimatum to Serbia, Europe was at war.

# 2. BRITISH POLICY DURING THE CRISIS OF JULY–AUGUST 1914

It was not until the terms of the ultimatum were known on 23 July that the British government paid any serious attention to the impending crisis. In the summer of 1914 all eyes were fixed on Ulster, where civil war threatened, rather than on the Balkans. The Cabinet discussed the Balkan crisis for the first time on 24 July. The British Foreign Minister, Sir Edward Grey, did his utmost to localise the conflict. On Saturday, 25 July he urged the Austrian government to extend the time limit of the ultimatum given to Serbia. On 26 July he suggested a four-power conference, and on 27 July he urged the German government to induce Austria to accept the Serbian reply to the ultimatum as a basis for negotiation, all to no avail. On 29 July he warned the German Ambassador, Prince Lichnowsky, that Britain could not stand aside indefinitely should France and Russia become involved in the Austro-Serbian conflict.

But Grey did not speak for the Cabinet as a whole. Five ministers, Burns, Morley, Simon, Beauchamp and Harcourt, threatened to resign when Grey mooted the possibility of intervention on Monday, 27 July. On 1 August the French Ambassador, Paul Cambon, failed to gain any assurance of British support in an awkward interview with Grey. The turning point came on 2 August, when the Cabinet agreed that Britain could not tolerate a German naval presence in the Channel (Source 13). Later that day Grey had news of the German ultimatum to Belgium, and at a second Cabinet meeting it was agreed that if there was a substantial violation of Belgian neutrality, Britain would have to act. On the morning of 3 August Grey outlined to the Cabinet the speech he intended to make that afternoon (Source 23). Four members of the Cabinet offered their resignations: Simon, Beauchamp, Morley and Burns. By the end of the day, Beauchamp and Simon had been prevailed on to stay. When Germany duly invaded Belgium on 4 August Grey sent an ultimatum requiring the withdrawal of all German troops within twelve hours. When it expired at midnight (German time, it was 11.00 p.m. in England) Asquith could count on a virtually united Cabinet and a virtually united country. As late as 2 August he had commented in a letter to Venetia Stanley: 'I suppose a good three quarters of our party are for non-intervention at any price.' The story of Britain's entry into the First World War is therefore not as simple as it has sometimes been portrayed.

This case study is designed to explore the nature of Britain's commitments to the Triple Entente (Sources 1–8); the conduct of British foreign policy between 23 July and 4 August, 1914 (Sources 9–14); the divisions within the Cabinet and the contrasting views of some of its members (Sources 15–24); and finally, the divisions in the country as represented by the views of rival newspapers, one Conservative, the other Liberal (Sources 25–7). The evidence consists of official documents, such as Foreign Office telegrams; politicians' memoirs; private correspondence; parliamentary speeches; newspaper editorials; and cartoons. Questions the reader should bear in mind relate both to the historical problems raised by this case study and to the nature of the evidence to be considered. To what extent did Britain's commitments to France limit her freedom of action in 1914? How was it that a Cabinet so divided at the outset of the crisis could reach an almost unanimous decision to go to war at the end of it? Did the critics of Sir Edward Grey's policy have a reasonable case? Where the evidence is concerned, the reader should apply to each document the criteria indicated in the Introduction: origin, selection, motive and bias.

# FURTHER READING

## Background

F.C. Bridge, *1914: The Coming of the First World War* (Historical Association, 1983)
J. Joll, *The Origins of the First World War* (Longman, 1984)
A.J.P. Taylor, *The Struggle for Mastery in Modern Europe* (OUP, 1954)
L.C.F. Turner, *The Origins of the First World War* (Arnold, 1970)

## British Policy

C. Hazlehurst, *Politicians at War* (Cape, 1971)
F.H. Hinsley, *The Foreign Policy of Sir Edward Grey* (CUP, 1977)
C.J. Lowe and M.L. Dockrill, *The Mirage of Power, British Foreign Policy, 1902–22* (Routledge & Kegan Paul, 1972)
M.C. Morgan, *Foreign Affairs, 1886–1914* (Collins, 1973)
K.S. Robbins, *Sir Edward Grey* (Cassell, 1971)
W.O. Simpson, *Changing Horizons* (Stanley Thornes, 1986)
Zara S. Steiner, *Britain and the Origins of the First World War* (Macmillan, 1977)

## Articles

K.M. Wilson, 'The British Cabinet's Decision for War', *British Journal of International Studies,* I, 1975
D.C. Watt, 'British Press Reaction and the Assassination at Sarajevo', *European Studies Review,* 1971

# SOURCE MATERIAL 1
# Britain's Obligations under the Anglo-French Conversations, 1905-12

*Sources 1–8 relate to three separate episodes: A. the inauguration of military conversations between French and British military staffs in December 1905–January 1096 (Sources, 1, 2); B. the revelation to the Cabinet in November 1911 of these conversations (Sources 3, 4); and C. the naval arrangements made in 1912, under which France undertook to keep the bulk of her fleet in the Mediterranean, thus enabling the British fleet to be concentrated in the North Sea (Sources 5–8).*

## 1A  The Inauguration of Military Conversations

**SOURCE 1**   Colonel Repington's Letter to Sir Edward Grey, 29 December, 1905

*Colonel Repington was military correspondent of* The Times. *Sir Edward Grey had been appointed Foreign Secretary on 8 December, 1905, following the resignation of Balfour's Conservative government on 4 December. Major Huguet was at the time the French military attaché in London. Prior to seeing Repington he had met General Grierson, Director of Military Operations, on 20 and 22 December to discuss the possibility of British military assistance in the event of war between France and Germany. M. Cambon was the French Ambassador in London.*

I had a confidential talk with the French military attaché last night lasting some five hours . . .

Major Huguet confessed that his Embassy felt anxious upon the question of the attitude of the new Government in England. His people, he said, had nothing to complain of, since the speeches of Sir Henry Campbell-Bannerman as well as yours, had produced an excellent effect. It was not a question of sympathies but rather of acts, of what the British government were prepared to do . . . There is another matter, he continued. M. Cambon cannot speak a word of English; he has tried to learn but says he is too old. Sir Edward Grey is believed not to be so perfect in French as Lord Lansdowne [Grey's predecessor] and Cambon feels he will have difficulty in seizing all the nuances of a conversation in such a difficult matter.

> J. Wilson, *A Life of Sir Henry Campbell-Bannerman* (Constable, 1973) pp. 523–4

# SOURCE 2 Sir Edward Grey's Correspondence with Sir Francis Bertie, 10 and 31 January, 1906

*Grey was immersed in the General Election of 1906 from 8 January until 22 January. Bertie was British Ambassador in Paris at the time. Rouvier was the French Foreign Minister. Count Metternich was the German Ambassador in London. The Morocco Agreement referred to in Grey's second letter was part of the Anglo-French entente of 1904, under which France recognised Britain's interests in Egypt, while Britain recognised France's interests in Morocco.*

FOREIGN OFFICE,
10 January, 1906

. . . M. Cambon said that he had spoken to this effect to M. Rouvier, who agreed in this view. It was not necessary, nor indeed expedient that there should be any formal alliance; but it was of great importance that the French Government should know beforehand whether in the event of aggression against France by Germany, Great Britain would be prepared to render to France armed assistance.

I replied that at the present moment the Prime Minister was out of town, and that the Cabinet were all dispersed seeing after the elections; that we were not yet aware of the sentiments of the country as they would be expressed at the polls; and that it was impossible therefore for me, in the circumstances to give a reply to his Excellency's question. I could only state as my personal opinion that, if France were to be attacked by Germany in consequence of a question arising out of the Agreement which our predecessors had recently concluded with the French Government, public opinion would be strongly moved in favour of France.

M. Cambon said he understood this, and that he would repeat his question after the elections . . .

In the meantime, he thought it advisable that unofficial communications between our Admiralty and War Office and the French Naval and Military Attachés should take place as to what action might advantageously be taken in case the two countries found themselves in alliance in such a war. Some communications had, he believed, already passed, and might, he thought, be continued. They did not pledge either Government.

I did not dissent from this view. – I am, etc.

EDWARD GREY

FOREIGN OFFICE,
31 January, 1906

*Sir Edward Grey to Sir F. Bertie*
Sir, – The French Ambassador asked me again today whether France would be able to count upon the assistance of England in the event of an attack upon her by Germany.

I said that I had spoken on the subject to the Prime Minister, and discussed it with him, and that I had three observations to submit. In the first place, since the ambassador had spoken to me a good deal of progress has been made. Our military and naval authorities had been in communication with the French, and I assumed that all preparations were ready, so that if a crisis arose, no time would have been lost for want of a formal engagement.

In the second place, a week or more before M. Cambon had spoken to me, I had taken an opportunity of expressing to Count Metternich my personal opinion, which I understood Lord Lansdowne had also expressed to him as a personal opinion, that in the event of an attack upon France by Germany arising out of the Morocco Agreement, public feeling in England would be so strong that no British Government could remain neutral.

In the third place, I pointed out to Monsieur Cambon that at present French policy in Morocco, within the four corners of the Declaration exchanged between us, was absolutely free, and that we did not question it, that we suggested no concessions and no alterations in it, that we left France a free hand and gave unreservedly our diplomatic support on which she could count . . .

He eventually repeated his request for some form of assurance which might be given in conversation. I said that an assurance of that kind could be nothing short of a solemn undertaking. It was one which I could not give without submitting it to the Cabinet, and that were I to submit the question to the Cabinet I was sure that they would say this was too serious a matter to be dealt with by a verbal engagement but must be put in writing. As far as their good disposition to France was concerned, I should have no hesitation in submitting such a question to the present Cabinet. Some of those in the Cabinet who were most attached to peace were those also who were the best friends of France; but, though I had no doubt about the good disposition of the Cabinet, I did think there would be difficulties in putting such an undertaking in writing . . . I told him also that should such a defensive alliance be formed, it was too serious a matter to be kept secret from Parliament. The Government could conclude it without the assent of Parliament, but it would have to be published afterwards. No British Government could commit the country to such a serious thing and keep the engagement secret . . .

Viscount Grey, *Twenty-Five Years,* vol. I (Hodder & Stoughton, 1925) pp. 72–4, 79–81

## 1B  Informing the Cabinet

*In 1911 a further crisis in Franco-German relations occurred, following the despatch of a German gunboat, the* Panther, *to Agadir on the Moroccan coast. At an important meeting of the Committee of Imperial Defence (CID) on 23 August, 1911, British plans to send an expeditionary force of six divisions to the Continent in the event of war with Germany were discussed and approved. News of these discussions leaked to certain members of the Cabinet, notably Lord Morley, who was strongly opposed to any military agreement with France, and who had not been present at the meeting of the CID on 23 August. In consequence, the military and naval conversations were discussed at Cabinet meetings on 1 and 15 November, 1911. Records of these meetings are to be found in Asquith's letters to George V, and there are references to them in Grey's and Lloyd George's memoirs.*

# SOURCE 3 Asquith to George V, 1 and 15 November, 1911

*1 November*

Lord Morley raised the question of the inexpediency of communications being held or allowed between the General Staff at the War Office and the General Staff of foreign states, such as France in regard to possible military and naval co-operation, without the previous knowledge and direction of the Cabinet. Lord Haldane [Minister for War] explained what had actually been done, the communications in question having been initiated as far back as 1906 with Sir Henry Campbell-Bannerman's sanction, and resumed in the Spring and Summer of the present year. The Prime Minister pointed out that all questions of policy have been and must be reserved for the decision of the Cabinet, and that it is quite outside the function of military or naval officers to prejudge such questions. He added that he believed (and Sir Edward Grey concurred) that this was fully recognised by the French Government. Considerable discussion ensued and no conclusion was come to, the matter being adjourned . . .

*15 November*

. . . a prolonged and animated discussion. Sir E. Grey made it clear that at no stage of our intercourse with France since 1906 had we either by diplomatic or military engagements compromised our freedom of decision or action in the event of war between France and Germany. On the other hand there was a prevailing feeling in the Cabinet that there was a danger that communications of the kind referred to might give rise to expectations, and that they should not, if they related to the possibility of concerted action, be entered into without the sanction of the Cabinet. In the result, at the suggestion of the Prime Minister, unanimous approval was given to the two following propositions:

    1. That no communications should take place between the General Staff here and the Staffs of other countries which can, directly or indirectly, commit this country to military or naval intervention.

    2. That such communications, if they relate to concerted action by land or sea, should not be entered into without the previous approval of the Cabinet.

Asquith Papers, cited in J. Macintosh, *The British Cabinet* (Methuen, 1968) pp. 338–9

# SOURCE 4

## (a) Grey's Recollections of these Cabinet Meetings

The Agadir affair had thus brought the military conversations into prominence. They must have been familiar to several members of the Cabinet in discussion at the Committee of Imperial Defence, and in 1912 the fact of their taking place became known to other members of the Cabinet . . .

Grey, *Twenty-Five Years*, vol. I, p. 96

### (b) Lloyd George's Recollections of the Meetings

There is no more conspicuous example of this kind of suppression of vital information than the way in which the military arrangements we entered into with France were kept from the Cabinet for six years. They came to my knowledge, first of all, in 1911 during the Agadir crisis, but the Cabinet as a whole were not acquainted with them before the following year. There is abundant evidence that both the French and the Russians regarded these military arrangements as practically tantamount to a commitment to come to the aid of France in the event of her being attacked by Germany . . .

When in 1912 (six years after they had been entered into) Sir Edward Grey communicated these negotiations and arrangements to the Cabinet the majority of its members were aghast. Hostility barely represents the strength of the sentiment which the revelations aroused: it was more akin to consternation. Sir Edward Grey allayed the apprehensions of his colleagues to some extent by emphatic assurances that these military arrangements left us quite free, in the event of war, to decide whether we should or should not participate in the conflict. The Prime Minister also exercised his great authority with the Cabinet in the same direction. In spite of these assurances a number of Cabinet Ministers were not reconciled to the action taken by the Foreign Office, the War Office and the Admiralty, and these commitments undoubtedly added a good deal to the suspicions which made the task of Sir Edward Grey in securing unanimity in 1914 very much more difficult.

D. Lloyd George, War Memoirs, vol. I (Ivor Nicholson & Watson, 1933) pp. 49–50

## 1C  The Naval Arrangements of 1912 and their Consequences

*In October 1911 Winston Churchill replaced Reginald McKenna as First Lord of the Admiralty. The growing naval strength of Austria and Italy in the Mediterranean, coupled with the increase in the size of the German High Seas Fleet, convinced Churchill that a redeployment of British naval force was necessary. As Britain could no longer hope to match the combined naval strength of Austria and Italy in the Mediterranean without seriously depleting the Channel fleet a new naval strategy was necessary. This would require a greater degree of co-operation with France. Churchill set out his views in a secret memorandum dated 15 June, 1912, but he evidently had some second thoughts, as indicated in the letter sent to Grey and Asquith on 23 August. The Cabinet also reaffirmed its unwillingness to see any advance in Britain's commitments to France, as indicated in the Grey–Cambon correspondence of 22–3 November, 1912.*

### SOURCE 5  Memorandum by Winston Churchill (Admiralty) 15 June, 1912

*In this Memorandum Churchill argued that if Britain was to maintain her naval superiority over Germany a margin of thirty-three British to twenty-five German fully commissioned battleships was necessary. To achieve this margin the Mediterranean squadron of six battleships would have to be brought home. To make good the gap thus created in British defences in the Mediterranean, he put forward various suggestions, including the following ones.*

7. A new submarine and torpedo station will have to be established at Alexandria. Another new flotilla of submarines, possessing sufficient radius of action to enable them to threaten the Dardanelles, or cover the approaches to the Suez Canal will also be needed . . . It seems to the Admiralty very probable that these arrangements may be made to fit conveniently into any scheme for strengthening the British force in Egypt . . .

8. It should be noted that these arrangements stand by themselves and are put forward as the best we can make in the circumstances. The situation would, however, become entirely favourable if France is taken into account. The French fleet supported by an adequate naval force, and enjoying the use of our fortified and torpedo-defended bases as well as their own, would be superior to any Austro-German alliance. An Anglo-French combination in a war would be able to maintain full control of the Mediterranean, and afford all necessary protection to British and French interests, both territorial and commercial, without impairing British margins in the North Sea. A definite naval arrangement should be made with France without delay.

This arrangement would come into force only if the two Powers were at any time allies in a war. It would not decide the question of whether they should be allies or not. No sound or effective disposition can be made without it, and many contingencies must be left unsatisfied . . .

*Winston Churchill,* Companion Volume II, Part 3: 1911–14 (Heinemann, 1969) p. 1567

# SOURCE 6   Winston Churchill to Sir Edward Grey and H.H. Asquith

*This letter was written from HMS* Enchantress, *the Admiralty yacht on which Churchill was enjoying a working holiday.*

HMS Enchantress<br>23 August

Secret

The point I am anxious to safeguard is our freedom of choice if the occasion arises, and consequent power to influence French policy beforehand. That freedom will be sensibly impaired if the French can say that they have denuded their Atlantic seaboard and concentrated in the Mediterranean on the faith of naval arrangements made with us. This would not be true. If we did not exist, the French could not make better dispositions than at present. They are not strong enough to face Germany alone, still less to maintain themselves in two theatres. They therefore rightly concentrate their Navy in the Mediterranean where it can be safe and superior, where it can assure their African communications, and overawe Italy. Neither is it true that we are relying on France to maintain our position in the Mediterranean. We have greatly strengthened our forces there and the Government have decided to strengthen them further as occasion may require. If France did not exist, we should make no other disposition of our forces.

Circumstances might arise which in my judgment would make it desirable and right for us to come to the aid of France with all our force by land and sea. But we ask nothing in return. If we were attacked by Germany we should not make it a charge of bad faith against the French that they left us to fight it out alone; and nothing in naval and military arrangements ought to have the effect of exposing us to such a charge if when the time comes we decide to stand out.

This is my view, and I am sure I am in line with you on the principle. I am not at all particular how it is to be given effect to; and I make no point about what document it is set forth in. But I don't think Bertie understands it a bit, nor how tremendous would be the weapon which France would possess to compel our intervention if she could say 'on the advice of and by arrangement with your naval authorities we have left our Northern Coasts defenceless. We cannot possibly come back in time'. Indeed it would probably be decisive whatever is written down now. Everyone must feel who knows the facts that we have the obligations of an alliance without its advantages and above all without its precise definitions.

*Notes by Sir Edward Grey and the Prime Minister:*

We must wait till Cambon returns. E.G.

Yes. H.H.A.

*Winston Churchill,* Companion Volume II, Part 3: 1911–14, pp. 1638–9

## SOURCE 7   Letters Exchanged by Sir Edward Grey and Paul Cambon, 22–3 November, 1912

*Grey explains the origin of these letters as follows: 'I had made it so plain to Cambon that the Government must remain absolutely free and uncommitted, that I anticipated no difficulty whatever in getting a satisfactory exchange of notes with him on behalf of ourselves and the French Government . . . I therefore agreed, readily and at once, to the proposal that this condition be put in writing.*

*'We proceeded to draft the letter in Cabinet, and again I thought I was conscious of a little surprise that words unqualified and explicit were agreed to. The letter, as approved by the Cabinet, was signed and given by me to Cambon, and I received one in similar terms from him in exchange. From that time onwards every Minister knew how we stood, and the letters became familiar to the public but they may be repeated here.'*

*Sir Edward Grey to M. Cambon, French Ambassador in London*

FOREIGN OFFICE,
22 November, 1912

MY DEAR AMBASSADOR, – From time to time in recent years the French and British naval and military experts have consulted together. It has always been understood that such consultation does not restrict the freedom of either Government to decide at any future time whether or not to assist the other by armed force. We have agreed that consultation between experts is not, and ought not to be, regarded as an engagement that commits either Government to action in a contingency that has not arisen and may never arise. The disposition, for instance, of the French and British fleets respectively at the present moment is not based upon an engagement to co-operate in war.

You have, however, pointed out that if either Government had grave reason to expect an unprovoked attack by a third Power it might become essential to know whether it could, in that event, depend upon the armed assistance of the other.

I agree that, if either Government had grave reason to expect an unprovoked attack by a third Power, or something that threatened the general peace, it should immediately discuss with the other whether both Governments should act together to prevent aggression and to preserve peace, and, if so, what measures they would be prepared to take in common. If these measures involved action, the plans of the general staffs would at once be taken into consideration, and the Governments would then decide what effect should be given to them.

Yours, etc.,

E. GREY

*M. Cambon to Sir Edward Grey (Translation)*

FRENCH EMBASSY, LONDON,
23 November, 1912

DEAR SIR EDWARD, – You reminded me in your letter of yesterday, November 22, that during the last few years the military and naval authorities of France and Great Britain had consulted with each other from time to time; that it had always been understood that these consultations should not restrict the liberty of either Government to decide in the future whether they should lend each other the support of their armed forces; that, on either side, these consultations between experts were not, and should not be, considered as engagements binding our Governments to take action in certain eventualities; that, however, I had remarked to you that, if one or other of the two Governments had grave reason to fear an unprovoked attack on the part of a third Power, it would become essential to know whether it could count on the armed support of the other.

Your letter answers that point, and I am authorized to state that, in the event of one of our two Governments having grave reason to fear either an act of aggression from a third Power, or some event threatening the general peace, that Government would immediately examine with the other the question whether both Governments should act together in order to prevent the act of aggression or preserve peace. If so, the two Governments would deliberate as to the measures which they would be prepared to take in common; if those measures involved action, the two Governments would take into immediate consideration the plans of their General Staffs and would then decide as to the effect to be given to those plans.

Yours, etc.,

PAUL CAMBON

Grey, *Twenty-Five Years,* vol. I, pp. 97–8

# SOURCE 8 Zara S. Steiner, *Britain and the Origins of the First World War*

*This is an authoritative secondary source on British foreign policy before 1914, based on an extensive use of Foreign Office documents. It was first published in 1967.*

By April 1913 agreements had been reached on the defence of the Straits of Dover and the Western Channel and for joint operations in the Mediterranean. A signal log book for the allied fleet had been sent to the printers; war orders for contingency of an alliance with France were sealed and sent to appropriate commanders. During the early part of 1914, the French navy tried to extend these arrangements, but their British counterparts were wary of any step which might be interpreted as a tightening of the Entente. The British were particularly dubious about further *pourparlers* between the two navies in the Mediterranean. Prince Louis of Battenburg [the First Sea Lord] would not receive a French representative nor would he make a public visit to Paris. Even when some details were settled, the ultimate question of whether the British would enter the war and whether they would remain a significant naval factor in the Mediterranean were left purposely unanswered. It is incorrect to speak of either a military or a naval alliance or even of a defensive *entente*. Nevertheless, the government's freedom of action had been compromised.

Zara S. Steiner, *Britain and the Origins of the First World War* (Macmillan, 1977) p. 104

---

# QUESTIONS ON SOURCES 1–8

1. Why should Colonel Repington have felt it necessary to write to Sir Edward Grey on 29 December, 1905 (Source 1)? (C)

2. How far was Grey prepared to go, prior to the General Election of 1906, in offering support to France (Source 2)? (C)

3. Why did Grey refuse to give a verbal assurance of British support to Cambon (Source 2)? (C)

4. What can be inferred about the respective attitudes of Britain and France towards the Anglo-French *entente* from Sources 1 and 2? (S)

5. What discrepancies can you detect between Asquith's account of the Cabinet discussions of November 1911 and those of Grey and Lloyd George (Sources 3 and 4)? How do you account for them? (E)

6. Why was Churchill so anxious for a 'definite naval arrangement' with France (Source 5)? (C)

7. Do you see any contradiction between Churchill's Memorandum of 15 June, 1912 and his letter to Grey and Asquith (Sources 5, 6)? (S)

8.  Does Source 8 support Grey's interpretation of 'the disposition . . . of the French and British fleets' (Source 7)? (S)

9.  Is Grey justified in saying that, after the publication of the Grey–Cambon letters of 22–3 November, 1912, 'every Minister knew how we stood' (Source 7)? (S)

10. Would you concur with Zara Steiner's view of Anglo-French relations between 1904 and 1914: 'It is incorrect to speak of either a military or a naval alliance or even of a defensive *entente*' (Source 8)? (S)

# SOURCE MATERIAL 2
# British Policy during the Crisis of July–August 1914

*Sources 9–27 relate to three aspects of the 1914 crisis: A. official British policy between the delivery of the Austrian ultimatum to Serbia on 23 July, 1914 and the British declaration of war on Germany on 4 August (Sources 9–14); B. divisions within the British Cabinet on Britain's proper response to the crisis, and contrasting views within the Cabinet (Sources 15–24); and C. public reaction to the crisis as it was reflected in the views of Conservative and Liberal newspapers, and in the cartoons of* Punch *(Sources 25–7).*

## 2A  Official British Policy

*It can safely be said that while no country positively wanted war in 1914, Grey did his best to avert it. He urged Austria to modify the terms of the ultimatum to Serbia; he suggested a four-power conference to mediate between Austria and Serbia; and he asked Germany to use her influence to induce Austria to accept the Serbian reply to the Austrian ultimatum as a basis for negotiation. But a question mark persisted over Britain's likely conduct in the event of war throughout the crisis. Grey refused to commit Britain to the support of France and Russia, while at the same time he would give Germany no guarantee of British neutrality. Uncertainty over Britain's attitude has been held to have contributed to the outbreak of war, on the one hand by encouraging Germany to gamble on the prospect of British neutrality, on the other because Britain failed to restrain Russian mobilisation. Sources 9–14 illustrate these uncertainties, and the changes in British policy as war approached. The Chart of Events below summarises the development of the crisis in Europe and British reaction to these events.*

| | *Chart of Events, June–August 1914* | |
| | *Europe* | *Britain* |
| --- | --- | --- |
| Sunday, 28 June | Assassination of Franz Ferdinand | |
| Sunday, 5 July | German promise of support to Austria | |
| Thursday, 23 July | Austrian ultimatum delivered to Serbia | |
| Friday, 24 July | Russian Council of Ministers requests partial mobilisation | Cabinet discusses Balkan crisis for the first time |

| | | |
|---|---|---|
| Saturday,<br>25 July | Russia introduces 'The Period<br>Preparatory to War' | Grey suggests extending time<br>limit to Vienna |
| Sunday,<br>26 July | Grey's suggestion of four-power<br>conference rejected by Germany | Grey suggests four-power<br>conference |
| Monday,<br>27 July | Austria decides to declare war<br>on Serbia<br>Kaiser returns to Berlin | Cabinet considers intervention<br>Five members threaten<br>resignation |
| Tuesday,<br>28 July | Austria declares war on Serbia | |
| Wednesday,<br>29 July | Tsar orders general mobilisation,<br>later amended to partial<br>mobilisation | Cabinet refuses to make<br>pledges to Germany or France |
| Thursday,<br>30 July | Tsar orders general mobilisation | Parliamentary Labour party<br>votes to stay out of war |
| Friday,<br>31 July | Germany orders mobilisation<br>Ultimatum to Russia | |
| Saturday,<br>1 August | German declaration of war on<br>Russia | Cambon requests British<br>support<br>Asquith non-committal |
| Sunday,<br>2 August | Ultimatum presented to<br>Belgium | Cabinet agrees to defend<br>French coasts if attacked by<br>Germany |
| Monday,<br>3 August | German declaration of war on<br>France<br>Invasion of Luxembourg | Cabinet agrees to defend<br>Belgium<br>Grey's speech to House of<br>Commons |
| Tuesday,<br>4 August | German invasion of Belgium | 11.00 a.m.   British ultimatum<br>to Germany<br>11.00 p.m.   British declara-<br>tion of war on Germany |
| Thursday,<br>6 August | Austrian declaration of war on<br>Russia | |

# SOURCE 9  Prince Lichnowsky to Jagow, 24 July, 1914

*Prince Lichnowsky became German Ambassador in London in 1911. Jagow was the German Foreign Minister in 1914. The marginal notes were in the Kaiser's handwriting.*

Lichnowsky to Jagow

Telegram 151                                         London, 24 July, 1914
D.D. 157                                                    D. 9.12 p.m.
                                                    R. 25 July, 1.16 a.m.

Sir E. Grey asked me to call on him just now. The Minister was evidently greatly affected by the Austrian note, which, according to his view, exceeded anything he had ever seen of this sort before. He said that he had so far had no news from St Petersburg, and consequently did not know what they thought of the matter there. But he very much doubted whether it would be possible for the Russian Government to recommend to the Serbian Government the unconditional acceptance of the Austrian demands. Any nation that accepted conditions like that would really cease to count as an independent nation. It was very difficult for him, Sir E. Grey, to offer advice of any sort to St Petersburg at the present moment. He could only *hope* that a *mild* and pacific view of the situation would gain ground there. As long as the matter concerned a localised quarrel between Austria and Serbia, such as Your Excellency laid stress on in despatch 1055 which I employed in talking to Sir E. Grey, he, Sir E. Grey, had nothing to do with it; but it would be a different matter should public opinion in Russia force the Government to proceed against Austria.

*This would be very desirable. It is not a nation in the European sense, but a band of robbers!*

*Right.*

To my remark that one could not measure the Balkan peoples by the same standard as the *civilised nations* of Europe, and that therefore one had to use another kind of language with them – that had been proved by their barbaric manner of warfare – than one used, say, towards Britons or Germans, the Minister replied that even if he were able to share this opinion, he did not believe that it would be accepted in Russia. The danger of a European war, should Austria *invade Serbian territory,* would become immediate. The results of such a war between *four* nations – he expressly emphasised the *number four,* and meant by it Russia, Austria-Hungary, Germany and France – would be absolutely incalculable. However the affair might come out, one thing would be certain: that would be total exhaustion and impoverishment; industry and trade would be ruined, and the power of capital destroyed. Revolutionary movements, like those of the year 1848, due to the collapse of industrial activities would be the result. What Sir Edward Grey

*Right for they aren't!*

*Right.*

*Then the Russians are not any better themselves.*

*Which will certainly happen.*

*He forgets Italy.*

most deplored, beside the tone of the note, was the brief time-limit, which made war almost unavoidable. He told me that he would be willing to join with us in pleading for a prolongation of the time-limit at Vienna, as in that way *perhaps a way out* might be found. He requested me to transmit this proposal to your Excellency. He further suggested that in the event of a dangerous tension between Russia and Austria, the four nations not immediately concerned – England, Germany, France and Italy – should undertake to mediate between Russia and Austria. This proposal, also, he requested me to submit to Your Excellency.

The Minister is evidently endeavouring to do everything to avoid European complications, and could not conceal his great regret at the challenging tone of the Austrian note and at the brief time-limit.

I am told from another quarter in the Foreign Office that there is reason for the assumption that Austria is very much under-estimating Serbia's power of self-defence. In any event it will be a long and desperate fight, in which Austria will be excessively weakened and in which she will be *bled white*. They also claim to know that Roumania's attitude is more than uncertain, and that they were saying in Bucharest that they would be against anybody who attacked.

*Marginal notes:*

Useless.

This is superfluous, as Austria has already made matters plain to Russia, and Grey has nothing else to propose. I will not join in it unless Austria expressly asks me to, which is not likely. In *vital* questions and those of honour, one does not consult with others.

Nonsense.

It may give Persia to England.

I. Geiss, *July 1914* (Batsford, 1967) pp. 183–4

## SOURCE 10   Grey to Buchanan, 25 July, 1914

*Buchanan was the British Ambassador to Russia; Count Benckendorff was the Russian Ambassador to Britain.*

Decree 295                                            London, 25 July, 1914
Confidential
B.D. 132

I told Count Benckendorff today of what I had said to the German Ambassador this morning as to the possibility of Germany, Italy, France and ourselves working together in Vienna and St Petersburg to secure peace after Austria and Russia had mobilised.

Count Benckendorff was very apprehensive that what I said would give Germany the impression that France and England were detached from Russia.

I said that France and ourselves, according to my suggestion, would be no more detached from Russia than Germany would be detached from her ally Austria. I had emphasised to Prince Lichnowsky that the participation of Germany in any such diplomatic mediation was an essential condition, and surely the situation was not made unsatisfactory for Russia if France and England held their hands, provided that Germany also held hers.

Count Benckendorff urged that I should give some indication to Germany to make her think that we would not stand aside if there was a war.

I said that I had given no indication that we would stand aside; on the contrary, I had said to the German Ambassador that, as long as there was only a dispute between Austria and Serbia alone, I did not feel entitled to intervene, but that, directly it was a matter between Austria and Russia, it became a question of the peace of Europe, which concerned us all. I had furthermore spoken on the assumption that Russia would mobilise, whereas the assumption of the German Government had hitherto been, officially, that Serbia would receive no support; and what I had said must influence the German Government to take the matter seriously. In effect, I was asking that, if Russia mobilised against Austria, the German Government, who had been supporting the Austrian demand on Serbia, should ask Austria to consider some modification of her demands, under the threat of Russian mobilisation. This was not an easy thing for Germany to do, even though we would join at the same time in asking Russia to suspend action. I was afraid, too, that Germany would reply that mobilisation with her was a question of hours, whereas with Russia it was a question of days; and that, as a matter of fact, I had asked that if Russia mobilised against Austria, Germany, instead of mobilising against Russia, should suspend mobilisation and join with us in intervention with Austria, thereby throwing away the advantage of time, for, if the diplomatic intervention failed, Russia would meanwhile have gained time for her mobilisation. It was true that I had not said anything directly as to whether we would take any part or not if there was a European conflict, and I could not say so; but there was absolutely nothing for Russia to complain of in the suggestion that I had made to the German Government, and I was only afraid that there might be difficulty in its acceptance by the German Government. I had made it on my own responsibility, and I had no doubt it was the best proposal to make in the interests of peace.

Geiss, *July 1914*, pp. 206–7

# SOURCE 11   Goschen to Grey, 29 July, 1914

*Goschen was the British Ambassador in Berlin. The Chancellor referred to is Bethmann-Hollweg. The Minute added is by Eyre Crowe, Assistant Under-Secretary at the Foreign Office and well known for his anti-German views.*

| | |
|---|---|
| Telegram 102 | Berlin, 29 July, 1914 |
| Secret. Urgent | D. 30 July, 1.20 a.m. |
| B.D. 293 | R. 30 July, 9.00 a.m. |

Chancellor having just returned from Potsdam sent for me again tonight and made the following strong bid for British neutrality in the event of war. He said he was continuing his efforts to maintain peace, but that in the event of a Russian attack on Austria, Germany's obligation as Austria's ally might, to his great regret, render a European conflagration inevitable, and in that case he hoped Great Britain would remain neutral. As far as he was able to judge key-note of British policy, it was evident that Great Britain would never allow France to be crushed. Such a result was not contemplated by Germany. The Imperial Government was ready to give every assurance to the British Government provided that Great Britain remained neutral that, in the event of a victorious war, Germany aimed at no territorial acquisitions at the expense of France.

In answer to a question from me, His Excellency said that it would not be possible for him to give such an assurance as regards colonies.

Continuing, his Excellency said he was, further, ready to assure the British Government that Germany would respect neutrality and integrity of Holland as long as they were respected by Germany's adversaries.

As regards Belgium, His Excellency could not tell to what operations Germany might be forced by the action of France, but he could state that, provided that Belgium did not take sides against Germany, her integrity would be respected after the conclusion of the war.

Finally, His Excellency said that he trusted that these assurances might form basis of a further understanding with England which, as you well know, had been the object of his policy ever since he had been Chancellor.

An assurance of British neutrality in conflict which present crisis might possibly produce would enable him to look forward to a general neutrality agreement between the two countries, the details of which it would, of course, be premature to discuss at the present moment.

His Excellency asked me how I thought you would view his request. I replied that I thought that you would like to retain full liberty of action, and that personally I did not consider it likely that you would care to bind yourself to any course of action at this stage of events.

After our conversation I communicated to His Excellency the contents of your telegram 227, and he begged me to convey to you his best thanks.

*Minute*
The only comment that need be made on these astounding proposals is that they reflect discredit on the statesman who makes them.

Incidentally it is of interest to note that Germany practically admits the intention to violate Belgian neutrality but to endeavour to respect that of Holland (in order to safeguard German imports via the Rhine and Rotterdam).

It is clear that Germany is practically determined to go to war, and that the one restraining influence so far has been the fear of England joining in the defence of France and Belgium. – E. A. C. 30 July.

Geiss, July 1914, pp. 300–1

# SOURCE 12   Grey to Goschen, 30 July, 1914

*This is Grey's reply to the German request for British neutrality referred to in Source 11.*

Telegram 231                                                London, 30 July, 1914
B.D. 303                                                              D. 3.30 p.m.
Your telegram 102
You must inform the German Chancellor that his proposal that we should bind ourselves to neutrality on such terms cannot for a moment be entertained.

He asks us in effect to stand by while French colonies are taken and France is beaten so long as Germany does not take French territory as distinct from colonies.

From the material point of view such a proposal is unacceptable, for France could be so crushed as to lose her position as a Great Power, and become subordinate to German policy without further territory in Europe being taken from her.

But apart from that, for us to make this bargain with Germany at the expense of France would be a disgrace from which the good name of this country would never recover.

The Chancellor also in effect asks us to bargain away whatever obligation or interest we have as regards the neutrality of Belgium. We could not entertain that bargain either . . .

You should add most earnestly that the one way of maintaining the good relations between England and Germany is to continue to work together to preserve the peace of Europe; if we succeed in this object, the mutual relations of Germany and England will, I believe, be *ipso facto* improved and strengthened. For that object His Majesty's Government will work with all sincerity and goodwill . . .

Geiss, *July 1914*, pp. 315–16

## SOURCE 13   Britain's Assurance to France, 2 August, 1914

*In response to Cambon's query on 1 August as to Britain's likely response should French coasts be attacked by the German navy, Grey gave this statement to the French Ambassador on the afternoon of 2 August.*

I am authorised to give an assurance that if the German fleet comes into the Channel or through the North Sea to undertake hostile operations against the French coasts or shipping, the British fleet will give all the protection in its power. This assurance is, of course, subject to the policy of His Majesty's Government receiving the support of Parliament, and must not be taken as binding His Majesty's Government to take any action until the above contingency of action by the German fleet takes place.

Grey, *Twenty-Five Years*, vol. II, p. 301

## SOURCE 14   Sir Edward Grey to Goschen, 4 August, 1914

*This is the text of the ultimatum delivered to the German Foreign Minister by Goschen on the instructions of the British government. It was German failure to comply with its terms that led to the British declaration of war.*

We hear that Germany has addressed a note to the Belgian Minister for Foreign Affairs stating that the German Government will be compelled to carry out, if necessary by force of arms, the measures considered indispensable.

We are also informed that Belgian territory has been violated at Gemmenich.

In these circumstances, and in view of the fact that Germany declined to give the same assurance respecting Belgium as France gave last week in reply to our request made simultaneously at Berlin and Paris, we must repeat that request and ask that a satisfactory reply to it and to my telegram No. 266* of this morning be received here by 12 o'clock tonight. If not, you are instructed to ask for your passport and to say that His Majesty's Government feel bound to take all steps in their power to uphold the neutrality of Belgium and the observance of a Treaty to which Germany is as much a party as ourselves.

*Telegram 266, also despatched on 4 August, protested against the ultimatum delivered by Germany to Belgium, and requested an explanation.

G.P. Gooch and H. Temperley (eds.), *British Documents on the Origins of the War, 1898–1914*, vol. XI (HMSO, 1926) p. 314

---

## QUESTIONS ON SOURCES 9–14

1. Compare the responses of Prince Lichnowsky and the Kaiser to Grey's proposals for averting conflict (Source 9). (C)

2. How reliable as a guide to the Kaiser's own views are the marginal notes he makes on Lichnowsky's despatch (Source 9)? (E)

3. Was Count Benckendorff justified in the apprehensions he voiced to Grey in Source 10? (S)

4. What can be inferred about Sir Eyre Crowe's attitude to Germany from his Memorandum in Source 11? (E)

5. How do Grey and Crowe differ in their interpretations of German policy (Sources 11 and 12)? (S)

6. Did the pledge to France made on 2 August (Source 13) go beyond the requirements of the Grey–Cambon letters of 1912 (Source 7)? (S)

7. Did the German government have any grounds for assuming that Britain would remain neutral should Belgium be invaded (Sources 11 and 12)? (S)

8. Is it correct to say that Britain declared war on Germany simply to uphold the neutrality of Belgium (Sources 9–14)? (S)

---

## 2B Changing Views within the Cabinet

*The Cabinet first considered the Balkan crisis on Friday, 24 July, the day after the delivery of the Austrian ultimatum to Serbia. Cabinet meetings were subsequently held on Monday, 27 July and Wednesday, 29 July, and then on every day from Saturday, 1 August to Tuesday, 4 August.*

*There were two meetings on Sunday, 2 August at which critical decisions were taken, first to oppose the entry of the German fleet into the Channel and second to defend the integrity of Belgium. At the outset opinions were very divided. Asquith, Grey, Churchill and Haldane were clear that if France were attacked Britain would have to come to her assistance, both on grounds of interest and obligation. Morley and Burns were equally strongly opposed to British involvement. Most of the others were undecided. Simon, Beauchamp and Harcourt sided initially with Morley and Burns. Lloyd George's position was equivocal. He had been strongly anti-German at the time of the Agadir Incident in 1911, but was reluctant to sever his links with the anti-war group in the Liberal party. Three factors appear to have influenced the waverers: the threat of German naval action in the Channel; the German ultimatum to Belgium; and the knowledge that should a Liberal government fail to respond to the German challenge, it would almost certainly be replaced by a War Ministry made up of pro-war Liberals and the Conservative leaders. On 2 August Bonar Law sent word to Asquith that 'it would be fatal to the honour and security of the United Kingdom to hesitate in supporting France and Russia at the present juncture' and offered the unqualified support of the Opposition in the event of war. Whatever the reasons, when Britain declared war on Germany on 4 August, only two members of the Cabinet, Burns and Morley, resigned. Sources 15–17 reflect the initial divisions of the Cabinet, and Sources 18–23 represent differing individual standpoints.*

## SOURCE 15   Sir Edward Grey's View of the Situation

Now, when the possibility of war appeared, there was an anti-war party in the Cabinet. As possibility became probability this party naturally became at first not less but more active and determined. It did not appear in Cabinet discussions, for neither I nor anyone tried to force a decision while there was still any hope of peace . . . But outside the Cabinet I felt sure that the anti-war group were meeting, were arranging concerted action, if need be, to keep this country out of war or to resign if they failed in doing so . . . This group included more than one of the names that came next after that of the Prime Minister in authority and influence within the Liberal Party inside and outside. It is needless to enquire whether the group included half or less or more than half the Cabinet; it was sufficient in number and influence to have broken up the Cabinet . . . It was clear to me that no authority would be obtained from the Cabinet to give the pledge for which France pressed more and more urgently, and that to press the Cabinet for a pledge would be fatal; it would result in the resignation of one group or the other, and the consequent break-up of the Cabinet altogether.

Grey, *Twenty-Five Years*, vol. I, pp. 333–5

## SOURCE 16   Asquith to Venetia Stanley, 1 August, 1914

We had a Cabinet wh. lasted from 11 to ½ past 1. It is no exaggeration to say that Winston occupied at least half of the time. We came every now and again, near to the parting of the ways: Morley & I think the Impeccable (Simon) are on what may be called the *Manchester Guardian* tack – that we shd. declare now and at once that *in no circumstances* will we take a hand. This no doubt is the view for the moment of the bulk of the party. Ll. George – all for peace – is more sensible & statesmanlike, for keeping the position still open . . . The main controversy pivots upon Belgium & its neutrality. We parted in a fairly amicable mood, and are to sit again tomorrow (Sunday) an almost unprecedented event.

M. and E. Brock (eds.), *The Letters of H.H. Asquith to Venetia Stanley* (Macmillan, 1982) p. 141

# SOURCE 17 Harold Samuel to his Wife, 2 August, 1914

*Samuel was one of the moderate waverers. It was at his suggestion that the Cabinet agreed to endorse the undertakings in relation to the German fleet and the integrity of Belgium.*

Had the matter come to an issue, Asquith would have stood by Grey, in any event, and three others would have remained. I think all the rest of us would have resigned. The consequences would have been either a Coalition Government or a Unionist Government, either of which would have been a war ministry.

K.M. Wilson, 'The British Cabinet's Decision for War', *British Journal of International Studies*, I, 1975, pp. 154–5

# SOURCE 18 Winston Churchill's Assessment of Cabinet Divisions

On Monday began the first of the Cabinets on the European situation, which thereafter continued daily or twice a day. It is to be hoped that sooner or later a detailed account of the movement of opinion in the Cabinet during this period will be compiled and given to the world. There is certainly no reason for anyone to be ashamed of honest and sincere counsel given either to preserve peace or enter upon a just and necessary war. Meanwhile it is only possible, within the bounds of constitutional propriety, to deal in the most general terms with what took place.

The Cabinet was overwhelmingly pacific. At least three-quarters of its members were determined not to be drawn into a European quarrel, unless Britain were herself attacked, which was not likely. Those who were in this mood were inclined to believe first of all that Austria and Serbia would not come to blows; secondly, that if they did, Russia would not intervene; thirdly, if Russia intervened, that Germany would not strike; fourthly, they hoped that if Germany struck at Russia, it ought to be possible for France and Germany to neutralize each other without fighting. They did not believe that if Germany attacked France, she would attack her through Belgium or that if she did the Belgians would forcibly resist; and it must be remembered, that during the whole course of this week Belgium not only never asked for assistance from the guaranteeing Powers but pointedly indicated that she wished to be left alone.

So here were six or seven positions, all of which could be wrangled over and about none of which any final proof could be offered except of events. It was not until Monday, 3 August, that the direct appeal from the King of the Belgians for

French and British help raised an issue which united the overwhelming majority of Ministers and enabled Sir Edward Grey to make his speech that afternoon to the House of Commons.

Winston S. Churchill, *The World Crisis,* vol. I (Thornton Butterworth, 1922), p. 199

## SOURCE 19    Winston Churchill to his Wife, 28 July, 1914

Midnight

My darling one & beautiful,

Everything tends towards catastrophe and collapse. I am interested, geared up and happy. Is it not horrible to be built like that? The preparations have a hideous fascination for me. I pray to God to forgive me for such fearful levity. Yet I wd do my best for peace, & nothing wd induce me wrongfully to strike the blow. I cannot feel that we in this island are in any degree responsible for the wave of madness wh. has swept over the mind of Christendom. I wondered whether those stupid Kings and Emperors cd not assemble together and revivify kingship by saving the nations from hell but we all drift on in a kind of cataleptic trance. As if it was somebody else's operation! . . . God guard us and our long accumulated inheritance. You know how willingly & proudly I wd risk – or give – if need be my period of existence to keep this country great & famous & prosperous & free. But the problems are vy difficult. One has to measure the indefinite and weigh the imponderable.

I feel sure however that if war comes we shall give them a good drubbing . . .

*Winston Churchill,* Companion Volume II, Part 3, pp. 1989–90

## SOURCE 20    John Burns's Diary, 27 July, 1914

*Burns was the only working-class member of the Cabinet. He had first been elected to Parliament in 1892 as an independent Labour candidate. He subsequently joined the Liberal party and in 1905 was made President of the Local Government Board, a post he still held in 1914.*

Why 4 great powers should fight over Servia no fellow can understand . . . It must be averted by all the means in our power. Apart from the merit of the case it is my especial duty to dissociate myself and the principles I hold and the trusteeship for the working classes which I carry from such a universal crime as the contemplated war will be.

Burns MSS, cited in K. Robbins, *Sir Edward Grey* (Cassell, 1971) p. 291

## SOURCE 21  Asquith to Venetia Stanley, 30 July, 1914

Happily I am quite clear in my own mind as to what is right and wrong. I put it down for you in a few sentences:

(1) We have no obligation of any kind to France or Russia to give them military or naval help.

(2) The despatch of the Expeditionary Force to help France at this moment is out of the question and wd serve no object.

(3) We mustn't forget the tie created by our long-standing and intimate friendship with France.

(4) It is against British interests that France should be wiped out as a great power.

(5) We cannot allow Germany to use the Channel as a hostile base.

(6) We have obligations to Belgium to prevent her being utilised and absorbed by Germany.

M. and E. Brock (eds.), *The Letters of H.H. Asquith to Venetia Stanley*, pp. 146–7

## SOURCE 22  Lloyd George to his Wife, 3 August, 1914

I am moving through a nightmare world these days. I have fought hard for peace & succeeded so far in keeping the Cabinet out of it but I am driven to the conclusion that if the small nationality of Belgium is attacked by Germany all my traditions & even prejudices will be engaged on the side of war. I am filled with horror at the prospect. I am even more horrified that I should ever appear to have a share in it but I must bear my share of the ghastly burden though it scorches my flesh to do so.

K.O. Morgan (ed.), *Lloyd George Family Letters, 1885–1936* (OUP, 1973) p. 167

## SOURCE 23  Grey's Speech to the House of Commons, 3 August, 1914

*Grey evidently won the support of the House with this speech; the opponents of intervention, who followed him, E.D. Morel, Arthur Ponsonby and Ramsay MacDonald, were given an unsympathetic hearing. In his speech Grey outlined the government's policies since 1912, but he confined his arguments for British intervention to the naval threat from Germany and the neutrality of Belgium. Grey referred to the promise of British protection given to Cambon, should the German fleet enter the Channel (Source 13), and continued as follows:*

I read that to the House, not as a declaration of war on our part, not as entailing immediate aggressive action on our part, but as binding us to take aggressive action should that contingency arise. Things move hurriedly from hour to hour. Fresh news comes in, and I cannot give this in any formal way; but I understand that the German Government would be prepared, if we would pledge ourselves to neutrality, to agree that its fleet would not attack the Northern Coast of France. I have only heard that shortly before I came to the House, but it is far too narrow an engagement for us. And, Sir, there is the more serious consideration –

becoming more serious every hour – there is the question of the neutrality of
Belgium.

No, Sir, if it be the case that there has been anything in the nature of an
ultimatum to Belgium, asking her to compromise or violate her neutrality,
whatever may have been offered to her in return, her independence is gone if
that holds. If her independence goes, the independence of Holland will follow. I
ask the House, from the point of view of British interests, to consider what may
be at stake. If France is beaten in a struggle of life and death, beaten to her knees,
loses her position as a great power, becomes subordinate to the will and power of
one greater than herself – consequences which I do not anticipate, because I am
sure that France has the power to defend herself with all the energy and ability
and patriotism which she has shown so often – still, if that were to happen, and if
Belgium fell under the same dominating influence, and then Holland, and then
Denmark, opposite to us then would not Mr Gladstone's words come true, that
just opposite to us there would be a common interest against the aggrandisement
of any Power?

It may be said, I suppose, that we might husband our strength, and that,
whatever happened in the course of this war, at the end of it intervene with
effect to put things right, and to adjust them to our own point of view. If, in a
crisis like this, we run away from those obligations of honour and interest as
regards the Belgian Treaty, I doubt whether, whatever material force we might
have at the end, it would be of very much value in face of the respect that we
should have lost. And do not believe, whether a great Power stands outside this
war or not, it is going to be in a position at the end to exert its superior strength.
For us, with a powerful fleet, which we believe able to protect our commerce, to
protect our shores, and to protect our interests, if we are engaged in war, we shall
suffer but little more than we shall suffer even if we stand aside . . .

Grey, Twenty-Five Years, vol. II, pp. 301–6

# SOURCE 24  John, Viscount Morley, *Memorandum on Resignation*

*Morley, the disciple and biographer of Gladstone, first entered a Liberal Cabinet in 1886, as
Secretary for Ireland. In 1905 he became Secretary of State for India, a post which he
relinquished in 1912 for the non-departmental office of Lord President of the Council. He
wrote this Memorandum after the outbreak of war. It is based on the notes he took during the
ten days of hurried negotiations and Cabinet deliberations that preceded it. The memorandum was published unaltered in 1925.*

We were all first alarmed on the Saturday evening [1 August]. Burns himself
took the lead, to good purpose, and intimated in his most downright tones that
the warning to Germany not to try it on against French coasts or ships in the
Channel was more than he could stand, not only because it was practically a
declaration of war on sea, leading inevitably to a war on land, but mainly because
it was the symbol of an alliance with France with whom no such understanding
had hitherto existed . . .

. . .

*Sunday, 2 August*

The Belgian question took its place in today's discussion, but even now only a secondary place. Grey very properly asked leave to warn the German ambassador that, unless Germany was prepared to give us a reply in the sense of the reply we had from France, it would be hard to restrain English feeling on any violation of Belgian neutrality by either combatant. This leave of course we gave him . . . There was a general, but vague, assent to our liabilities under the Treaty of 1839, but there was no assent to the employment of a land force, and, I think, no mention of it.

The plain truth, as I conceive the truth to be, is this. The German line on Belgian neutrality might be met in two ways. One, we might at once make it a *casus belli;* the other, we might protest with direct energy, as the British Government protested on the Russian repudiation in 1870 of the Black Sea Articles of the Treaty of Paris, and push on by diplomatising. What was the difficulty of the second course? Why, our supposed entanglement with France, and nothing else. The precipitate and peremptory blaze about Belgium was due less to indignation at the violation of a treaty than to natural perception of the plea it would furnish for intervention on behalf of France, for expeditionary force, and all the rest of it. Belgium was to take the place that had been taken before as pleas for war, by Morocco and Agadir . . .

. . .

The significance of the French Entente had been rather disingenuously played with, before both Cabinet and Parliament. An entente was evidently more dangerous for us than an alliance. An alliance has definite covenants, an entente is vague, rests on points of honour to be construed by accident and convenience. The Prime Minister and Grey had both of them assured the House of Commons that we had no engagement unknown to the country, yet here we were confronted by engagements that were vast indeed because indefinite and undefinable. The same two Ministers and others had deliberately and frequently, in reply to anxious protests from Harcourt and myself, minimised the significance of the systematic conferences constantly going on between the military and naval officers of these two countries. Then the famous letter to Cambon of 1912 [Source 7] which we had extorted from Grey – what a singularly thin and deceptive document it was turning out.

Grey's firm character had achieved an influence in Europe that was the noblest asset for the fame of England and the glory of peace. In a few hours it would be gone. I could not but be penetrated by the precipitancy of it all. What grounds for expectation that the ruinous waste and havoc of war would be repaired by peace and better terms than were already within reach of reason and persistent patience. When we counted our gains, what would they amount to when reckoned against the ferocious hatred that would burn with inextinguishable fire, for a whole generation at least, between two communities better fitted to understand one another than any other pair in Europe?

John, Viscount Morley, *Memorandum on Resignation* (Macmillan, 1925) pp. 7, 17, 19

## QUESTIONS ON SOURCES 15–24

1. How many distinctive viewpoints within the British Cabinet during the crisis from 27 July to 4 August can you identify (Sources 15–24)? (C)

2. Whose account of these divisions would you regard as most reliable, and why (Sources 15–18)? (E)

3. Would it be correct to say that it was only the invasion of Belgium by Germany that enabled the Cabinet to agree on a declaration of war (Sources 15–24)? (S)

4. 'Churchill was of course for any enterprise which gave him a chance of displaying his navy as an instrument of destruction.' (C. Hobhouse, *Diary*) Hobhouse was Postmaster-General in the Asquith Cabinet in 1914. Is his statement a fair comment on Churchill's attitude to the outbreak of the First World War (Source 19)? (S)

5. 'My own opinion is that L.G.'s mind was really made up from the first, that he knew we would have to go in, and that the invasion of Belgium was, to be cynical, a heaven-sent opportunity for supporting a declaration of war.' (Frances Lloyd George, née Stevenson, Lloyd George's mistress and personal secretary at the time) Do you prefer this explanation of Lloyd George's views to the one he gave to his wife (Source 22)? (E)

6. Do you see any contradictions in the 'few sentences' which Asquith addressed to Venetia Stanley on July 30 (Source 21)? (C)

7. What were the 'obligations of honour and interest as regards the Belgian Treaty' to which Grey referred in Source 23? (S)

8. What does Morley mean by his comment on 'the famous letter to Cambon of 1912' – 'what a singularly thin and deceptive document it was turning out' (Source 24)? (C)

9. What were the chief differences between the policy adopted by Grey and the Cabinet on 3–4 August and the policy advocated by Morley (Source 24)? (C)

10. Compare the predictions made by Grey and Morley as to the likely outcome of British participation in the First World War (Sources 23, 24)? Whose proved to be the more accurate? (S)

---

## 2C   **Press Reaction to the Crisis**

*In 1914 Britain had a lively and politically conscious press. The quality papers included* The Times, *the* Manchester Guardian, *the* Daily Telegraph, *the* Morning Post, *the* Daily News *and the* Daily Chronicle. *These newspapers tended to reflect the political opinions of their proprietors and editors. At one end of the political spectrum the* Morning Post, *owned by Lady Bathurst and edited by Mr H. Gwynne, was strongly conservative. At the other end the*

Daily News, *owned by the Quaker Cadbury family and edited by Mr A.G. Gardiner, represented the radical strand in the Liberal party.* Punch, *though primarily a humorous weekly magazine, has always had a serious side to it, and its cartoons provide a perceptive commentary on current political issues.* Punch *had a radical outlook when it was founded in 1841, but by 1914 under the editorship of Sir Owen Seaman, very much a member of the establishment, it had come to reflect the views of its primarily upper-class readership, if not in any partisan sense. Sources 25–7 include excerpts from all three publications, and illustrate their different interpretations of events from the delivery of the Austrian ultimatum to Serbia on 23 July up to the British declaration of war on 4 August, 1914.*

# SOURCE 25 Press Reaction to the Austrian Ultimatum

### (a) *Morning Post*, Saturday, 25 July

This is not an ordinary ultimatum. It is a demand to Servia to surrender her independence and abandon her sovereignty. If she does not agree to that within forty eight hours notice Austria-Hungary proposes to conquer her . . .

The just cause is always the best. It seems to us that the other powers would do right to point out to the Austro-Hungarian government that the terms of the ultimatum infringe the principles of the equal rights of nations, and are inconsistent with the independence of Servia . . .

### (b) *Morning Post*, Monday, 27 July

In our judgment the Austro-Hungarian ultimatum went beyond the bounds of any legitimate demands. In so far as it did so it was not defensive but an act of aggression. If Austria-Hungary persists in it and uses force she will not only have made herself an aggressor; any action taken to defend Servia from the destruction threatened in that way cannot but be regarded as resistance to aggression. If the alliance with Germany requires support of Austria in this vindictive policy then automatically the force of treaties leads to a war between Austria-Hungary, the ally of Germany and Russia, the ally of France. The desperate nature of such a war is universally understood. What in such an event is the duty of England? It is not defined by any treaty. It consists of moral obligation. England is one of the Powers in deference to whose advice and to whom Servia gave the undertaking quoted in the Austro-Hungarian note. She can therefore not escape the obligation to see that the undertaking is not made the excuse for an attempt to destroy Servia or to humiliate her beyond what is reasonable and just. She cannot quietly assent to one Power constituting herself judge, jury and witness in a case based on an undertaking given not to that Power but to a group of which she herself is one. The war which Austria-Hungary is preparing must put France in the position of having to fight for her very existence. But the existence of France as one of the Great Powers has long been recognised as one of her own vital interests. She cannot look on idle and see France engaged in a struggle for life. The war if it comes is not of France's making. How could Englishmen look Frenchmen in the face if they were in this case in which there is no French aggression, not even a direct French interest, to look on with folded arms?

The impression that England is paralysed or divided against herself or in-different to the fate of her neighbours or to the cause of right is completely erroneous. The policy of Great Britain has been more than once clearly put in general terms by members of the present government. It is essential in the highest interests of this country that Britain should maintain her place and her prestige among the countries of the world. National honour is no party question. If, therefore, matters are pushed, as we devoutly hope they will not be, to extremes, and if the peace of Europe is disturbed, England must take her place by the side of those who are, by the rash haste and immoderation of the policy which dictated the late ultimatum, to be drawn into the vortex of war. If the word mobilisation is pronounced in St Petersburg, Berlin and Paris, it will have to be pronounced in London, also.

### (c) *Daily News*, Saturday, 25 July

The best, indeed the only hope of avoiding yet a third war in the Balkans is the prompt submission of Servia to the demands of Austria-Hungary. Despite the lofty tone of the Note and the accompanying circular, there does not appear to be anything really intolerable in the Austrian demands in view of the undoubtedly grave evidence of cumulative provocation produced. Most of them, despite the needlessly high language in which they are couched, are such as any State has a right to ask of its neighbours. The right of asylum is one thing: the right of another country to make itself into a centre for plots and intrigues against the political integrity of another, culminating in a particularly vile murder is quite another. There is really only one clause in the Austrian demands which might legitimately cause trouble, and that is the demand that the Servian government 'should accept the collaboration in Servia of representatives of the Austro-Hungarian Government in the suppression of the subversive movement directed against the territorial integrity of the monarchy'. This, at least until [the Serbian Prime Minister] Mr Paschitch's professions have been given a fair trial, is scarcely a just demand and should be withdrawn.

But the best way to get it withdrawn so far as Servia is concerned is undoubtedly by prompt submission.

### (d) *Daily News*, Monday, 27 July

Our own task, as Sir John Simon said on Saturday, is that of mediator. We have no interest to serve except that of peace and justice. Sir Edward Grey played a distinguished and successful part in preserving peace through the anxious months of the Balkan Wars. His influence is great and the disinterestedness of this country is admitted. There was never a moment when greater issues hung in the balance than now, or when the detachment of this country from the European camps was a fact of more momentous consequence. If it should prove impossible at this late hour to prevent the outbreak of war between Austria and Servia, it is at least possible to isolate the struggle. If Great Britain, Germany, France and Italy, acting together in good faith, do not achieve that, they will be responsible for the greatest crime in history.

**(e)** *Punch,* **Wednesday, 29 July**

## THE POWER BEHIND.

AUSTRIA (*at the ultimatum stage*). "I DON'T QUITE LIKE
HIS ATTITUDE. SOMEBODY MUST BE BACKING HIM."

## SOURCE 26   Press Reaction to the Austrian Declaration of War on Serbia, 28 July

**(a)** *Morning Post,* **Wednesday, 29 July**

The mode chosen, of making the late assassination a pretext for a war, is provocative of Austria, and well known in Austria to be so. It is a quite deliberate 'daring' Russia to come on, and is apparently to be so extended to a challenge from the Dual Monarchy to the Triple Entente, or to a challenge of the reality or consistency of the Entente, at any rate so far as England is concerned. It is hard to know which would be the greater misfortune for Europe – the acceptance of the challenge and a great war, or the non-acceptance and the consequent domination of the Triple Alliance. It is for Englishmen as fast as they can, to realise the situation and to make up their minds as to the country's duty.

## (b) *Morning Post*, Thursday, 30 July

It is clear that a force which by appearing on time on the battlefield may decide the result might, if it appeared the day after the battle be powerless to change defeat, if defeat there had been, and superfluous if victory had already been gained. The function of England has always been to be the makeweight in the European balance . . .

   Not from motives of animosity to any nation but from a sense of duty to her neighbour, must not England, if war is forced upon Europe, stand by her friendships and play the game?

## (c) *Morning Post,* Friday, 31 July

*England's Clear Duty*
Austria-Hungary has undertaken to bring about by force a change in the conditions of South East Europe, a change which must be detrimental to Russian ideas, interests and policy, and she has declined to discuss the proposed changes with Russia, or indeed with any other power. Russia is placed in the position that she must either acquiesce or fight, and she has ordered the mobilisation of part of her army. If Germany should reply by mobilisation France is, so far as is known, bound to follow suit and a war to begin in which the military and political purpose of Germany would be to crush France. We believe that the general intention of Englishmen, the nation's will, is not to look on the crushing of France, but to take part in the war to prevent its accomplishment.

## (d) *Daily News*, Tuesday, 28 July

Left to herself Russia is not likely to take up that challenge. And as we have said, there is no just ground for doing so. No one has ever yet dared to claim that Russia is the champion of anybody. She has enslaved many, but she has freed none. Her claim to be the Protector of the Slav peoples has no historic basis. If it had she would have as much right to interfere in the interests of the Slavs of the Austrian empire as the Slavs of Servia. When she has interfered in Balkan issues it has been with no high motive, but for entirely selfish ends. And if she interferes now, it will not be for the sake of Servian freedom, which is not threatened, but in the interests of her own far reaching designs. With those designs, neither France nor this country have any sympathy or approval. France is not concerned for a Slav hegemony presided over by the most barbaric power in Europe, even though that Power is her ally. And we hope that she will have the courage to say firmly that she will have no part in saving Servia from chastisement in order to make Russia predominant in the Balkans. For ourselves, it is unthinkable that we should be drawn into any such quarrel. We have done much for the advancement of Russian interests in recent years. We have remained silent while the liberties of Finland have been trodden in the dust, and while Russia is defiant of her agreement with us to preserve the independence and integrity of Persia, has made the northern half of that country into a Russian province. But the suggestion that we should spend British lives and British treasure to establish Russia in the Balkans would be an inconceivable outrage to a democratic country. Our hands are free in this business and we must take care to keep them free. Let us work zealously to preserve peace, but let us remember that the most effective work for peace that we can do is to make it clear that not a British life should be sacrificed for the sake of a Russian hegemony of the Slav world.

### (e) *Daily News*, Thursday, 30 July

But in any case the free peoples of France, England and Italy should refuse to be drawn into the circle of this dynastic struggle. We must not have our civilisation submerged in a sea of blood in order to wipe out a Servian conspiracy.

### (f) *Daily News*, Friday, 31 July

Honour, principle and interest all alike dictate our course, to maintain an absolute neutrality should this lamentable dispute, in which we have neither lot nor part, bring war to the great continental Powers. By maintaining that attitude now and by making it plain to all the world, we shall do much to avert the colossal infamy of war; for we shall dissipate all suspicion as to the sincerity of our efforts for peace, and we shall disillusion any Power which is tempted to drive matters to a crisis because it counts on our aid. By standing apart from any conflict we preserve for Europe in the worst event the precious position of an impartial mediator.

### (g) *Daily News*, Saturday, 1 August

What is the duty of the Government? It is its duty not only to keep out of the war should war come, but to announce here and now its rigorous neutrality. That would be the greatest contribution it could make to the preservation of peace, for it is the hope of our support in arms which is encouraging Russia to draw the sword.

## SOURCE 27   Press Reactions to the Invasion of Belgium

*The* Morning Post, *having urged support for France and Russia throughout the crisis, naturally backed the government's stand over Belgium and the declaration of war. The* Daily News *continued to voice its reservations.*

### (a) *Daily News*, Tuesday, 4 August

Sir Edward Grey contends that we are bound to make a violation of the neutrality of Belgium a *casus belli*. We shall not ask whether he would have treated a similar violation of France as a *casus belli;* but we shall point out that Sir Edward did not assert that we are bound to defend Belgium's neutrality by force of arms. It is worth noting that all the Belgian government asked of us was diplomatic intervention . . . If we are under no treaty obligations in the matter of Belgium, then there is no question here of our honour. The real argument put forward here by Sir Edward is that of our interests. He declared that our vital interests are bound up with the neutrality of Belgium, and he drew a picture of all the neutral states of Northern Europe, – Belgium, Holland, Denmark, being absorbed by Germany. The picture does not persuade because we see no probability of its representing the facts, and while Sir Edward asserted our vital interest in Belgian neutrality he did not prove it, and with infinite regret we must confess ourselves unconvinced.

### (b) *Daily News*, Wednesday, 5 August

We place on record our conviction that it was possible, and that it would have been just and prudent and statesmanlike, for England to have remained neutral. We shall record that a mistaken course of foreign policy, pursued over ten years, the departure from our policy of splendid isolation, has led to the terrible conflict on which we are now engaged . . .

### (c) *Punch*, 12 August, 1914

BRAVO, BELGIUM!

**(d)** *Punch*, **12 August, 1914**

## FOR FRIENDSHIP AND HONOUR.

---

## QUESTIONS ON SOURCES 25–7

1. Compare the descriptions of the Austrian ultimatum to Serbia given by the *Morning Post*, the *Daily News* and *Punch* (Sources 25(a)–(c), (e)). How do you account for the differences? (C/S)

2. Why did the *Daily News* take such a hostile view of Russian intentions (Source 26(d))? Was there any justification for its view? (S)

3. How soon in the crisis of 1914 was the *Morning Post* prepared to advocate British participation in a European war, and on what grounds (Sources 25(a), (b); 26(a)–(c))? (C)

4. Does Source 27(c) fairly summarise German policy towards Belgium on 3–4 August, 1914? (E)

5. Compare the concepts of national honour held by the *Morning Post*, the *Daily News* and *Punch* during the 1914 crisis (Sources 25(b), 26(b), 26(f), 27(d)). (S)

6. Would you concur with the verdict of the *Daily News* on 5 August, 1914 on the conduct of British foreign policy in the previous ten years (Source 27(b))? (S)

# LOCATION OF SOURCES

1    J. Wilson, *A Life of Sir Henry Campbell-Bannerman* (Constable, 1973) pp. 523–4

2    Viscount Grey, *Twenty-Five Years,* vol. I (Hodder & Stoughton, 1925) pp. 72–4, 79–81

3    Asquith Papers, cited in J. Macintosh, *The British Cabinet* (Methuen, 1968) pp. 338–9

4    (a)  Grey, *op. cit.,* vol. I, p. 96

     (b)  D. Lloyd George, *War Memoirs,* vol. I (Ivor Nicholson & Watson, 1933) pp. 49–50

5    *Winston Churchill,* Companion Volume II, Part 3: 1911–14, (Heinemann, 1969) p. 1567

6    *Ibid.,* pp. 1638–9

7    Grey, *op. cit.,* vol. I, pp. 97–8

8    Zara S. Steiner, *Britain and the Origins of the First World War* (Macmillan, 1977) p. 104

9    I. Geiss, *July 1914* (Batsford, 1967) pp. 183–4

10   *Ibid.,*  pp. 206–7

11   *Ibid.,*  pp. 300–1

12   *Ibid.,*  pp. 315–16

13   Grey, *op. cit.,* vol. II, p. 301

14   G.P. Gooch and H. Temperley (eds.), *British Documents on the Origins of the War, 1898–1914,* vol. XI (HMSO, 1926) p. 314

15   Grey, *op. cit.,* vol. I, pp. 333–5

16   M. and E. Brock (eds.), *The Letters of H.H. Asquith to Venetia Stanley* (Macmillan, 1982) p. 141

17   K.M. Wilson, 'The British Cabinet's Decision for War', *British Journal of International Studies,* I, 1975, pp. 154–5

18   Winston S. Churchill, *The World Crisis,* vol. I (Thornton Butterworth, 1922) p. 199

19   *Winston Churchill,* Companion Volume II, Part 3, pp. 1989–90

20   Burns MSS, cited in K. Robbins, *Sir Edward Grey* (Cassell, 1971) p. 291

21   M. and E. Brock (eds.), *op. cit.,* pp. 146–7

22   K.O. Morgan (ed.), *Lloyd George Family Letters* (OUP, 1973) p. 167

23   Grey, *op cit.,* vol. II, pp. 301–6

24   John, Viscount Morley, *Memorandum on Resignation* (Macmillan, 1925) pp. 7, 17, 19

25–7 Microfilm copies of the *Morning Post* and the *Daily News,* July and August 1914, Bodleian Library, Oxford; *Punch,* July and August 1914

# Case Study 2

# THE BATTLE OF PASSCHENDAELE

## INTRODUCTION

The First World War was won and lost on the Western Front. It was here that the best of Europe's manhood was sacrificed in the pursuit of victory. The reasons for this lie in the strategy adopted by the German High Command in August 1914. Under the plan devised by Count von Schlieffen, Chief of the German General Staff from 1892 to 1905, German armies on the outbreak of war were to sweep round the north of France's defences and to take her armies in the flank and rear. Paris was to be occupied within six weeks. The plan was designed to knock France out of the war before her ally Russia had time to mobilise.

In the event, the Schlieffen Plan narrowly failed. German armies were halted at the battle of the Marne. British and German forces then engaged in a race to the sea which left Germany in control of Antwerp and the Belgian coast southwards as far as Ostend and Zeebrugge, while the British controlled the coast up to Nieuport. By the end of 1914 a line of trenches, 200 miles long, stretched from the English Channel to the Swiss frontier. The strategy of both sides was now geared to breaking this stalemate. Trench warfare and the weapons available at the time imposed their own constraints on the battlefield. This was a war dominated by artillery and the machine gun. Every battle on the Western Front developed into a killing match: a preliminary bombardment, followed by a painful advance across no man's land until the enemy trenches were reached.

The advantage usually rested with the defenders, who would remain protected in their trenches while the attacking infantry, weighed down with up to 40 kilograms of equipment, advanced in the open towards them, vulnerable to rifle and machine gun fire, and to the defenders' counter barrages. But the sheer weight of the artillery barrages which preceded an offensive, and the pressure from higher command to counterattack and recover any lost ground, meant that casualties were often as high on the defending as they were on the attacking side. This is what came to be meant by a war of attrition, which justified, in Haig's view, the appalling losses sustained by British armies in the offensives of 1916 and 1917.

The battle of Passchendaele epitomises the awful dilemma facing the British and French commanders on the Western Front. If Germany was to be forced to make

peace on terms acceptable to the Allies this could be done only by imposing unacceptable losses on the German army and forcing her to abandon the territory she occupied
in France and Belgium. Such losses could not be inflicted if both sides remained on the
defensive. Hence it was necessary, in Haig's view, to launch continuous offensives
which would compel the Germans to stand and fight. One of his reasons for preferring
Flanders in 1917 was because he knew this to be an area which Germany dare not
abandon.

By the end of 1916 the First World War had reached a critical stage. The German
attack on Verdun, lasting from February to December 1916, had cost each side
approximately 300 000 casualties (killed, wounded and missing). The British offensive
on the Somme, lasting from July to November, was even more expensive, British
casualties alone being reckoned at 415 000. Neither side could claim to have won a
decisive advantage – the front lines had barely changed and reserves of manpower
were still available to both sides.

In the early months of 1917 several new factors came into play. In January, Germany
announced a policy of unrestricted U-boat warfare. It was calculated that if 800 000
tons of shipping could be sunk every month Britain could be starved into surrender.
This total was achieved for the first time in April 1917. But German policy also helped
to provoke American entry into the war on the side of the *Entente* in the same month.
Although the United States was quite unprepared for war, her huge resources of men
and materials would sooner or later become available. This new threat was counter-
balanced, however, by the outbreak of the Russian Revolution in March 1917. Russia
was in a state of political turmoil from that date onward, and in no condition to
threaten Germany's eastern borders.

Thus the odds were evenly balanced. If Germany could sustain the submarine
offensive and hold out on the Western Front, she might force Britain and France to
make peace before the United States could make her presence felt. These were the
circumstances in which the battle of Passchendaele was conceived.

# 1. PLANNING THE CAMPAIGN

Planning for the battle has been traced back to a meeting of the British War Committee
on 20 November, 1916 (Source 1), when the desirability of denying Germany the use
of Ostend and Zeebrugge for her U-boats was first mooted. But the French had other
priorities. Their new Commander-in-Chief, General Nivelle, hoped for a quick
victory by launching a series of supposedly surprise attacks in the Aisne area (see
Map 1). At a conference held in London on 15–16 January, 1917, Nivelle succeeded in
getting Lloyd George's approval for the plan, and at a subsequent conference at Calais
on 26–7 February it was agreed that British military operations should conform to
Nivelle's plans. Accordingly, British forces put in a diversionary attack at Arras on
9 April, prior to the launching of Nivelle's offensive on 16 April. Though the British
gained their objectives, at a high cost, the French offensive went disastrously wrong,
and incurred some 180 000 casualties.

North Sea

ENGLAND

HOLLAND (NEUTRAL)

Folkestone

Ostend

English Channel

Passchendaele

Ypres

BELGIUM (OCCUPIED)

Boulogne

B.E.F. ZONE

GERMANY

Montreuil G.H.Q.

R. Somme

Arras

LUXEMBOURG

Albert

Amiens

N. FRANCE (OCCUPIED)

Rouen

R. Aisne

BATTLE OF
VERDUN

Rheims

Verdun

Paris

R. Seine

FRANCE

Arras  9 April–3 May

Aisne  16–29 April

Passchendaele  31 July–15 November

French front line
inside Germany

THE FRONT LINES

Belgian  — — —

British  - - - - -

French  ———

N

SWITZERLAND
(NEUTRAL)

0        50        100        150 km

0      25        50        75        100 miles

**Map 1**    Allied offensives in 1917 (based on M. Middlebrook, *The First*
*Day of the Somme, 1 July, 1916,* Penguin 1971, p. 45)

Two consequences followed. There was a dangerous collapse of morale in the French army, leading to an outright refusal in the case of some regiments to return to the Front. There were fifty-five mutinies in French units between 29 April and 10 June, 1917. But Nivelle's failure also freed Haig from any obligation to support a French offensive which had now come to a premature end. He was now in a position to carry out the independent offensive in Flanders on which he had set his heart.

Planning for this began in earnest in May. Haig's first objective was to extend the Ypres salient to absorb the high ground surrounding it to the north, east and south, currently in German hands. The salient (technically a piece of land jutting out into enemy-held territory) was overlooked by German artillery, and therefore its defence was a constant drain on manpower. Second, Haig hoped to break right through the German lines east and north of Ypres and, in combination with amphibious landings on the Belgian coast, sweep round to Ostend and Bruges. At best, Haig believed his offensive might pave the way for the invasion of Germany and bring the war to an end in 1917. At worst, he would have worn down much of the German army and won a much more easily defended salient round Ypres. Haig's plans were first seriously discussed by special committee of the War Cabinet on 19 June and discussions continued hotly until 25 June (see Sources 11(a)–(c)). Lloyd George had very serious reservations about the whole enterprise, as did many of his colleagues. Had it not been for the insistence of Jellicoe (First Sea Lord) that the war would be lost if German submarines continued to use Ostend and Zeebrugge, Haig might well have been overruled. As it was, the most that the War Cabinet would agree to was authorising Haig to continue with his preparations, pending the securing of support from the French, on which Lloyd George insisted.

Haig issued his operation orders on 5 July (Source 12) but it was not until 20 July that the War Cabinet gave their grudging and qualified approval for the offensive to go ahead (Source 14). Thus the Flanders offensive was conceived in confusion, and its parentage remains a matter of dispute.

# 2. MILITARY OPERATIONS

The battle of Passchendaele lasted from 31 July to 15 November, 1917, but the village from which its name derives was fought over only in the final phase. An alternative title is the Third Battle of Ypres (the first occurred in October 1914, the second in February 1915). In many ways this is a more appropriate description of the fighting that took place, for it was all concentrated within a radius of 5 miles of the shattered city. The breakthrough for which Haig hoped never occurred, and the battle essentially consisted of a series of assaults on the German strong points surrounding the British positions.

These were preceded by one of the few successes achieved by British attacks in 1917, the battle of Messines on 7 June. On this occasion General Plumer's Second Army launched their infantry advance just after the detonation of nineteen huge mines which had been successfully planted beneath the German front line. The shock produced by these explosions enabled the infantry to achieve all their objectives, and at least one of the ridges overlooking the Ypres salient was now in allied hands.

The Passchendaele offensive proper began with a barrage on German positions on 15 July. The first infantry assaults began on 31 July, and by the end of the day British forces had advanced on a broad front a distance of between 1 and 2 miles. Casualties were high, and heavy rain in the afternoon brought with it the hazard that was to dominate military operations thereafter. The artillery barrage had effectively destroyed the network of drainage ditches needed to carry away surface water from the heavy clay soil that predominated in the Flanders plain. Before long the battlefield became a sea of mud, in which all movement was difficult and, in the case of guns and tanks, virtually impossible. An unusually, but not unprecedentedly, wet August compounded the problem. Because of the weather, General Gough, commanding the Fifth Army, postponed his next offensive until 10 August, when an unsuccessful attempt was made to clear the area east of Ypres known as the Gheluvelt Plateau. On 16 August a full-scale offensive along the whole of the Fifth Army's front was launched. It resulted in the capture of Langemarck on the left, but few gains elsewhere. It was at this point in the battle that Gough advised the abandonment of the attack (Source 21). Haig would not agree, but conceded that further offensives should be delayed until the ground had dried out.

The next phase of the battle did not begin until 20 September, and was entrusted to General Plumer's Second Army, on the right of the British line. There followed in quick succession the battles of Menin Road (20 September), Polygon Wood (26 September) and Broodseinde (4 October). By the standards of the Western Front, these were accounted victories and achieved their limited objectives. General Harington, Plumer's Chief of Staff, reckoned that it was only after Broodseinde that conditions became really intolerable.

The last phase of the battle began on 9 October with an unsuccessful attempt by exhausted troops to capture the hamlet of Poelkapelle on the left flank. An attack on Passchendaele village on 12 October was successfully repulsed. A further attack with fresh Canadian troops took place on 26 October, and by 6 November Passchendaele village was finally occupied. The battle then petered out, Haig having given the order to end all offensive operations on the Flanders front on 15 November.

# 3. RESULTS OF THE BATTLE OF PASSCHENDAELE

The consequences of the battle, as will be seen in Sources 29–35, have been much disputed. The derisory territorial gains made by the British must be set against the diversion of German troops to Flanders at a time when the French armies were still recovering from the mutinies of April–June. Casualties, it has been claimed, were as high on the German as on the British side. To Haig, at General Headquarters 20 miles behind the line, German casualty figures and the capture of the high ground above Ypres made Passchendaele a success. To Lloyd George the British losses, which he had feared and anticipated, were proof of failure and of Haig's incompetence. Of the generals actually involved in the campaign, few besides Haig could escape a sense of remorse, while the troops who had to endure the fighting could see little purpose or reward in their sufferings.

In this case study the sources have been divided into three groups which cover respectively the concept and planning of the battle of Passchendaele (Sources 1–17); military operations between 31 July and 6 November, 1917 (Sources 18–28); and the consequences of the battle (Sources 29–35). Sources have been drawn from official records, diaries made at the time, the memoirs of the generals and politicians concerned, and personal reminiscences. The reconstruction of a battle is always a difficult exercise. In the fog of war confusion is only to be expected, and there is a marked disparity between the perceptions of commanders, isolated from the battlefield, and the experiences of those actually engaged in the fighting. Controversies surround the battle of Passchendaele. It was planned and undertaken against the wishes of Lloyd George, the British Prime Minister at the time. Haig's handling of the battle has been severely criticised. Its results have been disputed. For all these reasons it provides an object lesson in the use of evidence, as well as having the dubious distinction of being the scene of the ugliest fighting on the Western Front.

# FURTHER READING

## Background

B.H. Liddell Hart, *A History of the First World War* (Cassell, 1930)
J. Terraine, *The First World War, 1914–18* (Papermac, 1984)
Sir L. Woodward, *Great Britain and the War of 1914–18* (Methuen, 1967)

## The Politicians' View

Lord Hankey, *The Supreme Command,* vol. II (Allen & Unwin, 1961)
D. Lloyd George, *War Memoirs,* vol. IV (Ivor Nicholson & Watson, 1934)

## The Generals' View

R. Blake (ed.), *The Private Papers of Douglas Haig* (Eyre & Spottiswoode, 1953)
Duff Cooper, *Haig,* vol. II (Faber & Faber, 1936)
J. Terraine, *Douglas Haig, The Educated Soldier* (Hutchinson, 1963)
General Sir Hubert Gough, *The Fifth Army,* (Hodder & Stoughton, 1931)
Brigadier-General John Charteris, *At GHQ* (Cassell, 1931)

## The Soldiers' View

Guy Chapman, *A Passionate Prodigality* (Buchan & Enright, 1985)
E. Norman Gladden, *Ypres 1917* (William Kimber, 1967)
Lynn MacDonald, *They Called It Passchendaele* (Michael Joseph, 1978)

## Documentary Material

Sir James Edmonds (ed.), *The Official History of the War in France and Belgium, 1917,* vol. II
    (Macmillan, 1948)
J.H. Boraston (ed.), *Sir Douglas Haig's Despatches* (Dent, 1919)
J. Terraine, *The Road to Passchendaele* (Leo Cooper, 1977)

# SOURCE MATERIAL 1
# Planning the Campaign

*Sources 1–17 cover the inception and planning of the Flanders offensive and relate to: A. the period from November 1916 up to March 1917, and the launching of Nivelle's offensive (Sources 1–5); B. the period from April to June 1917, and Haig's plans and the arguments in the War Cabinet over their adoption (Sources 6–11); C. Haig's operation orders and the War Cabinet's response to them (Sources 12–17).*

## 1A The Idea of an Offensive in Flanders, November 1916–March 1917

**SOURCE 1**   Draft of a Letter Prepared for Asquith's Signature, and Addressed to Sir William Robertson, Chief of the Imperial General Staff (CIGS), 21 November, 1916

*There is a personal note at the top of the draft which reads: 'It was prepared by direction of the Prime Minister for him to send to the CIGS as a result of a discussion, between the Cabinet Ministers forming the War Committee, on Monday afternoon, 20th November. Before it was sent, however, Sir William Robertson stated that the matter was to be discussed between General Sir Douglas Haig, the First Sea Lord and CIGS on Thursday afternoon. Consequently, the Prime Minister decided not to send the letter. The draft, however, was sent to the CIGS on 22nd November in connection with the forthcoming conference.' Lloyd George comments: 'However, if the letter had been despatched it contains no "instructions" for a military offensive in Flanders. Here is the unfinished and unsigned draft.'*

10 Downing Street,
21 November, 1916

After you left the War Committee yesterday a very important discussion took place on the question of the submarine menace, and more particularly in regard to the protection of the routes through the Narrow Seas to France and Holland. The War Committee were absolutely unanimous on the very great desirability, if it is practicable, of some military action, designed either to occupy Ostend and Zeebrugge, or at least to render those ports useless as bases for destroyers and submarines . . . There is no operation of war to which the War Committee would attach greater importance than the successful occupation, or at least the deprivation to the enemy, of Ostend, and especially Zeebrugge. I desire therefore that the General Staff, in consultation with the Admiralty as necessary, shall give the matter their closest attention and that you will report to me personally at an early date what action you consider feasible.

*Lloyd George comments: 'Mr Asquith left Office on the 7th December, and if a report was ever presented to him, nothing seems to have been decided by him. There was no further discussion on the subject in the Asquith War Committee, nor did the War Cabinet consider the Project until June, 1917.'*

D. Lloyd George, *War Memoirs,* vol. IV (Ivor Nicholson & Watson, 1934) pp. 2119–20

## SOURCE 2   Letter from Sir William Robertson to Marshall Joffre, 1 December, 1916

*Joffre was still the French Commander-in-Chief at this time. After stressing the need to maintain good sea communications between Britain and France, Robertson continued:*

. . . and in these circumstances my Government desire that the occupation of Ostend and Zeebrugge should form one of the objectives of the campaign next year. I am accordingly instructing Sir Douglas Haig to place himself in communication with you with a view to this operation being given a place in the general plans of operations for next year, and to the necessary preparations being made to carry it out.

W. ROBERTSON

Lloyd George, *War Memoirs,* vol. IV, pp. 2116–17

## SOURCE 3   Haig's Diary, Sunday, 10 December, 1916

*Haig kept a diary throughout the war. It was usually written up on the evening of the day when the events he relates occurred.*

Gen. des Vallières [Chief of the French Mission at British HQ] brought me a plan of operations which he had received from Chantilly dated December 7th. Its objective is the capture of the Belgian Coast by a combined operation of the British Army and Fleet, French and Belgians, all to be under a British General. This is practically the scheme at which I have aimed for the past twelve months. There are some modifications in the number of divisions to be employed. It is most satisfactory that Gen. Joffre has at last come round to see the advantage of carrying out such an operation and has at last agreed that the Belgians and a French contingent should operate under me (or some other British General if circumstances require it).

R. Blake (ed.), *The Private Papers of Douglas Haig* (Eyre & Spottiswoode, 1953) p. 184

## SOURCE 4   Convention Agreed at a Meeting of the War Cabinet in London, 15–16 January, 1917

*It was at this meeting that Nivelle gained British approval for his offensive. Lloyd George was present. The operations referred to are those planned by Nivelle.*

5. In case these operations do not achieve the success which is expected and which ought to be very rapidly attained, the battle will be broken off by agree-

ment, in order to allow the British Armies to engage in other operations on a front further north, in co-operation with the Belgian Army and the French Nieuport Group.

Sir James Edmonds (ed.), *Official History of the War, 1917*, vol. I (Macmillan, 1940)
Appendix 8, p. 16

## SOURCE 5   Haig's Diary, 14 March, 1917

*In this entry Haig records a further meeting of the War Cabinet which he attended, and at which he explained 'the general plan agreed upon by Nivelle and myself'.*

This is to:

1. Continue pressing the enemy back with advanced guards wherever he is giving way.

2. To launch our attacks as soon as possible.

3. But in view of these attacks falling in the air, at once to prepare for attacks elsewhere.

As to the British Army, my plan based on the foregoing is:

1. To continue to make all preparations (as arranged) for 1st and 3rd Armies, keeping adequate reserves available either to support my 2nd Army (Ypres) or to exploit the success of our attacks near Arras. These Reserves are to be obtained from the 5th Army.

2. *If successful* at Arras, exploit with all Reserves and the Cavalry.

3. *If not successful*, prepare to launch attacks near Ypres to clear the Belgian Coast. All Cavalry will be required probably if this attack is successful. The attack on the Messines Ridge might be made in May if desirable.

Blake, *The Private Papers of Douglas Haig*, p. 212

## QUESTIONS ON SOURCES 1–5

1. Why was the letter in Source 1 sent to Robertson, but left unsigned by Asquith? Why does Lloyd George draw attention to this omission? (C)

2. Is Lloyd George correct in saying that it contains 'no instructions' for a military offensive in Flanders? (C)

3. What were the essential differences between the plan referred to by Haig in Source 3, and that referred to by him in Source 5? What had happened in the meantime to produce the change? (C/S)

4. Is Lloyd George correct to say that 'There was no further discussion on the subject in the Asquith War Committee, nor did the War Cabinet consider the Project until June, 1917.' (Source 1)? (S)

5. What further insight into Haig's views and motives in the Flanders offensive can be obtained from his diary entries for 10 December, 1916 and 14 March, 1917 (Sources 3 and 5)? (S)

6. How strongly committed was the War Committee, later the War Cabinet, to an offensive in Flanders, prior to the failure of Nivelle's offensive (Sources 1–5)? (S)

*Under Nivelle's plan, the British offensive at Arras was duly launched on 9 April, 1917. After some initial success, the advance became literally bogged down, and where Cavalry were employed the results were predictably disastrous. The French offensive on the Aisne began on 16 April. It was clear from the outset that German defences had not been subdued by the preliminary bombardment, and casualties were very high. On 29 April the first mutiny in a French front-line unit occurred. It was evident that Nivelle's high hopes had come to nought, and Haig's alternative plan for an attack in Flanders could now go ahead – but in circumstances that were hardly propitious. Not only had the French armies suffered a serious defeat, their reliability was now in question.*

## 1B   Arguments over the Planned Offensive, April–July 1917

### SOURCE 6   The General and Military Situation, particularly on the Western Front, 29 April, 1917

*This Memorandum was drawn up by General Smuts, a member of the Imperial War Cabinet highly regarded as a military strategist after his successes against the British in the Boer War.*

I feel the danger of a purely defensive policy so gravely that I would make the following suggestions in case the French carry out such a policy. In that case we should make them take back a substantial part of their line now occupied by us. As they would require no great reserve for offensive purposes, they would be in a position to do so. Our forces should then be concentrated towards the north, and part should go to the rear as a strategic reserve, while the rest should endeavour to recover the northern coast of Belgium and drive the enemy from Zeebrugge and Ostend . . .

J. Terraine, The Road to Passchendaele (Leo Cooper, 1977) p. 80

### SOURCE 7   Haig to War Cabinet, OAD, 428: 'The Present Situation and Future Plans', 1 May, 1917

*There is no record that this important paper was discussed by the War Cabinet, although it was addressed to them. In it Haig announced that 'Preliminary measures to enable me to undertake operations to clear the Belgian coast have been in hand for some time and are fairly well advanced'. He stressed the need for French reinforcements of men and heavy guns, and concluded with the following arguments for the coming offensive.*

The guiding principles on which my general scheme of action is based are those which have always proved successful in war from time immemorial, viz, that the first step must always be to wear down the enemy's power of resistance until he is so weakened that he will be unable to withstand a decisive blow; then to deliver the decisive blow; and finally, to reap the fruit of victory.

The enemy has already weakened appreciably; but a long time is required to wear down such great numbers of troops composed of fine fighting material, and he is still fighting with such energy and determination that the situation is not yet ripe for the decisive blow. Our action must therefore continue for the present to be of a wearing down character until his power of resistance has been further reduced . . .

Under the conditions I have stated success in this attempt is now, in my opinion, reasonably possible and would have valuable results on land and sea; while even if a full measure of success is not gained we shall be attacking the enemy on a front where he cannot refuse to fight, and where, therefore, our purpose of wearing him down can be given effect to – while even a partial success will considerably improve our defensive position in the YPRES Salient and thus reduce the heavy wastage which must otherwise be expected to occur there next winter as in the past.

Terraine, *The Road to Passchendaele*, p. 84

# SOURCE 8  Haig to Robertson, 28 May, 1917

*In this letter Haig refers to a previous one from Robertson, warning him that 'we could not expect to get any large numbers of men in the future, but only scraps'.*

As to what the effect of the curtailment of the Drafts in the future may be (as foreshadowed in your letter), it is difficult to estimate until we know what is meant by 'only scraps'. There seems little doubt, however, that victory on the Western Front means victory everywhere and a lasting peace. And I have further no doubt that the British Army in France is capable of doing it, given *adequate drafts and guns* [Haig's italics].

Another conclusion seems also clear to me, and that is that the Germans can no longer attack England by means of a landing on her coasts. Consequently the time has now arrived for sending every available man to reinforce the Divisions now in France.

Terraine, *The Road to Passchendaele*, p. 107

# SOURCE 9  General Sir Henry Wilson's Diary

*Wilson was Director of Military Operations from 1910 to 1914. He served on the Western Front from 1914 to 1916, and in March 1917 was made Liaison Officer to French military headquarters, a position he held until June 1917. He saw a good deal of Nivelle, the French Commander-in-Chief in the early part of 1917, and then of Pétain, Nivelle's successor. His diary was written up every night, and excerpts from it were incorporated in the biography of Wilson written by Sir C.E. Callwell, published in 1927.*

*20 May*
I had a very interesting interview with Pétain. I wanted to impress upon him the danger of allowing Haig to carry out his big offensive towards Ostend, an

operation which will cost him heavy losses over many months' fighting, if the French are not to do likewise. I told him that he must either do the same as Haig, or else must state now, and in the clearest and most emphatic manner, that he is not going to do so, and specify what he is going to do. This was all new to him. But he agreed and thanked me for speaking so openly.

He said that he could not attack like Haig, because he was already holding far too long a line and we were holding too short a line; that he entirely disagreed with any idea of distant objectives; that he was opposed to the Somme procedure; that he would make three or four small attacks for limited objectives and when the objectives were reached fighting would cease. In short, he made it clear that all I had written in my Memorandum to the War Cabinet on April 30 was absolutely correct. This pleased me. He told me that, in his opinion, Haig's attack towards Ostend was certain to fail, and that his effort to disengage Ostend and Zeebrugge was a hopeless one. So I replied that this made it all the more imperative for him to make his position and plans absolutely clear . . .

*2 June*
Foch [French Chief of Staff at the time] wanted to know who it was who wanted Haig to go 'on a duck's march through the inundations to Ostend and Zeebrugge'. He thinks the whole thing futile, fantastic and dangerous, and I confess I agree and always have. Haig always seems to think that when he has got to Roulers and Thorout he has solved the question. So Foch is entirely opposed to this enterprise, Jellicoe notwithstanding.

> Sir C.E. Callwell, *The Life of Field Marshal Sir Henry Wilson,* vol. I (Cassell, 1927)
> pp. 354–5, 359

## SOURCE 10   Haig to Robertson, OAD, 478: 'The Present Situation and Future Plans', 12 June, 1917

*In this despatch, Haig argues strongly for maintaining pressure on Germany on the Western Front, and for carrying on with plans to advance from Ypres.*

In conclusion, I desire to make it clear that, whatever force may be placed at my disposal, my undertaking will be limited to what it is reasonable to succeed in.

Given sufficient force, (provided no great transfer of German troops is made, in time, from East to West), it is probable that the Belgian coast could be cleared this summer, and the defeats on the German troops entailed in doing so might quite possibly lead to their collapse.

Without sufficient force I shall not attempt to clear the coast and my efforts will be restricted to gaining such victories as are within reach, thereby improving my position for the winter and opening up possibilities for further operations hereafter if and when the necessary means are provided.

A definition of 'sufficient force' must depend on developments in the general situation; but provided that does not grow less satisfactory than at present I estimate that even the full programme may not prove beyond reach with the number of divisions now at my disposal, if brought up to and maintained at establishment of men and guns. An increase in the forces available would, of course, give still greater prospects of complete success.

Terraine, *The Road to Passchendaele*, pp. 134–5

## SOURCE 11 Deliberations of the War Policy Committee and the War Cabinet, 11 June–18 July, 1917

*On 8 June a small committee of the War Cabinet, consisting of Lloyd George, Curzon, Milner, Smuts and Sir Maurice Hankey (Secretary to the Cabinet) was set up to consider war policy (subsequently referred to as the War Policy Committee). It met on sixteen occasions between 11 June and 18 July, when Hankey produced its final Report and Recommendations. The War Cabinet as a whole also continued to meet during this period, and authorised Haig to press ahead with preparations for his offensive on 25 June. It was not, however, until 21 July that Haig finally gained the War Cabinet's approval to launch the battle. The following three excerpts describe some of the discussions that took place, as seen from the point of view of the participants.*

### (a) Hankey's Diary, 30 June

For the last ten days I have been too desperately busy to write my diary at all. The heavy work of the Cabinet Committee on War Policy, which for reasons of secrecy I have had to work single handed, often without even my shorthand clerk, has been an overwhelming burden on top of the Cabinet work. Haig came over on the 19th and stayed for a week holding frequent conferences with the Committee on War Policy. There was a regular battle royal (conducted in the best possible spirit) between Lloyd George on the one hand and Robertson and Haig on the other . . . On the evening of the 20th there was a dinner at Curzon's attended by the Prime Minister, Milner, Smuts and myself, Bonar Law joining after dinner, when we adjourned to the terrace and thrashed the matter out until past midnight. It was a very interesting evening. All the week the controversy went on, but on Monday (June 25), after the Committee had adjourned to give Robertson and Haig time to think it over, they adhered to their opinion and Lloyd George felt that he could not press his amateur opinions and over-rule them, so he gave in, and Haig was authorised to continue his preparations. The final decision, however, was postponed until after a Conference with the French, as Lloyd George declines to agree until assured that the French will do their bit by attacking simultaneously . . .

Lord Hankey, *The Supreme Command*, vol. II (Allen & Unwin, 1961) pp. 682–3

### (b) Lloyd George's Memoirs

In the course of the discussions that took place between the War Policy Committee of the Cabinet and the Commander-in-Chief and the Chief of the Imperial General Staff and the conversations before and after the formal meetings, Ministers were misled on several critical points.

First of all we were misled as to the French attitude towards the offensive. This was vital, for without their active and whole-hearted cooperation the attack could not hope to succeed. When the Germans were almost equal in numbers and superior in artillery to the combined forces of the British and French, an offensive by one of them alone was doomed to failure. On this point the following facts were concealed:-

1. Ministers were told confidentially that the offensive was urged upon us in the first instance as the only means of saving France from collapse, just as the pressmen were subsequently informed in confidence that its continuance was attributable to French entreaties that we should keep on fighting. We were not informed that, so far from urging us on, the leading French generals had done their best to dissuade us, and had stated emphatically that they condemned the whole project and thought it a foolish venture, which must fail. They also made it clear to us that the greatest service we could render to them would be to take over more of their line. They had conveyed these opinions to Sir Douglas Haig and Sir William Robertson. These eminent Generals, in stating their case for the scheme, had concealed these important facts from the Government.

2. The salient facts as to the condition of the French Army and the extent of the demoralisation in its ranks were also withheld or minimised . . .

3. We were not informed that the new Commander-in-Chief of the French Army, and some of his leading Generals, favoured a combined attack on the Italian Front.

In order to persuade us that the time was opportune we were told by the Commander-in-Chief that we should have a superiority of two to one in infantry – it was untrue; that the enemy had no effective reserves – that was not in accordance with the facts; that the German morale was so broken that they would not put up anything like the resistance which they had hitherto offered – that was misleading; that they had inaccurate guns and inadequate ammunition – we found otherwise. He minimised the German reserve of manpower and informed the Cabinet that 'if the fighting was kept up at its present intensity for six months, Germany would be at the end of her available manpower'. . .

*Lloyd George goes on to examine the ground selected for the offensive, and the weather conditions that might have been anticipated in August.*

The War Committee were not made acquainted with this 'careful investigation' of the records and what they portended in the way of 'enhanced difficulties', and it will be found that in the whole discussions with the War Committee, not a word was said about the meteorological drawbacks and the peculiar conditions which rendered the terrain of the struggle especially disadvantageous for a sustained attack.

But the most reprehensible suppression of essential information was the withholding from the Government of the fact that all the Generals called into consultation by Sir Douglas Haig had serious misgivings about the whole project and had expressed their doubts to him . . .

Lloyd George, *War Memoirs*, vol. IV, pp. 2186–94

*Lloyd George made a powerful speech on 21 June in the War Policy Committee, urging Haig and Robertson to 'abandon this foolhardy enterprise', but, 'If, after hearing my views, and after taking time to consider them, they still adhered to their previous opinion, then, subject to the condition they have themselves suggested as to breaking off the attack if it did not work out in accordance with expectation, we would not interfere and prevent the attempt.'*

## (c) Haig's Diary

*Tuesday, 19 June*

Doris [Haig's wife] and I motored to the War Office. I saw the CIGS at 10.45 a.m. and then walked to Curzon's Office (Privy Council) for a meeting of the War Cabinet at 11 a.m. We discussed the military situation till 1 o'clock when the Prime Minister left to marry his daughter. The members of the War Cabinet asked me numerous questions, all tending to show that each of them was more pessimistic than the other. The Prime Minister seemed to believe the decisive moment of the war would be 1918. Until then we ought to husband our forces and do little or nothing, except support Italy with guns and gunners (300 batteries was the figure indicated). I strongly asserted that Germany was nearer to her end than they seemed to think, that **now** was the favourable moment for pressing her and that everything possible should be done to take advantage of it by concentrating on the Western Front **all** available resources. I stated that Germany was within six months of the total exhaustion of her available manpower, *if the fighting continues at its present intensity* [Haig's italics]. To do this more men and guns are necessary.

*Wednesday, 20 June*

A most serious and startling situation was disclosed today. At today's Conference, Admiral Jellicoe, as First Sea Lord, stated that owing to the great shortage of shipping due to German submarines, it would be impossible for Great Britain to continue the war in 1918. This was a bombshell for the Cabinet and all present. A full enquiry is to be made as to the real facts on which this opinion of the Naval Authorities is based. No one present shared Jellicoe's view, and all seemed satisfied that the food reserves in Great Britain are adequate. Jellicoe's words were, 'There is no good discussing plans for next Spring – we cannot go on.'

Blake, *The Private Papers of Sir Douglas Haig*, pp. 236–40

*Before Haig next attended a Cabinet meeting, both he and Robertson submitted papers to justify the forthcoming offensive in Flanders, reiterating their belief that it was vital to concentrate resources on the Western theatre; Robertson was less sanguine than Haig about the prospects of success: 'The ultimate objective is undoubtedly the Northern Coast, but I certainly do not advocate spending our last man and last round of ammunition in an attempt to reach that coast if the opposition which we encounter shows that the attempt will entail disproportionate loss.'* (Terraine, The Road to Passchendaele, *p. 169*)

*Monday, 25 June*

I attended a meeting of the War Cabinet at 11.30 a.m. The same people as before were present. As regards the main problem: Lloyd George said that he was much pleased with my notes. On the other hand, he criticised Robertson and tried to get a more definite statement of his views out of him as to the result which he expected. R. would not budge. All he would say was that my plan was the only thing to do. Eventually it was decided that I am to go on with my preparations; that in two weeks M. Albert Thomas [French Minister of Munitions] (who is in favour of my plan) will report on the state of feeling in France and on what the French Army can do. The British Government will then meet the French Government and decide on the extent of our operations.

*Thursday, 28 June*

*Haig had by now returned to his Headquarters at Montreuil in France.*

I had a long talk with Sir Henry Wilson. He thinks that by the British continuing the offensive is the only way to save France. The French Army is in a state of indiscipline not due to losses but to disappointment.

Blake, *The Private Papers of Sir Douglas Haig,* pp. 239–42

## QUESTIONS ON SOURCES 6–11

1. From Sources 7 and 10, what would you say were Haig's primary objectives in May–June 1917? (C)

2. How did he rate his prospects of success (Sources 8, 10)? (C)

3. How much can be reasonably inferred about French views of the projected Flanders offensive from Sources 6 and 9? (E)

4. What discrepancies can you detect in the various accounts given of the discussions held by the War Policy Committee between 11 June and 18 July (Source 11)? Whose account would you regard as most reliable? (E)

5. Is there any contradiction in the arguments advanced by Haig about German strength in Sources 7 and 11? (S)

6. From your reading of Sources 11(b) and 11(c) would you agree with Lloyd George that Haig and Robertson were guilty of deliberately misleading the War Policy Committee? (E)

## 1C  Haig's Plan of Campaign

**SOURCE 12**   Haig's Orders to his Army Commanders,
5 July, 1917

*Though he had not yet gained Cabinet approval for the Flanders offensive, as part of the
necessary preparations he was entitled to make Haig issued his orders on 5 July. The armies
concerned were the Fourth (under General Rawlinson), the Fifth (under General Gough)
and the Second (under General Plumer). The Orders begin with an optimistic summary
of the general international situation.*

Russia has resumed active operations, apparently with excellent results and on a
considerable scale.

We know that German faith in the submarine campaign must soon be abandoned entirely. Coming at a moment when the heavy attacks the enemy has been
making on the French front have failed to achieve success, and when he is
looking with grave anxiety to a resumption of the British offensive and to the
possibility of renewed attacks by our French and Italian allies, this sudden
resumption of a dangerous offensive on his Eastern front is a very heavy blow
to him.

We were justified in hoping for success with the possibility of great results
before we had this convincing evidence of Russia's intention and ability to fulfil
her whole duty to her allies. We are still more justified in this hope now, and our
plans must be laid to exploit the full possibilities of the situation.

With this object the following instructions are issued in confirmation and
amplification of those already given to Army Commanders:-

. . . 2. The Fifth Army, assisted on its right by the Second Army and
co-operating on its left with the French and Belgians, is first to secure the
PASSCHENDAELE–STADEN Ridge. To drive the enemy off that Ridge from
STIRLING CASTLE in the South to DIXMUDE in the North is likely to entail
very hard fighting lasting perhaps for weeks; but as a result of this we may hope
that our subsequent progress will be more rapid.

3. Subject to the modifications necessitated by developments in the situation,
the next effort of the Fifth Army, with the French and Belgians – after gaining
the Ridge mentioned above – will be directed north-eastwards to gain the line
(approximately) THOUROUT–COUCKELAERE.

4. Simultaneously with this advance to the THOUROUT–COUCKELAERE
line the Fourth Army, acting in combination with naval forces, will attack the
enemy about NIEUPORT and on the coast to the east of there.

5. The Fourth Army and the forces attacking the line THOUROUT–COUCKELAERE will afterwards operate to join hands on the general line THOUROUT–OSTEND and to push on to BRUGES.

6. Operations eastward, and towards LICHTERVELDE, from the PASSCHENDAELE–STADEN Ridge will be required to cover the right flank of the advance on THOUROUT; and possession of the high ground between THOUROUT and ROULERS will be of importance subsequently to cover the flank of the advance on BRUGES.

7. In the operations subsequent to the capture of the PASSCHENDAELE–STADEN Ridge opportunities for the employment of Cavalry in masses are likely to offer . . .

10. The above outline of possibilities is issued to enable Army Commanders to foresee and prepare for what may be required of them. The progress of events may demand modifications or alterations of plan from time to time and – especially in view of the comparatively short period of fine weather which we can count on – our progress before winter sets in may well fall short of what would otherwise have been within our power this year.

The general situation is such, however, that the degree of success gained and the results of it may exceed general expectations, and we must be prepared for the possibility of great developments and ready to take full advantage of them.

11. The extent of the success gained will depend much on the concentration and continuity of effort at the right time and place, and the necessary concentration must be obtained by a bold reduction of force at other points, and by ensuring that to the utmost possible extent every fit man takes his place in the ranks. Army Commanders will satisfy themselves that, during the coming offensive, no man fit to be employed in the ranks is employed elsewhere without the most urgent and necessary reason.

12. The drafts available to replace casualties are limited in number and in the great struggle before us it is essential that, without in the least degree relaxing the strength and continuity of our efforts, we shall conserve the energy of our officers and men so that we may outstay the enemy. For this the utmost use must be made of all means of offence and defence at our disposal. All ground must be held, by rifle and bayonet alone if no assistance is obtainable from other arms. In the attack, more especially in the earlier attacks, each step must be thoroughly prepared and organised. Each advance must be carried out steadily – but none the less vigorously – with thorough combination and mutual support between the troops employed. The tendency of isolated bodies of troops to dash forward beyond reach of support must be held in check. This tendency, springing from the finest motives, is of the greatest value if controlled and used for adequate objects, whereas if uncontrolled and misapplied it leads to the loss of many of the most gallant officers and men without the gain of compensating advantages.

Conducting our operations on these principles as has been done with such success on so many previous occasions during the past twelve months, we may look forward with confidence to still greater successes in the future.

Terraine, *The Road to Passchendaele*, pp. 185–7

# SOURCE 13

### (a) Map of Passchendaele Battlefield

*This map is to be found in Lloyd George's* War Memoirs. *Its ulterior purpose can perhaps be inferred.*

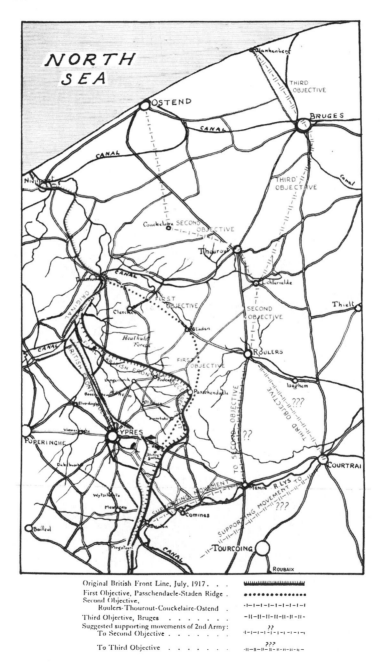

| | |
|---|---|
| Original British Front Line, July, 1917 . . . | |
| First Objective, Passchendaele-Staden Ridge . | |
| Second Objective, | |
|     Roulers-Thourout-Couckelaire-Ostend . | |
| Third Objective, Bruges . . . . . . . | |
| Suggested supporting movements of 2nd Army: | |
|     To Second Objective . . . . . . . | |
| | |
|     To Third Objective . . . . . . . . | |

Lloyd George, *War Memoirs,* vol. IV, p. 2240

## (b) Map to Illustrate the Offensive in Flanders

*This map is to be found in an account of Sir Douglas Haig's command by George A.B.*
*Dewar, assisted by Lieutenant-Colonel J.H. Boraston. Boraston, one of Haig's strongest*
*admirers, wrote the chapter on the Flanders offensive from which this map is taken.*

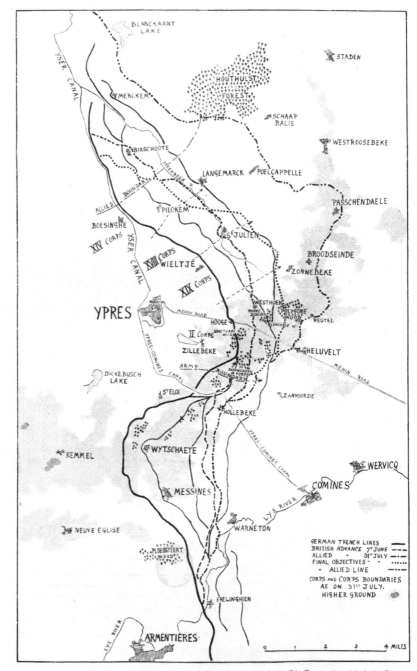

G.A.B. Dewar and Lieutenant-Colonel J.H. Boraston (eds.), *Sir Douglas Haig's Command,*
*December 1915 to November 1918,* vol. I (Constable, 1922) facing p. 365

# SOURCE 14  Report of the War Policy Committee, 19 July, 1917

*Between 25 June and 18 July the War Policy Committee continued to meet and consider the Flanders offensive. A dinner was held at 10 Downing Street on Monday, 16 July at which the decision was taken finally to authorise it. This was confirmed when the Committee met again on Wednesday, 18 July. Hankey was instructed to produce a Report of the Committee's findings, which he did by 5.00 p.m. on 19 July. This Report was considered by the War Cabinet on 20 July, and formed the basis for the instructions sent to Haig on 21 July. The Report is sixty pages long. These two excerpts are taken from Para. 125 of Part IV on Future Military Policy in the Main Theatres of Operations and from Part VI, the Summary of Recommendations.*

*Para. 125*
... the Committee have decided to recommend that this plan [Haig's] shall be commenced. They feel strongly, however, that the offensive must on no account be allowed to drift into costly and indecisive operations as occurred in the offensive on the Somme in 1916, as the effect might be disastrous on public opinion ... The Committee, therefore, attach the greatest importance to a frequent review of the results ...

*Recommendations 2(a)*
The Field-Marshal Commanding the British Expeditionary Force in France should be authorised to carry out the Plans for which he has prepared, as explained by him to the Cabinet Committee on War Policy on 19 June.

Terraine, *The Road to Passchendaele*, pp. 200–1

# SOURCE 15  Cabinet Papers CAB 23/13, War Cabinet No. 19a, 20 July, 1917: Military Policy in the Western and Southern Theatres

*This Minute records the conclusions reached by the War Cabinet on 20 July, and sent to Haig by Robertson on 21 July.*

2. The War Cabinet approved that the military policy in the Western and Southern Theatres should be as follows:
   (a) Report Recommendation No. 2(a) verbatim, as above [i.e. as in Part VI of the War Policy Committee recommendations].
   (b) If it appears probable in the execution of these plans that results are not commensurate with the effort made and the losses incurred, the whole question should be re-examined by the War Cabinet with a view to the cessation of this offensive and the adoption of an alternative plan.

Terraine, *The Road to Passchendaele*, p. 201

# SOURCE 16   Haig to Robertson, 22 July, 1917

*In this letter Haig acknowledges receipt of the draft conclusions of the War Cabinet. He comments on the lateness of the approval given to his plans, and on the grudging nature of that approval.*

The effect on the morale of officers and men might have been so serious if it had been decided, for no apparent reason to them, to abandon the attack at this stage, after all their efforts to prepare for it, after a fierce struggle for artillery and air supremacy has already been in progress for some days, and when the assault is almost on the verge of being launched, that I earnestly hope the War Cabinet may never again find it necessary to postpone such a decision to the last moment.

From sub-paragraph (b) I note that I may expect the cessation of the offensive to be ordered hereafter if, in the judgment of the War Cabinet, the results are not commensurate with the effort made and the losses incurred.

No doubt, before such an order is issued, the effort and losses of the enemy as well as on our side will be duly considered, as also the possible effect on both the enemy and our own Army of stopping the action, as foreshadowed in this Conclusion. On such points the judgment of the Commander on the spot, in close touch with the situation, is entitled to great weight, and I trust that my opinion may be taken and fully considered before a decision of such vital importance is arrived at.

From these sub-paragraphs, as well as from the Minutes generally, I have formed the impression that the plan of operations, although approved, has neither the full confidence nor the wholehearted support of the War Cabinet. Such an impression adds very greatly to the responsibilities and anxieties of a Commander in entering on such a serious undertaking; and if the impression is not justified I respectfully ask for an assurance to that effect.

Terraine, *The Road to Passchendaele*, pp. 202–3

# SOURCE 17   Telegram from Robertson to Haig, 25 July, 1917

Your OAD 564 of 22 July. War Cabinet authorises me to inform you that having approved your plans being executed you may depend on their wholehearted support and that if and when they decide to reconsider the situation they will obtain your views before arriving at any decision as to cessation of operations.

Terraine, *The Road to Passchendaele*, p. 203

# QUESTIONS ON SOURCES 12–17

1.  What evidence can you find in Sources 12 and 13 that (a) Haig still had a very unrealistic view of conditions on the Western Front, and (b) he was anxious to minimise casualties? (C)

2. Compare the objectives of the Passchendaele campaign as indicated in Sources 13(a) and (b). How closely do they conform to those spelt out by Haig in Source 12? (E)

3. How enthusiastically did the War Policy Committee endorse Haig's plans (Sources 14–15)? (C)

4. What do Sources 16 and 17 indicate about relations between generals and politicians in the First World War? (C)

5. How do you account for the reluctance of the War Cabinet to give their full support to Haig (Sources 14–16)? (C)

6. In the circumstances of the spring and summer of 1917 were they finally right to give their approval to Haig's plans? (S)

# SOURCE MATERIAL 2
# Military Operations

*Sources 18–28 cover military operations between 31 July and 6 November and relate to: A. the first days' fighting, as seen at different levels (Sources 18–20); B. subsequent points in the battle at which its suspension was considered (Sources 21–4); and C. conditions on the battle-field, and how much the higher command was aware of them (Sources 25–8).*

## 2A  The First Offensive, 31 July to 4 August, 1917

### SOURCE 18  *Official History of the War in France and Belgium*

*This work was written by Sir James Edmonds and others between 1922 and 1948. It runs to 14 volumes and is the best available source of factual information.*

Compared with the first day of the battle of the Somme, when the casualties were 68 816 (reduced later by the return of absentees to 57 540), the losses, 31 850 (for the three days 31st July–2nd/3rd August) were moderate, although in themselves severe.

A general advance of about three thousand yards had been made, whereas at the Somme only three divisions on the right had made fair, but less progress, and two others only achieved small isolated advances.

Although expectations had not been entirely realised and considerable casualties had been suffered, valuable results had been gained. The enemy's observation areas on the highest part of the Gheluvelt plateau (near Clapham Junction) and along the long rise via Bellewaarde to Pilckem and been captured, and nine of his divisions badly mauled. Apart from an unusually large number of German dead on the battlefield, over six thousand prisoners (including 133 officers) and 25 guns had been captured. It is now known, as might have been expected, that the front divisions had been so badly shattered that they had to be replaced within a few days by fresh divisions. This relief implied the provision of a new complement of counter-attack divisions in close support. Thus began that steady stream of German divisions to the Flanders front which was to drain the resources of the enemy during the next four months and keep him from attacking the French. The situation was, however, only relatively satisfactory. The nine leading divisions of the four corps of the Fifth Army had been intended to reach the third and fourth objectives on the first day, and then to carry out the subsequent advance to the Passchendaele–Staden ridge before relief. Actually, they were less than half-way to the first day's objectives, and had already lost 30 per cent to 60 per cent of their fighting strength . . .

Apart from the actual losses the conditions under which the battle was fought were most exhausting for all the troops concerned.

Sir James Edmonds (ed.), *Official History of the War, 1917,* vol. II (Macmillan, 1948) pp. 177–9

# SOURCE 19  Haig's Diary

Fighting on our right had been most severe. This I had expected. Our divisions had made good progress and were on top of the ridge which the Menin road crosses, but had not advanced sufficiently eastward to have observation into the valleys beyond. Further to the west, our troops had established themselves beyond the Steenbeck, and the French had taken Bixschoote and the Cabaret Kortakeer (which was so frequently attacked on October and November 1914). This was a fine day's work. Gough thinks he has taken over 5000 prisoners and 60 guns or more. The ground is thick with Germans, killed mostly by our artillery. I sent Alan Fletcher and Colonel Ryan round the casualty clearing stations. They report many slight cases, mostly shell fire. Wounded are very cheery indeed. Some 6000 wounded had been treated in ten hours up to 6 p.m.

As regards future operations, I told Gough to carry out the original plan; to consolidate ground gained and to improve his position, as he may deem necessary, for facilitating the next advance; the next advance will be made as soon as possible, *but only after adequate bombardment and after dominating the hostile artillery* [Haig's italics]. Heavy rain fell this afternoon and aeroplane observation was impossible. The going became very bad, and the ground was much cut up. This has hampered our progress and robbed us of much of the advantage due to our success.

Duff Cooper, *Haig,* vol. II (Faber & Faber, 1936) pp. 140–1

# SOURCE 20  *They Called It Passchendaele*

*In 1978 Lynn MacDonald published* They Called It Passchendaele, *a compilation of over 600 eye-witness accounts of the battle. Ideally, the whole book should be read to realise the conditions endured by the participants in the battle. The following excerpt gives a not untypical account of what might happen to one battalion of 600–700 men engaged in an apparently successful day's fighting. The eyewitness in this case is Company Quartermaster Sergeant G.W. Fish, 1st Battalion the Hertfordshire Regiment, which as part of the 39th Division was involved in the attack on the west of the line across the Steenbeck stream. The division captured two of its three objectives.*

I saw my company off, with extra bandoliers of ammunition and so on, and I remember shaking hands with the officer commanding the company, Captain Lowry, M.C. He shook hands with me, and I looked at him and he looked at me and I knew he wasn't coming back, and he knew that I knew he wasn't coming back. He said: 'I'll see you tonight up on the Green line' – that was their third objective. I said, 'I'll be there all right.'

Normally, the rations went up on limbers, but the mud was so bad that we had to take them up in paniers on pack mules. The conditions were so bad we saw some of the artillery people, who were taking their ammunition up that way, actually having to shoot some of their mules, for they were right up to their stomachs in mud. They just couldn't get them out. When we eventually got to what had been the first German line, the officer in charge of the transport said, 'Well, this is as far as I can take my mules. I am dumping the rations here. You must make contact with the companies and get carrying parties down to take the rations up.' So, he about turned with his mules and off he went. There were four Company Quartermaster Sergeants, myself and three others, and we decided between us that two of us should go forward to try to find the battalion, one would stay with the rations, and the other would try to find Brigade Headquarters to get some indication as to where the battalion might be. We tossed for the different jobs and it fell to my lot to find Brigade Headquarters, so I set off. There was a most tremendous bombardment going on all the while. After a long time, I found Brigade Headquarters. They were in an underground German concrete pillbox, just in front of St Julien. I went down the stairs, saluted the Brigadier, told him who I was, explained the position and said, 'Could you give me any instructions, sir, that would help me to find the battalion?' He just stood and looked at me. We were both standing on the steps, and the pillbox was rocking like a boat in a rough sea with explosions. After a while he said, 'I'm sorry, Quarters, I'm afraid there isn't *any* Hertfordshire Regiment.'

(Of the 650 who had attacked through St Julien to the Langemarck–Zinnebeke Road, 136 were killed and 400 wounded.)

Lynn MacDonald, *They Called It Passchendaele* (Michael Joseph, 1978) pp. 121–2

# 2B Suspension of the Campaign?

## SOURCE 21   General Sir Hubert Gough, *The Fifth Army*

*General Sir Hubert Gough commanded the Fifth Army, which bore the brunt of the fighting in the early part of the battle. His account of the First World War,* The Fifth Army, *was published in 1931; he intended it to be 'a plain tale of War as I saw it myself'. This excerpt describes the situation after the attack of 16 August in which the village of Langemarck had been captured by British troops.*

The state of the ground was by this time frightful. The labour of bringing up supplies and ammunition, of moving or firing the guns, which had often sunk up to their axles, was a fearful strain on the officers and men, even during the daily task of maintaining the battle front. When it came to the advance of the infantry for an attack across the water-logged shell-holes, movement was so slow and fatiguing that only the shortest advance could be contemplated. In consequence I informed the Commander-in-Chief that tactical success was not possible, or would be too costly, under such conditions, and advised that the attack should now be abandoned.

I had many talks with Haig during these days and repeated this information frequently, but he told me that the attack must be continued. He saw the possibilities of a German victory, a defeat for the whole Allied cause. There was only one Army in the field in a position to prevent this disaster, and that was the British Army in France. On it fell this heavy burden.

A comprehensive view of the general strategical situation showed that the French Army was in no position at that time to withstand a powerful offensive; at any moment, if the Germans sent some divisions to the Italian front, our Allies there would be driven back in rout – a danger the battle of Caporetto in October was shortly to bring home to the Allies; it was also important to prevent the Germans administering the final knock-out blow to the Russians, if such were possible.

General Sir Hubert Gough, GCMG, KCB, KCVO, *The Fifth Army*
(Hodder & Stoughton, 1931) p. 205

## SOURCE 22   Haig's Diary, 2 October, 1917

*This entry follows the relatively successful battles of the Menin Road (20 September) and Polygon Wood (26 September).*

*Tuesday, 2 October*
I held a Conference at my house at Cassel at 11 a.m. Kiggell [Haig's Chief of Staff], Davidson and Charteris [Haig's Chief Intelligence Officer] accompanied me. Generals Plumer [commanding Second Army] and Gough [commanding Fifth Army] were also present with their senior Staff Officers and General Nash (DGT). I pointed out how favourable the situation was and how necessary it was to have all necessary means for exploiting any success gained on the 10th, should the situation admit, e.g. if the enemy counter-attacks and is defeated, then reserve brigades must follow after the enemy and take the Passchendaele ridge at once. Both Gough and Plumer quite acquiesced in my views, and arranged whole-heartedly to give effect to them when the time came. At first they adhered to the idea of continuing our attacks for limited objectives.

Charteris emphasised the deterioration of German Divisions in numbers, morale and all-round efficiency.

Blake (ed.), *The Private Papers of Douglas Haig,* p. 256

## SOURCE 23   Brigadier-General John Charteris, At GHQ

*Brigadier-General Charteris was Haig's Chief Intelligence Officer from 1915 to 1918. His account of his experiences was not published until 1931, but was largely based on the records he kept at the time and the letters he sent: 'A most careful and painstaking secretary had seen to it that all the letters which I received and wrote, other than those to my own home, were carefully filed. From these records I have compiled this volume.'*

*5 October*
There was a conference late in the afternoon – D.H. and the Army Commanders. We are far enough on now to stop for the winter, and there is much to be said for that. Unless we get fine weather for all this month, there is now no chance of

clearing the coast. With fine weather we may still do it. If we could be sure that the Germans would attack us here, it would be far better to stand fast. But they would probably be now only too glad to remain quiet here and try elsewhere. Anyhow, there are reasons far more vital than our own interests here that give us no option. But it is a tremendous responsibility for D.H. Most of those at the Conference, though willing to go on, would welcome a stop.

*8 October*

We go on again tomorrow, and yesterday and today there have been heavy downpours of rain, a last effort. Documents taken on the 4th show that the Germans are very hard pressed to hold their ground. They have given up their new plan of thinly held front lines and gone back to their old scheme, which is all to the good; but unless we have a very great success tomorrow it is the end of the year so far as Flanders is concerned, and next year the Germans will have all their troops from Russia. With great success tomorrow, and good weather for a few more weeks, we may still clear the coast and win the war before Christmas. It is not impossible, but it is pouring again today.

*10 October*
*This entry follows the unsuccessful attacks launched at the village of Poelkapelle on 9 October.*

I was out all yesterday at the attack. It was the saddest day of this year. We did fairly well but only fairly well. It was not the enemy but mud that prevented us doing better. But there is no chance of complete success this year. We *must* fight on for a few more weeks, but there is no purpose in it now so far as Flanders is concerned. I don't think I ever really had great hope of a big success yesterday, but until noon there was, at least, still a chance. Moving about close behind a battle, when things are going well and when one is keyed up with hope of great results, one passes without much thought all the horrible part of it – the wounded coming back, the noise, the news of losses, the sight of men toiling forward through mud into great danger. But when one knows that the great purpose one has been working for has escaped, somehow one sees and thinks of nothing but the awfulness of it all. Yesterday afternoon was utterly damnable. I got back very late and could not work, and could not rest. D.H. sent for me about 10 to discuss things. He has to bear the brunt of it. He was still trying to find some grounds for hope that we might still win through this year, but there is none.

   The French were still appealing for the protection provided by our attacks . . .

Brigadier-General John Charteris, CMGF, DSO, *At GHQ* (Cassell, 1931) pp. 258–9

## SOURCE 24   Telegram from the War Cabinet to Haig, 16 October, 1917

The War Cabinet desire to congratulate you and the troops under your command upon the achievements of the British Armies in Flanders in the great battle which has been raging since July 31st. Starting from positions in which every advantage rested with the enemy and, hampered and delayed from time to time by most unfavourable weather, you and your men have nevertheless continuously driven the enemy back with such skill, courage and pertinacity, as have commanded the grateful admiration of the peoples of the British Empire and filled the enemy with alarm. I am personally glad to be the means of transmitting this message to you, and to your gallant troops, and desire to take this opportunity of renewing my assurance of confidence in your leadership, and in the devotion of those whom you command. Signed Lloyd George.

Blake, *The Private Papers of Douglas Haig,* p. 261

## QUESTIONS ON SOURCES 18-24

1. Does the *Official History* endorse Haig's view of the results of the fighting on 31 July (Sources 18, 19)? (C)

2. What light do Sources 19 and 20 shed on the attitude of the Higher Command to casualties? (S)

3. How convincing do you find General Gough's account of his opposition to the continuation of the campaign after the middle of August (Source 21)? (E)

4. Do Charteris' diary entries in Source 23 support his assessment of the deterioration in the fighting capacity of the Germans in Source 22? If not, why not? (E)

5. Compare the attitudes of Haig and Charteris towards the prospects of success in Flanders in October 1917 (Sources 22, 23). How are these differences to be explained? (S)

6. How do you explain Source 24 in the light of the reservations previously expressed by the War Cabinet in Source 14? (S)

7. On what grounds did Haig insist on persevering with the Passchendaele campaign, and with what justification (Sources 21-3)? (S)

## 2C | Fighting Conditions at Passchendaele

### SOURCE 25　E. Norman Gladden, *Ypres 1917, A Personal Account*

*Norman Gladden served in the Northumberland Fusiliers, both at the Somme and at Passchendaele. His account of his military service is based on a diary, kept at the time and subsequently written up and published in 1967. This episode describes his experiences as a Lewis gunner during the advance on the Menin Road on 20 September, 1917.*

Our barrage – a wave of inconceivable confusion – began to creep away from the edge of the wood, whose trees stood out even more clearly as the fumes gradually cleared. Now the whole situation changes as if by magic, evil magic for us! Zip-ping. Zip-ping. Snipers' bullets began their deadly work. Machine guns, opening out ahead began to traverse methodically across our front, like flails of death crossing and recrossing as they sprayed the advancing line. I felt the tearing lead swishing across as the muzzle slewed and could hardly believe I had not been hit. A man a few yards ahead slipped to the ground and lay in a heap. Sergeant Rhodes was still in front, there, urging the line forward. The machine-guns cut across again and single rifle shots syncopated their steadier rattle. The defenders were resisting with deadly effect. I heard screams around me. Agony and death seemed to be cutting into the attacking lines. From the edge of the wood, now much closer, flashes from rifles and machine-guns filled the air like venomous darts. Terror now ruled my dying world!

E. Norman Gladden, *Ypres 1917, A Personal Account* (William Kimber, 1967) p. 130

# SOURCE 26   Lieutenant J.W. Naylor, Royal Artillery

*This account of the Ypres salient is given by a junior officer, Lieutenant J.W. Naylor, who served as a gunner, providing artillery support.*

I came to hate that salient. Absolutely loathed it . . . I always used to think the names were so sinister – Zonnebeke – Hill 60 – Zillebeke – the names terrified you before you got there, they had such a sinister ring about them. Then to end up making for Passchendaele was the last straw. You could practically segregate the salient from the whole of the rest of the war-zone. It wore you down. The weather, the lack of rations, everything seemed to be against you. There didn't seem to be anything left. You were wet through for days on end. We never thought we'd get out alive. You couldn't see the cloud with the silver lining. There wasn't one.

We'd had an awful time getting the guns up the plank road on to Westhoek Ridge – and that was before the worst of the mud. Three weeks later we couldn't have done it at all. It was just sheets of water coming down. It's difficult to get across that it's a sea of mud. Literally a sea. You can drown in it. On the day I reached my lowest ebb I'd gone down from the gun position to meet the ammunition wagon coming up the supply road. It was my job to see that they got the wagons unloaded at the dump and to arrange carrying parties to take the shells and rations up to the battery. Oddly enough it was a quiet afternoon, but they must have seen some movement on the road because just as the wagon came up a heavy shell came over and burst very close. There were six horses pulling that wagon and they took fright at the explosion, veered right off the road and down they went into the mud. We had no possible way of getting them out. In any event they sank so fast that we had no chance even to cut them loose from the heavy wagon. We formed a chain and stretched out our arms and managed to get the drivers off, but the poor horses just sank faster and faster and drowned before our eyes. The wagon and horses disappeared in a matter of minutes. One of the drivers was absolutely incoherent with terror. It was the thought of being drowned in that awful stuff. It's a horrible thought. Anyone would rather be shot and know nothing about it.

MacDonald, *They Called It Passchendaele*, pp. 187–8

# SOURCE 27

### (a) Captain Liddell Hart, *A History of the First World War*

*This account of the First World War came out in 1930. Liddell Hart was one of Haig's fiercest critics. Lloyd George cites this passage in his* War Memoirs, *vol. IV, p. 2210. For the identity of the officer referred to see Source 27(b).*

Perhaps the most damning comment on the plan which plunged the British Army in this bath of mud and blood is contained in an incidental revelation of the remorse of one who was largely responsible for it. This highly placed officer from General Headquarters was on his first visit to the battle front – at the end of the four months' battle. Growing increasingly uneasy as the car approached the swamp-like edges of the battle area, he eventually burst into tears, crying, 'Good God! did we really send men to fight in that?' To which his companion replied that the ground was far worse ahead. If the exclamation was a credit to his heart it revealed on what a foundation of delusion and inexcusable ignorance his indomitable 'offensiveness' had been based.

B. Liddell Hart, *A History of the First World War* (Cassell, 1930) p. 454

### (b) Letter from Captain B.H. Liddell Hart to the *Spectator*, 3 January, 1958

Brigadier Desmond Young asks in his letter that I should now disclose the name of the 'highly placed officer from GHQ . . .' As there is no longer any justification for withholding the name of this officer, and the service demands it, I can state that it was General Kiggell, Haig's Chief of Staff.

### (c) Letter from E.A. Osborne to the *Spectator*, 3 January, 1958

*Major Osborne, as he then was, was a General Staff Officer II serving as a Liaison Officer at GHQ. His task was to go round Brigade and Battalion Headquarters, and keep GHQ informed of what was happening at the front. He spent much of the autumn of 1917 with Gough's Fifth Army.*

I did not keep a diary and at this distance in time it is hard to remember more than a few incidents, but I have a clear recollection of one day during the battle of Passchendaele.

It was in the latter part of October, 1917. The 34th Division was in action at Poelkapelle.

I went up and spent some time at brigade and battalion headquarters. I could see, and heard much about, the awful conditions. I felt very bad about it all, probably to an increased extent as so many valued friends were involved. On returning that evening I dictated and signed what could only be described as a violent report. After dinner I was sent for by the CGS, General Sir Launcelot Kiggell. He took me straight to the C. in C.'s room. There was nobody else there. Sir Douglas Haig took me across to a big wall map and told me to elaborate my report. I did so at considerable length and with great emphasis. As far as I remember, he made little or no comment. At the end, he said, 'Thank you Major Osborne, Good night.'

I left with a feeling of great relief. I had unburdened my soul to a great man and a real commander.

## SOURCE 28  Haig's War Despatches, 25 December, 1917

*Haig regularly forwarded to the War Cabinet an account of the most important features of the operations on the Western Front, on average twice a year. His account of the Passchendaele offensive was dated 25 December, 1917. Haig is here recalling the events of 31 July.*

43.  The weather had been threatening throughout the day, and had rendered the work of the aeroplanes very difficult from the commencement of the battle. During the afternoon, while fighting was still in progress, rain began, and fell steadily all night. Thereafter, for four days the rain continued without cessation, and for several days afterwards the weather remained stormy and unsettled. The low-lying, clayey soil, torn by shells and sodden with rain, turned to a succession of vast muddy pools. The valleys of the choked and overflowing streams were speedily transformed into long stretches of bog, impassable except for a few well-defined tracks which became marks for the enemy's artillery. To leave these tracks was to risk death by drowning, and in the course of the subsequent fighting on several occasions both men and pack animals were lost in this way . . .

J.H. Boraston (ed.), *Sir Douglas Haig's Despatches* (Dent, 1919) p. 116

## QUESTIONS ON SOURCES 25–8

1.  What do you infer about the effectiveness of the British artillery barrage which preceded the battle which Norman Gladden describes (Source 25)? (S)

2.  How much credence would you give to the story of General Kiggell (Source 27)? Why should Lloyd George quote it? (E)

3.  From your reading of Sources 25–8 do you get the impression that the High Command were really aware of conditions on the battlefield during the Passchendaele campaign? (S)

4.  What conclusions would you draw from these sources about the attitude of the High Command to the suffering endured by the front-line soldier? (S)

# SOURCE MATERIAL 3
# Results of the Battle of Passchendaele

*Few battles have been as controversial as Passchendaele. The following sources speak for them-selves in most cases, and have been chosen to illustrate different viewpoints. They include the conclusions of Haig (Commander-in-Chief); Lloyd George (Prime Minister); Maurice Hankey (Cabinet Secretary); and Guy Chapman (an infantry subaltern, who later became a distin-guished historian in his own right). Two German sources are also cited. Finally there are the rival assessments of casualty figures on both sides.*

## SOURCE 29 Haig's Despatches, 25 December, 1917

This offensive, maintained for three and a half months under the most adverse conditions of weather, had entailed almost superhuman exertions on the part of the troops of all arms and services. The enemy had done his utmost to hold his ground, and in his endeavours to do so had used up no less than seventy-eight divisions, of which eighteen had been engaged a second or third time in the battle, after being withdrawn to rest and refit. Despite the magnitude of his efforts, it was the immense natural difficulties, accentuated manifold by the abnormally wet weather, rather than the enemy's resistance, which limited our progress and prevented the complete capture of the ridge . . .

Notwithstanding the many difficulties, much has been achieved. Our captures in Flanders since the commencement of operations at the end of July amount to 24 065 prisoners, 74 guns, 941 machine-guns and 138 trench mortars. It is most certain that the enemy's losses considerably exceed ours. Most important of all, our new and hastily trained Armies have shown that they are capable of meeting and beating the enemy's best troops, even under conditions which favoured his defence to a degree which it required the greatest endurance, determination and heroism to overcome . . .

The British Armies have taken their full share in the fighting on the Western Front. Save for such short intervals as were enforced by the weather or rendered necessary for the completion of the preparation for our principal attacks, they have maintained a vigorous and continuous offensive throughout practically the whole period covered by this Despatch. No other example of offensive action on so large a scale and so successfully sustained, has yet been furnished by the war . . .

Without reckoning, therefore, the possibilities which have been opened up by our territorial gains in Flanders, and without considering the effect which a less vigorous prosecution of the war by us might have had in other theatres, we have every reason to be satisfied with the results of this year's fighting.

Boraston (ed.), *Sir Douglas Haig's Despatches,* pp. 133–5

# SOURCE 30   Lloyd George, *War Memoirs*

The fighting went on until the first week in December. When it was finally concluded the attack had failed in all the purposes for which it was originally designed. We had not cleared the Flemish coast. We had not broken through the enemy's defences into open country. The cavalry charge had not come off. Not a single cavalry horse had wetted his hooves in the slush. If the reader will refer back to the plan of attack, he will understand better how this dreadfulness had ended in an utter fiasco. He will see marked on that map [Source 13(a)] the stages by which we were to reach our final objective. The Passchendaele–Staden Ridge was only the first stage. At its utmost limit it was only five miles from where we started. The last objective was 25 miles distant. The ridge which constituted the first stage in our advance was 18 miles in length. After four months of terrible fighting, resulting in casualties which reached nearly 400 000 and an enormous expenditure of ammunition – the greatest blaze of high explosive ever yet fired on any battlefield – we had only captured five miles of that ridge, that is about a fourth of our first line or projected advance . . .

When it was realised some time in September that a breakthrough was impracticable and that the clearing of the Flemish coast this year was out of the question, GHQ substituted the policy of 'wearing down the enemy' as the primary purpose of their strategy. How did that thrive? We lost 400 000 men in our direct and subsidiary attacks. The enemy did not lose on the whole British front during that period 250 000 men. Our losses were nearly five to every three of the German . . . The balance of attrition, which was already heavily in favour of the enemy, was, by this offensive, tipped still more definitely in his favour . . .

As I have already pointed out in the previous chapter, not even the first objective had been attained. The fight came to be known as the 'Battle of Passchendaele', but the capture of this village gave us only a fourth of the first ridge which the Army had to occupy as a starting point. It left the Army with a narrower salient than the deadly salient of Ypres which had already cost us so much . . .

The Passchendaele fiasco imperilled the chances of final victory. Had it not been for the effect of the blockade on the German people, the disappointment caused by the failure of the submarine campaign, combined with the arrival of the American troops in France in swelling numbers, the failure of the Flanders offensive in 1917 might well have been fatal to Allied prospects in 1918. It weighed down the balance of man-power still further to the Central Powers. The desertion of Russia and the defeat of Roumania had already created an adverse balance. The gigantic casualties of Passchendaele pressed appreciably down the Allied end of the grisly scales. Our military leaders had acquired the habit of prodigality in their expenditure of life.

Lloyd George, *War Memoirs*, vol. IV, pp. 2232–42

# SOURCE 31   Lord Hankey, *The Supreme Command*

The question whether the results of the battle of Flanders justified the effort and tremendous casualties has been and will remain a matter of controversy.

Haig to the end of his days believed that the battle had been an essential factor in winning the war. Not long after the war the Field Marshal was invited to London to advise a sub-committee of the Committee of Imperial Defence on certain technical issues. Before leaving for the night train to the north he gave a small dinner party at which were present Hubert Gough, James Edmonds, author of so many volumes of the Official History, another military officer and myself. I took the opportunity of a very frank discussion with the Field Marshal to ask whether after hearing all the criticism of the battle, he still felt that the decision had been the right one. He replied without any note of hesitation that he had not the slightest doubt on the matter. Already by 1916, when the Germans failed to break through the French lines at Verdun and we had similarly failed at the Somme, the war had become a *guerre d'usure* [war of attrition]. Flanders he described as simply a continuation of the battle of the Somme and an essential factor in wearing down German resistance. On the whole it was less costly in casualties to attack than to defend as was shown in the battle in March 1918, when the Germans, with the aid of reinforcements released from their Eastern Front, had made their last bid for victory. Nevertheless they were so exhausted by the remorseless hammering they had received in the previous two years that their efforts in the spring of 1918 had finished them. This had enabled the Allies, reinforced by American troops to reap the harvest sown on the Somme and in Flanders. Whether he was right or wrong in this appreciation (which has had to be given from memory) I felt a sense of satisfaction as I bade him goodbye, for the last time as it turned out, that Haig's mind was so completely free from anything in the nature of self-reproach. On the other hand, no one can read Lloyd George's own account on the other side without realizing that there is a tremendous case on the other side.

Hankey, *The Supreme Command,* vol. II, pp. 700–1

# SOURCE 32  Guy Chapman, *A Passionate Prodigality*

*Guy Chapman served in the 13th Battalion, the Royal Fusiliers; during the battle of Passchendaele he was its adjutant.*

Each day the necessity of economising men became the first problem for a battalion headquarters. Here in the Salient where a battalion never went into an attack without fifty to eighty per cent casualties, where holding the line was scarcely easier, where ration carriers and digging parties were knocked out far behind the line, and when losses were never completely made good, and what was made up, was inferior material, a kernel of the best (so far as might be) was always husbanded . . .

But no man in all these armies could by an act of faith save one life. From the line came those tired desperate voices: ''E cawn't do it, Ser'eant; 'e's finished'; 'The platoon's all in, old boy, we'll only make a balls of it'; 'I've only sixty men left in the company, sir; it's too few for the job'; 'My battalion's been in the line for ten days, general; it's had 80 per cent casualties. We no longer exist'; 'unless

my brigade's relieved, I'll not answer for the consequences'. Those desperate
voices never carried to England, or if they did, they were drowned by the full-fed
bawling of such patriots as Lord Northcliffe and Mr Punch.

Guy Chapman, *A Passionate Prodigality* (Buchan & Enright, 1985) pp. 206–7

# SOURCE 33   German Views of the Battle

## (a) Crown Prince Rupprecht of Bavaria, Order of the Day, 5 December, 1917

Sons from all parts of Germany have shown heroic bravery and powers of
endurance and brought to nought the attempts by the British and French to
achieve the breakthrough which, had it succeeded, would have brought about a
decision because it would have meant the capture of Flanders and our U-boat
bases. Despite the use of unheard of masses of men and material the enemy has
not achieved this. A narrow strip of completely destroyed crater land is his only
gain. He has bought this with extremely high losses while our own casualties
have been less than in any previous defensive battle.

Thus the Battle of Flanders is a severe defeat to the enemy and is for us a great
victory. He who was present can be proud to have been a Flanders warrior.

## (b) Hermann von Kuhl, *Der Weltkrieg, 1914–18*

Above everything else the battle had led to a vast consumption of German
strength. Losses had been so high that they could no longer be replaced and the
fighting strength of battalions, already reduced, was further reduced. That the
enemy, despite the most thorough preparation, numerical superiority, bravery
and perseverance had been able to achieve so little, was partly due to the adverse
weather conditions which made movement in the Flanders soil extremely
difficult. But water and mud were no less a disadvantage to the defenders . . .
These conditions, more than the bloody fighting, led to a rapid wearing out of
the troops and were, along with the lower numerical strength of the German
divisions and the serious inferiority in guns and ammunition, among the reasons
why the German defence required a more rapid relief of divisions than during
the enemy's attacks [*sic.* 'the attacking enemy'?].

Terraine, *The Road to Passchendaele*, p. 332

# SOURCE 34   Casualty Figures

*These have been, and continue to be, widely disputed. British estimates are based on two
main accounts:* The Official History of the War, 1917, *vol. II, written by Sir James
Edmonds and published in 1948; and* Statistics of the Military Effort of the British
Empire, *compiled by the War Office and published in 1922. The* Official History *relies
upon the casualty returns of the Second and Fifth Armies, submitted weekly, and on the
figures submitted to the Supreme War Council on 25 February, 1918; the* Statistics of

the Military Effort of the British Empire *are derived from the casualties sustained by each of the main contingents serving in the British Expeditionary Force. German casualty figures have been taken from Hermann von Kuhl's* Der Weltkrieg, 1914–18, *cited in* Terraine, The Road to Passchendaele.

## (a) Official History of the War

The total battle and trench wastage casualties in the Second and Fifth Armies for the period of the 'Third Battle of Ypres', 31st July–10th November, 1917, were, as rendered week by week at the time, 238 313. Except in the case of the report of one Army for one week, this total includes 'Missing' (of whom there were 29 036), some of whom subsequently returned. The figures submitted to the Supreme War Council on the 25th February, 1918, by the British Section of the Military Representatives were:

| | |
|---|---|
| 31st July–3rd October | 138 787 |
| 4th October–12th November | 106 110 |
| Total | 244 897 |

The clerk-power to investigate the exact losses was not available. It will be recalled that on the first day of the Battles of the Somme, the total casualties originally reported were 61 816, with 17 758 missing. Later investigation – requiring 6 months for a single day – reduced these figures to 57 470, with 2152 missing and 585 prisoners of war.

Edmonds (ed.), *Official History of the War, 1917,* vol. II, pp. 360–1

## (b) Statistics of the Military Effort of the British Empire

TABLE (xiv)   CASUALTIES IN THE EXPEDITIONARY FORCE, FRANCE (EXCLUDING SICK)

*Period of the Third Battle of Ypres, 31st July to 19th September, 1917*

| Force | Officers | Other ranks |
|---|---|---|
| Regular Forces | 4 774 | 84 873 |
| Territorial Force | 1 267 | 27 341 |
| Canadian Contingent | 436 | 11 794 |
| Indian Natives | | 59 |
| Australian Contingent | 164 | 3 125 |
| New Zealand Contingent | 75 | 1 736 |
| Newfoundland Contingent | 1 | 178 |
| South African Contingent | 3 | 115 |
| British West Indies Contingent | | 145 |
| Royal Naval Division | 21 | 340 |
| Total | 6 741 | 129 706 |

| Period of the Third Battle of Ypres, 20th September to 31st December, 1917 | | |
| --- | --- | --- |
| Force | Officers | Other ranks |
| Regular Forces | 7 827 | 140 464 |
| Territorial Force | 2 615 | 52 455 |
| Canadian Contingent | 743 | 17 666 |
| Indian Natives | 18 | 406 |
| Australian Contingent | 1 319 | 26 693 |
| New Zealand Contingent | 344 | 7 558 |
| Newfoundland Contingent | 19 | 672 |
| South African Contingent | 75 | 1 721 |
| British West Indies Contingent | 8 | 283 |
| Royal Naval Division | 110 | 2 378 |
| Total | 13 078 | 250 296 |

*Statistics of the Military Effort of the British Empire* (War Office, 1922) p. 326

### (c) Hermann von Kuhl, *Der Weltkrieg, 1914–18*

The German Fourth Army (which bore the brunt of the fighting in Flanders) lost from 21 July to 31 December, 1917, about 217 000, of which 35 000 were killed and 48 000 missing.

Terraine, *The Road to Passchendaele*, pp. 328, 343–7

# SOURCE 35   Recent Glosses on these Figures

### (a) A.J.P. Taylor

The British casualties were something over 300 000; the German under 200 000 – a proportion slightly better than on the Somme.

A.J.P. Taylor, *The First World War* (Hamish Hamilton, 1963) p. 148

### (b) J. Terraine

The casualties have given rise to endless controversy which there is no way of definitely settling. The Official History (published in 1948) gives corrected British casualties as 244 897. This total has been disputed, and it has been said that the official historian 'cooked' the figures. To those who are disposed to believe this, it can only be suggested that they read the appropriate volume of the Official History with great care, and study the remarkable documentation with which the British casualties are presented. If Sir James Edmonds was really 'cooking' the figures, he set about it in an astonishingly open and above-board way. Personally, this author after a very long and sincere consideration, does not find the Official total surprising or suspicious . . .

What of the German losses? The British Official History states frankly: 'They must be conjectural.' Not everyone will follow Sir James Edmonds in his estimate that they totalled 400 000. But that they at least equalled those of the Allies, and probably exceeded them seems a safe assumption.

J. Terraine, *Douglas Haig, The Educated Soldier* (Hutchinson, 1963) pp. 371–2

## QUESTIONS ON SOURCES 29–35

1. On what grounds did Haig feel that 'we have every reason to be satisfied with the results of this year's fighting' (Source 29)? (C)

2. Why does Lloyd George use the term 'fiasco' about Passchendaele (Source 30)? (C)

3. Were the reasons advanced by Haig in defence of the Flanders campaign in Source 31 the same as those he used to secure its approval by the War Policy Committee (Sources 7, 8, 10)? (S)

4. With reference to Sources 31–3, assess the validity of Lloyd George's indictment of the Passchendaele campaign. (E)

5. How might the discrepancies in the British casualty figures be explained (Source 34)? (E)

6. Why should A.J.P. Taylor prefer a higher estimate and John Terraine a lower estimate of British casualties (Source 35)? (E)

# LOCATION OF SOURCES

1     D. Lloyd George, *War Memoirs,* vol. IV (Ivor Nicholson & Watson, 1934) pp. 2119–20

2     *Ibid.,* vol. IV, pp. 2116–17

3     R. Blake (ed.), *The Private Papers of Douglas Haig* (Eyre & Spottiswoode, 1953) p. 184

4     Sir James Edmonds (ed.), *Official History of the War, 1917,* vol. I (Macmillan, 1940) Appendix 8, p. 16

5     Blake (ed.), *op. cit.,* p. 212

6     J. Terraine, *The Road to Passchendaele* (Leo Cooper, 1977) p. 80

7     *Ibid.,* p. 84

8     *Ibid.,* p. 107

9     Sir C.E. Callwell, *The Life of Field Marshal Sir Henry Wilson,* vol. I (Cassell, 1927) pp. 354–5, 359

10    Terraine, *op. cit.,* pp. 134–5

11    (a) Lord Hankey, *The Supreme Command,* vol. II (Allen & Unwin, 1961) pp. 682–3
        (b) Lloyd George, *op cit.,* vol. IV, pp. 2186–94
        (c) Blake (ed.), *op. cit.,* pp. 236–42

12    Terraine, *op. cit.,* pp. 185–7

13    (a) Lloyd George, *op. cit.,* vol. IV, p. 2240
        (b) G.A.B. Dewar and Lieutenant-Colonel J.H. Boraston (eds.), *Sir Douglas Haig's Command, December 1915 to November 1918,* vol. I (Constable, 1922) facing p. 365

14    Terraine, *op. cit.,* pp. 200–1

15    Terraine, *op. cit.,* p. 201

16    Terraine, *op. cit.,* pp. 202–3

17    Terraine, *op. cit.,* p. 203

18    Sir James Edmonds (ed.), *Official History of the War, 1917,* vol. II (Macmillan, 1948) pp. 177–9

19    Duff Cooper, *Haig,* vol. II (Faber & Faber, 1936) pp. 140–1

20    Lynn MacDonald, *They Called It Passchendaele* (Michael Joseph, 1978) pp. 121–2

21    General Sir Hubert Gough, *The Fifth Army* (Hodder & Stoughton, 1931) p. 205

22    Blake (ed.), *op. cit.,* p. 256

23    Brigadier-General John Charteris, *At GHQ* (Cassell, 1931) pp. 258–9

24    Blake (ed.), *op. cit.,* p. 261

25    E. Norman Gladden, *Ypres 1917, A Personal Account* (William Kimber, 1967) p. 130

26    MacDonald, *op. cit.,* pp. 187–8

27    (a) B. Liddell Hart, *A History of the First World War* (Cassell, 1930) p. 454
      (b) *Spectator,* 3 January, 1958
      (c) *Ibid.*

28    J.H. Boraston (ed.), *Sir Douglas Haig's Despatches* (Dent, 1919) p. 116

29    *Ibid.,* pp. 133–5

30    Lloyd George, *op. cit.,* vol. IV, pp. 2232–42

31    Hankey, *op. cit.,* vol. II, pp. 700–1

32    Guy Chapman, *A Passionate Prodigality* (Buchan & Enright, 1985) pp. 206–7

33    Terraine, *op. cit.,* p. 332

34    (a)  Edmonds (ed.), *op. cit.,* vol. II, pp. 360–1
      (b) *Statistics of the Military Effort of the British Empire* (War Office, 1922) p. 326
      (c) Terraine, *op. cit.,* pp. 328, 343–7

35    (a) A.J.P. Taylor, *The First World War* (Hamish Hamilton, 1963) p. 148
      (b) J. Terraine, *Douglas Haig, The Educated Soldier* (Hutchinson, 1963) pp. 371–2

# Case Study 3

# BRITAIN AND IRELAND, 1912–22

## INTRODUCTION

The years 1912–22 were vital ones in the long and generally unhappy story of Britain's relationship with Ireland. The political framework which emerged during this decade has endured, while its inadequacies help to explain the continuing problem of Ulster today. This case study is focused on three particular episodes:

(a) the attempt to provide Ireland with Home Rule from 1912–14;

(b) the Easter Rising of April 1916 and its repercussions; and

(c) the period known as 'the Troubles', from 1919 to 1922, which culminated in the emergence of Ulster as a separate but constituent part of the United Kingdom, and the birth of the Irish Free State.

At the outset in 1912, Asquith's Liberal government, with the aid of the Irish Nationalist party under John Redmond, was attempting to negotiate a Home Rule Bill that would have resulted in a united Ireland, still firmly within the British Empire. By 1922 two wholly unexpected developments had taken place. Ulster had broken away from the rest of Ireland, and though granted its own Parliament, was still closely linked to the United Kingdom; and the Irish Free State, given Dominion status under the treaty signed in 1921, was well on its way to independence, an outcome which few would have predicted in 1912.

But the Irish problem was by no means solved. The terms of the Irish Treaty of 1921 were so unacceptable to a large minority in the South that they led to a civil war between pro- and anti-Treaty elements, and this division was perpetuated in the pattern of Irish party politics thereafter. The permanent exclusion of Ulster from the rest of Ireland left a void in the Irish Free State that still demands to be filled. Redmond's words, spoken in 1913, still have a contemporary resonance: 'Ireland for us is one entity. It is one land. Tyrone and Tyrconnell are as much a part of Ireland as Munster or Connaught . . . Our ideal in this movement is a self-governing Ireland in the future, where all her sons, and all races and creeds, within her shores will bring their tribute, great or small, to the great total of national enterprise, national statesmanship, and national happiness . . .'

The substantial minority of Catholics in the North found themselves members of a political entity to which they had never wanted to belong, and in which they were deprived of an effective voice.

The question raised by this case study is whether the solution achieved in 1922 was already inevitable in 1912, or whether with wiser counsels and greater moderation on all sides a better alternative might have been found.

There were essentially two aspects to the Irish problem facing Britain in 1912. First was the relationship of Britain to Ireland as a whole. It had long been evident that the majority of the Irish people were not content with the Act of Union of 1801, even if the Irish were now overrepresented in the House of Commons. (Ireland had 101 MPs in 1912. Simply on the basis of population she was entitled to about 60.) Gladstone's two Home Rule Bills of 1886 and 1893 were a belated recognition of that fact. By 1912 the barrier which the House of Lords had erected to Home Rule in 1893 could be circumvented, and while the Conservative party was still violently against Home Rule, the Liberal party and its allies, the Irish Nationalists and the Labour party, had a comfortable majority in the House of Commons. But in the north-east of Ireland a Protestant enclave, made up of the descendants of the English and Scots who had settled in Ulster in the seventeenth century, was equally opposed to Home Rule, if for different reasons. When Gladstone's Home Rule Bill was introduced in 1886 it led to violent riots in Belfast in which several people were killed, and to Randolph Churchill's inflammatory remark that 'Ulster will fight and Ulster will be right.' The Ulster Defence Union kept opposition to Home Rule alive after 1886 and was strengthened by the formation in 1905 of the Ulster Unionist Council. As the prospect of Home Rule approached, so resistance to it could be expected to increase. The ultimate question was whether any British government would be prepared to use force to impose the wishes of the Catholic majority in Ireland as a whole on the Protestant majority in Ulster.

# 1. THE FAILURE OF HOME RULE, 1912–14

In 1909 the House of Lords rejected Lloyd George's 'People's Budget'. This was the final provocation in a series of encounters between the Liberal government and the Conservative-dominated Upper House. It persuaded Asquith that the time had come to trim the powers of the House of Lords. Under the terms of the Parliament Act passed in 1911 the Lords lost all power over money bills, and their powers to delay ordinary legislation were limited to two years. Two General Elections in 1910 had deprived the Liberal party of its overall majority, and Asquith's government was henceforth dependent on the support of the Irish Nationalists with their 82 seats. Although, so far as is known, there was no specific agreement between Asquith and Redmond, it was clear that a Home Rule Bill for Ireland was the price Asquith would have to pay for this support. Anticipating such a move, and in the knowledge that the House of Lords could no longer come to the rescue, the Ulster Unionists, led by Sir

Edward Carson, MP, took steps to defend themselves. In January 1912 the Ulster Volunteers were formed to resist, by force if necessary, the imposition of Home Rule. In England Bonar Law, leader of the Conservative party, pledged his unqualified support for resistance to Home Rule in Ulster, whatever form it might take (Source 1). In September over half a million Ulster Loyalists signed the Covenant (Source 2) pledging themselves to use 'all means which may be found necessary to defeat the present conspiracy to set up a Home Rule Parliament in Ireland'.

Between 1912 and 1914, while the Home Rule Bill made its slow but inexorable progress through Parliament, opposition to it mounted in Ulster, which provoked in its turn attempts to reach a compromise that might win over the Ulster Unionists without forfeiting Redmond's support. The crisis came to a head in 1914. In March, in the so-called 'Curragh Mutiny', 57 out of 70 officers in the 3rd Cavalry Brigade stationed at the Curragh Camp near Dublin, threatened to resign their commissions rather than undertake military operations against their Protestant co-religionists in Ulster. In April the Ulster Volunteers succeeded in smuggling 20 000 rifles and 3 million rounds of ammunition into Ulster. Taking a leaf out of Carson's book, the Nationalist Movement in Southern Ireland also prepared to adopt a policy of physical force. In November 1913 the Irish Volunteers, a citizen army, was launched 'to secure and maintain the rights and liberties common to all the people of Ireland'. In July 1914 they too succeeded in smuggling in a boatload of arms, though not without a scuffle with British troops in which three civilians were killed. By the summer of 1914 there were three armies in Ireland: the British army, whose loyalty in any encounter with the Ulster Volunteers was at best doubtful; the Ulster Volunteers, now 100 000 strong, and well-armed; and the Irish Volunteers, by May a force of 75 000.

In the face of these developments, Asquith sought a compromise. Outright opposition to Home Rule, both in Ulster and in the Conservative party, might be overcome by a policy of exclusion. The province of Ulster consisted of nine counties: Donegal, Cavan and Monaghan, where the Catholics were in a substantial majority; Antrim, Armagh, Londonderry and Down, where the Protestants predominated; and Fermanagh and Tyrone, where Catholics slightly outnumbered Protestants. It is safe to say that by this time all Protestants virtually were Unionist, all Catholics supporters of Home Rule. Various proposals were canvassed. In June 1912 Agar-Robartes, a Liberal MP, proposed that the four Protestant counties of Antrim, Armagh, Londonderry and Down should be allowed to opt out of Home Rule. The amendment was easily defeated. But in March 1914 Asquith himself introduced a White Paper which would have permitted any county in the province of Ulster to be excluded from the Home Rule government for a period of three, later raised to six, years. Redmond gave his reluctant assent to this proposal, but it was rejected both by Bonar Law and Carson, who remarked: 'We do not want sentence of death with a stay of execution for six years' (Source 9). Despite their objections, Asquith persevered with an Amending Bill, along these lines, but when introduced into the House of Lords in June 1914, it was savagely amended to provide for the permanent exclusion of all nine counties, without even a plebiscite, which made it clearly unacceptable to the Irish Nationalists.

In these circumstances George V summoned an all-party conference which met at Buckingham Palace from 21 to 24 July, in a final effort to avert civil war. It was attended by Asquith and Lloyd George for the Liberals; Bonar Law and Lord Lansdowne for the Conservatives; John Redmond and John Dillon represented the Irish Nationalists, Sir Edward Carson and Captain Craig the Ulster Unionists. Discussion centred upon both the area of Ulster to be excluded and the time limit for which this exclusion would operate. No agreement could be reached on either issue, and the conference broke up without achieving anything (Sources 10–12).

What finally brought about a temporary agreement was the outbreak of the First World War. On 30 July, at the height of the crisis, Bonar Law and Carson requested that both the Home Rule Bill and the Amending Bill should be postponed. When war was declared on 4 August Redmond in an impromptu gesture volunteered his party's support to the British government (Source 13); in return, the Home Rule Bill was finally put on the Statute Book on 18 September, despite Conservative objections. The Amending Bill, providing for Ulster's exclusion, was dropped, but a Suspending Bill was passed at the same time providing that the Home Rule Act (as it had now become)

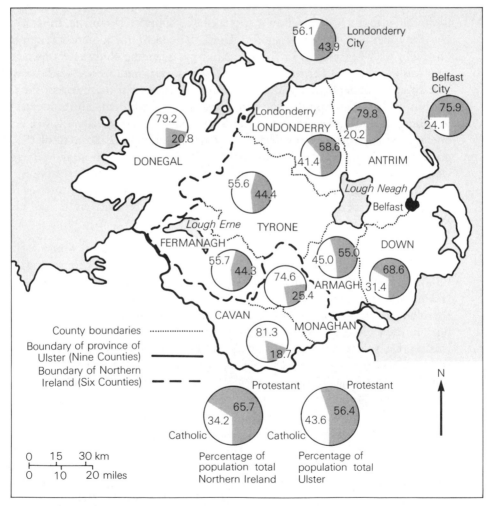

**Map 2**   Northern Ireland and Ulster, Religious Affiliations 1911 (based on O. Woodward, *Divided Ireland*, Heinemann, 1976, p. 34)

must not come into operation until one year after the conclusion of the war. Asquith also promised Carson that the coercion of Ulster was 'unthinkable,' and gave a further assurance 'that the Home Rule Bill will not, and cannot come into operation until Parliament has had the fullest opportunity, by an Amending Bill, of altering, modifying or qualifying its provisions in such a way as to secure the general consent both of Ireland and of the United Kingdom'. After two years of negotiation the Irish and Ulster problems were thus no nearer solution in 1914 than they had been in 1912 and the First World War came almost as a relief, offering as it did a temporary way out of the impasse.

# 2. THE EASTER RISING, 1916

Redmond's appeal to his fellow-nationalists to support Britain in the war against Germany met with a ready response. Until the end of 1915 there were more Irish Catholics than Protestants in the British army, including Redmond's own brother, who was killed in 1917 at the battle of Messines. But there were also those who saw Britain's predicament as Ireland's opportunity, as their Fenian predecessors had done. Within the broad grouping, two factions may be distinguished. The moderates, while unwilling to lend active support to the British, saw their role primarily as a defensive one against any threats from Ulster, or any backsliding on the part of the British government. They formed the bulk of the Irish Volunteers, whose military activities were allowed to continue under the benign eye of the Chief Secretary, Augustine Birrell. But within the Irish Volunteers a splinter group emerged, known as the Irish Republican Brotherhood, who began actively plotting a rebellion as soon as war broke out.

They included Padraic Pearse, founder of two successful schools, whose nationalism was based on a romantic view of Irish history and culture (Source 14); Joseph Plunkett, son of the Papal Count George Noble Plunkett, a member of one of Ireland's most distinguished Catholic families; Thomas Clarke, who had already served a fifteen-year gaol sentence in England for terrorist activities; and Eamon de Valera, born in the United States to a Spanish father and an Irish mother, but brought up in Ireland. De Valera, like Pearse, was motivated by a romantic vision of Ireland, free and independent. More remarkable, perhaps, was the support given to the Irish rebellion by Sir Roger Casement, formerly a member of the British Consular Service, and Countess Markiewicz, who prior to her marriage was Constance Gore-Booth, daughter of Sir Henry Gore-Booth, a prominent Irish landowner. They were to be joined in 1916 by James Connelly, a committed socialist and trade union organiser, who had his own Citizen Army in Dublin to add to the cause (Source 16). Two conditions were essential if a rebellion was to succeed; first the rebels would need to be adequately armed; secondly, they would have to be able to count on a wide measure of public support. Neither condition applied to the Easter Rebellion, and these weaknesses were to be compounded by bitter divisions within the nationalist movement.

In July 1915 the Supreme Council of the Irish Republican Brotherhood set up a Military Council, consisting initially of Pearse, Plunkett and Eamonn Ceannt, whose task it was to plan the Rising. Financial assistance was obtained from Clan na Gael, a militant Irish nationalist movement in the United States. Sir Roger Casement had meanwhile obtained a promise of support from the German government. But the moderates in the Irish Volunteers, who were very sceptical about the prospects of success for an armed rising (Source 17) were kept in ignorance of these preparations. Eoin MacNeill, their Chief of Staff, was deceived by means of a forged document into believing that the British authorities were about to disarm the Volunteers; it was only that threat which persuaded MacNeill to give his initial and reluctant assent to the Rising, when he was finally told about it.

The Rising was planned to take place on Easter Sunday, 23 April, 1916, a day with symbolic overtones. It was to be preceded by the landing of a shipload of German arms (40 000 rifles and ten machine guns) in Tralee Bay, between 20 and 22 April. Casement, who had been unsuccessful in his attempts to recruit an Irish brigade from Irish prisoners of war captured on the Western Front, was to land in Ireland at the same time.

Everything went wrong. British naval intelligence had intercepted the wireless messages through which the arms shipment had been arranged. The *Aud*, carrying the arms, was successfully intercepted off the Irish coast and, rather than surrender his cargo, her captain scuttled his ship at the entrance to Queenstown harbour on Saturday, 22 April.

Casement, who had been landed the previous day from a German submarine, was arrested and identified within hours. Finally, MacNeill discovered that the document purporting to announce the disarming of the Volunteers was a forgery. This, coupled with the news of Casement's arrest and the sinking of the *Aud*, convinced him that the Rising should be called off. On the evening of Saturday, 22 April, instructions were sent out to that effect. But the intransigents in the Military Council were not to be deterred. The Rising planned for Easter Sunday, 23 April, was indeed cancelled, but it was now to take place on Easter Monday, 24 April, instead.

Quite what the rebels now hoped to achieve is far from clear. All copies of their plan have disappeared. It seems likely that they hoped to hold a number of strategically placed buildings in Dublin for long enough to provoke a sympathetic response in the rest of Ireland, and to attract the support of international opinion for the cause of Irish independence; but for Pearse, the gesture was more important than the prospect of success (Source 15).

On Easter Monday rebel detachments occupied a number of buildings north and south of the River Liffey, of which the most important was the General Post Office. The birth of the Irish Republic was proclaimed (Source 18). Despite being heavily out-numbered (there were about 1600 rebels against 12 000 British troops) the rebels fought with such determination that it took a week to dislodge them, and casualties on both sides were severe, amounting to about 450 killed and 2614 wounded in all. By Saturday, 29 April, Pearse recognised the inevitability of defeat, and surrendered unconditionally.

Resistance in the rest of Ireland was confined to a few isolated demonstrations and skirmishes. The only success recorded was in County Dublin, where a rebel force captured four police barracks. In Dublin itself there was little evident sympathy for the rebels. Irish regiments played a leading part in the suppression of the Rising, and rebel prisoners were jeered at on their way to gaol.

But the aftermath of defeat led to ultimate victory for the rebels. Public opinion in Britain was outraged by the Rising (Sources 21–2), and the British government's response was to use force and exemplary punishments. Between 3 and 12 May fifteen rebel leaders were tried by court martial in Dublin and shot. Casement was tried in England for treason, and was also executed. Seventy-nine women and 3430 men were arrested, of whom 1841 were subsequently interned in England. The sympathy evoked by these events for the Easter rebels meant that before long John Redmond's moderate nationalism was outflanked by the appeal of the Sinn Fein movement, now sanctified by the blood of its martyrs. Sources 23–8 reflect British and Irish responses to the executions.

# 3.  IRELAND, 1916–22

Between 1916 and 1918 Anglo-Irish relations grew steadily worse. Lloyd George was despatched in May 1916 to negotiate the immediate granting of Home Rule, but once again he ran into the obstacle of Unionist intransigence. Carson was now willing to limit the excluded area of Ulster to the Six Counties, but two members of the Cabinet, Walter Long and Lord Lansdowne, insisted that this exclusion must be permanent, and not left to be determined by an imperial conference, as Redmond would have been prepared to accept. Redmond felt that he had been deceived, and repudiated the government's proposals.

In July 1917 a further effort at a negotiated settlement was made with the summoning of an Irish Convention, to be attended by all the political groupings in Ireland. The Sinn Fein party refused to send any representatives, and the Ulster Unionists again dug in their heels on the question of a time limit for Ulster's exclusion. The convention lingered on until 1918, but achieved nothing.

Then, in March 1918, the British Cabinet made perhaps its worst blunder in deciding to extend conscription to Ireland. Though never implemented, the threat provoked a furious response. The Catholic Church which had hitherto condemned all forms of violence now urged resistance to conscription 'by every means consonant with the Law of God'. The Nationalist party withdrew their members from the House of Commons in protest. A final insult was the arrest in May 1918 of 73 Sinn Fein leaders on suspicion of having dealings with Germany, though no evidence was provided to support these accusations.

These developments and the failure of the Nationalist party to make any progress towards Home Rule between 1914 and 1918 played into the hands of Sinn Fein, whose candidates began to win by-elections as early as January 1917. In the 1918 General Election Sinn Fein won 73 out of 105 Irish seats, with 47 per cent of the popular vote.

True to their election promises the Sinn Fein members refused to take their seats at Westminster (47 were still in gaol) and the 26 remaining at liberty established their own Parliament (Dáil) in Dublin on 21 January, 1919. Consciously reaffirming the Republic which had been proclaimed in April 1916 the Dáil then adopted 'The Democratic Programme of Dáil Éireann', and assumed responsibility for governing the whole of Ireland.

The British government was now faced by another direct challenge to its authority, this time backed by a popular mandate. Its response took three forms. At first there was a final attempt to solve the problem with Home Rule, but now based on the principle of partition, with separate parliaments in Belfast and Dublin. The Government of Ireland Act which gave effect to these proposals was passed in December 1920 (Source 30). It was grudgingly accepted in the North, but dismissed in the South as 'a scheme for the plunder and partition of Ireland'. At the same time the government did its best to reassert imperial authority. Sinn Fein parties were banned in many Irish counties, the Dáil forbidden to meet, and an army of occupation, strengthened by the notorious Auxiliaries and Black and Tans (recruited from British ex-servicemen), was sent over to maintain law and order. A guerilla war, euphemistically known as 'the Troubles', ensued. It was marked by atrocities on both sides. In 1920 alone, the British forces suffered 203 deaths and 369 wounded, while Irish losses between January 1919 and July 1921 are calculated at 752 killed and 866 wounded.

By the summer of 1921 Lloyd George had decided on a third course of action: negotiation with his opponents. A truce was called, and an Irish delegation came to London. The chief negotiators on the British side were Lloyd George himself, Lord Birkenhead and Winston Churchill. The Irish were represented mainly by Arthur Griffith and Michael Collins. De Valera took part in the early stages, but, significantly, remained in Dublin as the talks neared a climax, understanding that any terms reached would have to be approved by the Dáil.

Two main issues dominated the proceedings: the status of the new Irish state and the exclusion of Ulster. Less controversial was the question of Britain's right to use Irish ports for the purpose of defence. Lloyd George was ready to concede Dominion status (i.e. Ireland should enjoy the same constitutional position as Canada), but insisted that Ireland remain within the British empire. De Valera was equally determined that Ireland should become a sovereign republic.

Controversy therefore centred upon the Oath of Allegiance that would be required of all Irish ministers and officials. If it meant recognising the monarchical authority of George V, then Ireland could hardly claim to be a republic. The solution devised in 1949, under which India and Pakistan became republics who recognised the King as Head of the Commonwealth, was not conceivable in 1921. Eventually, a formula was produced that was acceptable to Griffith, if not to De Valera (Source 34).

Where Ulster was concerned, Lloyd George proposed a two-part solution: the Six Counties given Home Rule under the Government of Ireland Act (Armagh, Antrim, Down, Londonderry, Tyrone and Fermanagh) were to be given the option of withdrawing from the new Irish Free State should they choose to do so. In this case, a Boundary Commission would be required to revise the boundary of Northern Ireland 'so as to make the boundary conform as closely as possible to the wishes of the population' (Source 31). Griffith gave some form of assent to this proposal when it was presented to him on 12 November, and Lloyd George reminded him of this at the final negotiating session on 5 December. Griffith acknowledged his commitment: 'I have never let a man down in my life, and I never will.'

Other members of the Irish delegation, Barton and Duffy in particular, were less willing to agree to the terms. But when Lloyd George threatened that, should they refuse, 'It is war, and war within three days', they did so.

There is little doubt that some of the Irish delegates, Michael Collins in particular, believed that a Boundary Commission would report in their favour and that the counties of Tyrone and Fermanagh would rejoin the Irish Free State, thus rendering Ulster so small as not to be economically viable. How far Lloyd George encouraged them in this belief is a matter for speculation (Source 32).

The Irish Treaty, finally signed at 2.10 a.m. on 6 December, 1921 did not solve the Irish problem (Sources 35–6). It was approved by only 4 votes to 3 in the Irish Cabinet, and by 67 votes to 57 in the Dáil. In June 1922 a civil war broke out between the pro- and anti-Treaty forces in the South, while in the North the Catholic minority's allegiance went to the Irish Free State, as to a great extent it still does. What can be said in defence of the Treaty is that it finally enabled the 26 counties that made up the Irish Free State to go their own way, no longer hindered by an alien government.

The Boundary Commission agreed under Article XII of the Treaty (Source 34) eventually met in 1925. The Irish Free State's representative on this occasion was Eoin MacNeill, himself an Ulster Catholic, and a prominent Irish Nationalist, as we have seen. The Northern Ireland government refused to nominate a member, and the British government nominated on its behalf J.R. Fisher, a newspaper editor and close associate of Sir James Craig, the Ulster Prime Minister at the time. The Commission was presided over by Justice Feetham of the South African Supreme Court.

From the start, it was clear that Feetham and Fisher were only prepared to discuss minor rectifications to the frontier, and when the commission's findings (Source 37) were prematurely published in the *Morning Post* on 7 November, MacNeill resigned in protest. This led to a crisis in Anglo-Irish relations that could only be resolved by high-level negotiations between Baldwin, the British Prime Minister, and representatives of the Southern and Northern Irish governments. In December 1925 an agreement was reached providing that: (i) the existing border between Ulster and the Irish Free State was to remain unchanged; (ii) the Irish Free State was to be released from its liabilities for a share of the British National Debt (the sum was not specified); and (iii) the Council of Ireland, which was envisaged in the Government of Ireland Act of 1920 but had never actually met, was brought officially to an end. Thus, untidily and unsatisfactorily, Ulster's frontiers were finally decided. The consequences of these arrangements are still with us.

# FURTHER READING

## Sources

E. Curtis and R.B. MacDowell (eds.), *Irish Historical Documents* (Methuen, 1943)

## General

G. Dangerfield, *The Damnable Question* (Constable, 1977)
F.S.L. Lyons, *Ireland since the Famine* (Weidenfeld & Nicolson, 1971)
N. Mansergh, *The Irish Question, 1840–1921* (Allen & Unwin, 1965)
P. O'Farrell, *Ireland's English Question, Anglo-Irish Relations 1534–1970* (Batsford, 1971)

## The Ulster Problem, 1912–14

D. Gwynn, *The History of Partition, 1912–25* (Brown & Nolan, 1950)
A.T.Q. Stewart, *The Ulster Crisis, Resistance to Home Rule, 1912–14* (Faber & Faber, 1969)
A.T.Q. Stewart, *The Narrow Ground, Aspects of Ulster 1609–1969* (Faber & Faber, 1977)

## The Easter Rising

T. Coffey, *Agony at Easter* (Penguin, 1969)
Owen D. Edwards and Fergus Pyle (eds.), *1916: The Easter Rising* (MacGibbon & Kee, 1968)
K.B. Nowlan (ed.), *The Making of 1916* (Stationery Office, Dublin, 1969)

## Ireland, 1919–22

F. Pakenham, *Peace by Ordeal* (Jonathan Cape, 1935)
C. Townshend, *The British Campaign in Ireland* (OUP, 1978)
D. Williams (ed.), *The Irish Struggle, 1916–26* (Routledge & Kegan Paul, 1966)

## Articles

D.G. Boyce, 'British Conservative Opinion, the Ulster Question and the Partition of Ireland', *Irish Historical Studies*, 1970–1
R. Murphy, 'Faction and the Home Rule Crisis, 1912–14', *History*, June 1986

# SOURCE MATERIAL 1
# The Failure of Home Rule, 1912-14

*Sources 1–13 cover: A. the objections of Conservatives and Ulster Unionists to Home Rule (Sources 1–4); B. the various proposals canvassed to meet these objections (Sources 5–9); C. the Buckingham Palace conference of July 1914 (Sources 10–12); and D. Redmond's attitude to Britain on the outbreak of the First World War (Source 13).*

## 1A   Conservative and Ulster Unionist Opposition to Home Rule

### SOURCE 1   Bonar Law's Speech to the Conservative Party at Blenheim Palace, 29 July, 1912

In our opposition to them [the Liberal Government] we shall not be guided by the consideration or bound by the restraints which would influence us in an ordinary constitutional struggle. We shall take the means, whatever means seem to us most effective, to deprive them of the despotic power which they have usurped and compel them to appeal to the people whom they have deceived. They may, perhaps they will, carry their Home Rule Bill through the House of Commons but what then? I said the other day in the House of Commons and I repeat here that there are things stronger than Parliamentary majorities.

Before I occupied the position which I now fill in the party I said that, in my belief, if an attempt were made to deprive these men of their birthright – as part of a corrupt Parliamentary bargain – they would be justified in resisting such an attempt by all means in their power including force. I said it then, and I repeat it now with a full sense of the responsibility which attaches to my position, that if such an attempt is made, I can imagine no length of resistance to which Ulster can go in which I should not be prepared to support them, and in which, in my belief, they would not be supported by the overwhelming majority of the British people.

R. Blake, *The Unknown Prime Minister: The Life and Times of Andrew Bonar Law*
(Eyre & Spottiswoode, 1955) p. 130

### SOURCE 2   Ulster's Solemn League and Covenant

*This document was approved by the Ulster Unionist Council on 23 September, 1912, and signed publicly on 28 September, 'Ulster Day'. Over half a million people added their signatures.*

Being convinced in our consciences that Home Rule would be disastrous to the material well-being of Ulster, as well as the whole of Ireland, subversive of our civil and religious freedom, destructive of our citizenship, and perilous to the unity of the Empire, we, whose names are underwritten, men of Ulster, loyal subjects of His Gracious Majesty King George V, humbly relying on the God whom, our fathers in days of stress and trial confidently trusted, do hereby pledge ourselves in solemn Covenant throughout this time of threatened calamity to stand by one another in defending for ourselves and our children our cherished position of equal citizenship in the United Kingdom, and in using all means which may be found necessary to defeat the present conspiracy to set up a Home Rule Parliament in Ireland. And in the event of such a Parliament being forced upon us we further and mutually pledge ourselves to refuse to recognise its authority. In sure confidence that God will defend the right, we hereto subscribe our names. And further we individually declare that we have not already signed this Covenant. God Save the King.

E. Curtis and R.B. MacDowell (eds.), *Irish Historical Documents* (Methuen, 1943) p. 304

## SOURCE 3 *Punch,* 8 October, 1913

## SECOND THOUGHTS.

MR. JOHN REDMOND. "FULL SHTEAM AHEAD! (*Aside*) I WONDHER WILL I LAVE THIS CONTRAIRY LITTLE DIVIL LOOSE, THE WAY HE'D COME BACK BY HIMSELF AFTHERWARDS?"

## SOURCE 4   Letter from Sir Edward Carson to Asquith, 10 January, 1914

*This letter from the leader of the Ulster Unionists was written in reply to one from Asquith, in which the Prime Minister had asked Carson to state 'what is the precise form of "exclusion" which you have in mind?'*

My dear Prime Minister,

I am in receipt of your letter of the 8th inst. I thought it was always apparent that when the exclusion of Ulster was discussed, I meant that Ulster should remain as at present under the Imperial Parliament and that a Dublin Parliament should have no legislative powers within the excluded area. Ulster would therefore send no members to the Dublin Parliament, but would continue as at present to send members to the Imperial Parliament.

This would of course involve that the administration of Ulster should be under the control of the Imperial Parliament.

I do not think I can say anything more specific.

I remain,

Sincerely yours,

Edward Carson

D. Gwynn, *The History of Partition, 1912–25* (Brown & Nolan, 1950) p. 76

## 1B   Proposals to Exclude Ulster and their Reception

## SOURCE 5   Memorandum of an Interview between Asquith and John Redmond, 2 February, 1914

*This interview took place after Asquith had received news of a Unionist plot to amend the Army Bill in the House of Lords in such a way that the use of the army in Ulster would be prevented until given approval after a General Election. Asquith predicted that were such an election to be held, the Unionists might sweep the country. The Memorandum is Redmond's own account of what transpired.*

Mr Asquith said he had reason to believe that the crisis might arise on the Army Annual Bill. This Bill must be passed into law by a certain date in March or April, otherwise the Army is disbanded and there is no power to pay it or continue its existence. He expects the Opposition in the House of Commons will take up the position that they won't sanction the Army Bill until they know how the Army is going to be used in Ulster. He thinks they will fight the Army Bill in the House of Commons, and possibly resort to extreme disorder of such a character that the whole business of the House will be held up.

These considerations have led Mr Asquith to the conclusion that for the safety of Home Rule it is essential that he should make an offer to Ulster of such a character that in the event of their refusal of it – and he thinks that at this stage any offer he makes short of the exclusion of Ulster would be rejected – it would deprive them of all moral force.

I argued generally against the making of any proposals whatever at the present time. I said it would mean to his opponents very largely an abandonment of his Bill, that the months intervening between now and the discussions of the Bill when it comes up would be spent in most destructive criticism, that the Ulster leaders would not accept any proposals whatever, that it would be quite impossible for us to accept or support suggestions of this character . . .

Gwynn, *The History of Partition*, pp. 79–80

## SOURCE 6 Speech by Sir Edward Carson in the House of Commons, 11 February, 1914

*This speech was delivered during the debate on the Address to the Throne. Carson announced that if there was a proposal to exclude Ulster from the Home Rule Bill in order to avoid civil war and bloodshed, then it would be his duty to put the question of exclusion to his supporters. He concluded his speech as follows:*

Believe me, whatever way you settle the Irish question, there can be only two ways to deal with Ulster. It is for statesmen to say which is the best and right one. She is not part of the community which can be bought. She will not allow herself to be sold. You must therefore either coerce her if you go on, or you must, in the long run, by showing that good government can come under the Home Rule Bill, try and win her over to the case of the rest of Ireland. You probably can coerce her – though I doubt it. If you do, what will be the disastrous consequences not only to Ulster, but to this country and the Empire?

Will my fellow countryman, the leader of the Nationalist party have gained anything? I will agree with him – I do not believe he wants to triumph any more than I do. But will he have gained anything if he takes over here and then applies for what he used to call the enemies of the people, to come to coerce them into obedience? No, Sir, one false step taken in relation to Ulster will in my opinion, render for ever impossible a solution of the Irish problem . . .

I say then to my nationalist fellow-countrymen, and indeed to our government: you have never tried to win over Ulster. You have never tried to understand her position . . . I say to the leader of the Nationalist party, if you want Ulster, go and take her, or go and win her. You have never wanted her affection, you have wanted her taxes.

Curtis and MacDowell (eds.), *Irish Historical Documents*, pp. 306–7

## SOURCE 7 Lloyd George's Memorandum to the Cabinet

*This was submitted in February 1914, and formed the basis of the White Paper which Asquith introduced on 9 March.*

I am far from suggesting that proposals designed to promote compromise ought to be treated as admissions that the original Bill is defective; but I fear it would be difficult to induce the general public to draw the distinction. I am, therefore, earnestly opposed to offers which might be interpreted into a confession of blemishes in the Home Rule Bill as passed by the House of Commons, and I am convinced that it would be almost impossible for the Government to undertake the responsibility of ordering troops to fire on an Ulster riot if the Bill were forced through after the rejection of these proposed modifications.

I am, therefore, strongly of the opinion that the proposal must have two essential characteristics:

(1) It must be an offer the rejection of which would put the other side entirely in the wrong, as far as the British public is concerned; and,

(2) It must not involve any alteration in the scheme of the Bill; so that if it is rejected, the Unionists cannot say, 'Why, you yourselves admitted that your Bill needed amendment.'

I can only think of one suggestion which would meet these two fundamental conditions. Mr Bonar Law in his speech made it clear that a General Election would involve a complete change in the attitude of the Tory Party towards the measure. If the General Election resulted in favour of the Government he undertook on behalf of his party, to withdraw every encouragement to resistance. Sir Edward Carson, in much more cautious terms, practically admitted that an election would make a substantial difference in his attitude. They have no right to demand an election in respect of those areas in Ireland which are in favour of the Bill; their demand must logically be confined to the resisting areas. Why not say to them: 'We will concede your demand in respect of that portion of Ireland which is hostile to Home Rule. The rest of Ireland do not ask for it; in fact, they are opposed to it. They want Home Rule now, as soon as the measure can be carried.'

I would therefore suggest that any county in Ireland that wished to submit its case once more to the British electorate for decision should be allowed to contract out of the Act. The opinion of the counties would be taken by means of a plebiscite of the electors in each county, taken on some such plan as has been incorporated in the Scottish Temperance Act of last year. A poll would be taken in the county on a requisition demanding it, say one-tenth of the voters on the register. If the poll should be in favour of exclusion that particular county would be excluded from the operation of the Act for X years; at the end of that term it would, unless the Imperial Parliament in the meantime provided otherwise, be incorporated with the rest of Ireland in the area governed by the Dublin Parliament.

As this House of Commons cannot last beyond December 1915 an election must intervene before the end of the period X, however short its term. The excluded counties would, therefore have the decision of the United Kingdom upon their case for permanent exclusion. If the appeal goes against them they come in at the end of the X years without any further legislation in their favour. A Unionist Parliament would deal with the case of Ireland as it sees fit, and nothing which is now enacted would interfere with the power of that Parliament . . .

Gwynn, The History of Partition, pp. 85–6

# SOURCE 8   Redmond's Memorandum in Response to the Lloyd George Proposals

*There were lengthy consultations between the Irish Nationalist leaders and the Cabinet, culminating in this Memorandum which indicated the limits of concession to which the Irish Nationalist party was prepared to go.*

We adhere to the pledges we have consistently made that we should give all our help towards any reasonable attempt to have the question settled by general consent. We may add, as strong confirmation of the sincerity and consistency of this attitude on our part, that we are ready to take considerable risks in getting a fair consideration by our people, even of proposals which we know will be both unwelcome and disappointing to them.

*Redmond then listed the possible solutions that had been suggested, and indicated his preference for the Plunkett plan, which would have allowed Ulster to vote itself out of a Home Rule Parliament after ten years. He accepted that the third suggested solution – namely the right of any county in Ulster, by plebiscite, to vote itself temporarily out of the jurisdiction of the Irish Parliament – was the one offering the best tactical advantages, and concluded as follows:*

To sum up: we are ready to give our acquiescence to the solution of the standing out for three years by option of the counties of Ulster as the price of peace, and to recommend it as the price of peace to our people.

Gwynn, The History of Partition, pp. 93–5

# SOURCE 9   Debate on the White Paper, 9 March, 1914

*The White Paper put forward what was in essence Lloyd George's scheme. Under its terms any Ulster county might, by a majority of its parliamentary electors, vote itself out of the operation of the Home Rule Bill for six years. Asquith had secured Redmond's reluctant assent to the extension of the three-year limit to six years.*

*Bonar Law:* Does the right hon. gentleman mean that at the end of six years the counties which have the option now are not to have it for themselves?

*Asquith:* Yes, they would come in at the end of six years unless the Imperial Parliament otherwise decides.

*Bonar Law:* If you think it is wrong to compel them to come in today, how can you think it is right to compel them to come in tomorrow?

*Carson:* So far as Ulster is concerned, be exclusion good or bad and I think we are only driven into exclusion from the exigencies of the case and of the facts – but be exclusion good or bad, Ulster wants this question settled now and for ever. We do not want sentence of death with a stay of execution for six years.

I. Colvin, The Life of Lord Carson, vol. II (Gollancz, 1934) pp. 297–8

# 1C  Deadlock at the Buckingham Palace Conference

*On 23 June, 1914 an Amending Bill was introduced into the House of Lords providing for exclusion by option of any of the counties which wished to vote themselves out of the Home Rule Bill. A further Amendment to the Amending Bill was passed by Unionist peers, providing for the exclusion of all nine Ulster counties, without option or time limit. An impasse had been reached. On 18 July Asquith asked King George V to use his influence, and an all-party conference was duly summoned to meet at Buckingham Palace on 21 July. It sat for three days, without achieving any result.*

## SOURCE 10   Letter from Walter Long to Lord Lansdowne, 19 July, 1914

*Walter Long had been Chief Secretary for Ireland in 1905, and represented a Dublin constituency from 1906–10. He was a respected and influential figure in the Tory party, and was considered for the Tory leadership when Balfour retired from that post in 1911. Lord Lansdowne was leader of the Conservative peers in the House of Lords, and had extensive properties in Ireland.*

Conference will be very unpopular with our friends . . . Is it too late for you to ask for an audience with HM? Our men do not believe in the reality of any arrangement save the Clean Cut [i.e. the permanent exclusion of Ulster]. They say 'The Party has supported Ulster with votes, speeches and money and should not now at the last moment be sacrificed. The Government are in a hole, must face civil war or an Election, therefore will choose the latter unless we give in. If we stand firm there can be no settlement. Conference cannot last more than one day.' Do let me implore you to save the party from disruption.

R. Murphy, 'Faction and the Home Rule Crisis, 1912–14', History,<br>June 1986, p. 231

# SOURCE 11   John Redmond's Memorandum at the Buckingham Palace Conference

*No official record of the conference proceedings was kept, in order to allow complete freedom of discussion. Redmond, however, dictated his personal memoranda each day after the meeting. The following material is taken from his account of the first two days' proceedings.*

The Irish National Party have all along been, and still are, strongly of the opinion that no satisfactory settlement of the Irish question can be obtained by the exclusion of any portion of Ireland from the operation of the Home Rule Bill.

They are, further, of opinion that there is no considerable section of any political party in Ireland in favour of such a settlement, and that view has been strongly confirmed by the frank condemnation of that method on its merits by the Unionist peers in the recent debate in the House of Lords.

The Irish Party only consented to negotiate on the basis of exclusion because the leaders of the Ulster Unionists repeatedly and flatly refused to consider any other proposal, and the Irish Party were, and are, genuinely and deeply anxious to do everything within their power to obtain a settlement by consent.

Having once agreed to negotiate on the basis of exclusion, the principle which recommended itself to them, and the only principle which appears defensible, was that, so far as is practicable, those districts should be *ex*cluded in which the population was predominantly Unionist and those districts should be *in*cluded in which the population was predominantly Nationalist.

Having examined carefully all possible methods of carrying out that principle, the Nationalist Party came to the conclusion that the only practical method, and the one by which the nearest approximation to the carrying out of this principle could be reached, was by giving each administrative county an option to exclude itself by ballot from the operation of the act.

All other conceivable methods of determining the districts to be excluded, when examined, turned out to be, in their judgment, impracticable . . .

Let us examine how the principle of county option would work out, so far as the different political creeds and religious creeds in Ulster are concerned.

On a county plebiscite, let it be assumed, for the sake of argument, that four of the nine counties of Ulster and the borough of Belfast would *ex*clude themselves; and that five counties and also the borough of Derry would vote for inclusion.

If the counties of Antrim, Down, Derry and Armagh and the borough of Belfast were excluded by the operation of county option, then 293 483 Catholics would be excluded from the operation of the Home Rule Bill, and these some of the most passionate Nationalists in Ireland; whereas in Cavan, Donegal, Fermanagh, Monaghan, Tyrone and Derry Borough, which presumably, would be included in voting, only 179 113 Protestants would be included within the jurisdiction of the Irish Parliament.

If it be contended that it is an injustice to the Protestant minority in the five counties to be included, surely it cannot be contended that it is not an equal injustice to the Catholic minority in the four counties to be excluded? And the injustice is greater in the latter case than in the former; for, while the number of the Protestant minority in the included counties would be, as has been said, 179 113, the number of Catholics in the excluded counties would be 293 483. We append a table:

| | *Catholics Excluded in the Four Counties* | | |
|---|---|---|---|
| *County* | *Protestant* | *Catholics* | *Total* |
| Antrim | 154 113 | 39 751 | 193 864 |
| Armagh | 65 765 | 54 526 | 120 291 |
| Belfast Borough | 293 704 | 93 243 | 386 947 |
| Down | 139 818 | 64 485 | 204 303 |
| Derry County | 58 367 | 41 478 | 99 845 |
| Total | 711 767 | 293 483 | 1 005 250 |

| | *Protestants Included in Rest of Ulster* | | |
|---|---|---|---|
| *County* | *Protestant* | *Catholics* | *Total* |
| Derry Borough | 17 857 | 22 923 | 40 780 |
| Cavan | 16 902 | 74 271 | 91 173 |
| Donegal | 35 516 | 133 021 | 168 537 |
| Fermanagh | 27 096 | 34 740 | 61 836 |
| Monaghan | 18 092 | 53 363 | 71 455 |
| Tyrone | 63 650 | 79 015 | 142 665 |
| Total | 179 113 | 397 333 | 576 446 |
| In the four counties | 711 767 | 293 483 | 1 005 250 |
| Grand Total | 890 880 | 690 816 | 1 581 696 |

Sir Edward Carson agreed that, in view of Mr Redmond's statement, nothing was to be gained by discussing any further proposal for the total exclusion of Ulster.

At this point the Conference adjourned until 11.30 a.m. the following day.

*Secret Wednesday, 22 July, 1914*
*After considering the division of Ulster on the basis of Poor Law Unions, it became apparent that 'no arrangement of this kind could possibly be devised which would meet with the approval of either Sir Edward Carson on the one side or of Mr Redmond on the other. Any such scheme would involve a system of what might be called swapping districts in different parts of Ulster, which was generally agreed to be an impossible thing.'*

Sir Edward Carson repeatedly stated that, so far as Tyrone was concerned, he was unable, even if his judgment led him in that direction, to agree to the INclusion of any part of the county in the jurisdiction of the Home Rule Parliament.

Mr Redmond made a similar declaration with reference to the EXclusion of any part of Tyrone.

The same situation, in substance, arose with regard to Fermanagh and, eventually, Sir Edward Carson substituted, for his demand for the EXclusion of the whole of Ulster, the EXclusion of a *block* consisting of the Six Counties: Antrim, Down, Armagh, Derry, Tyrone and Fermanagh, INcluding Derry City and Belfast: *all to vote as one unit.*

Mr Redmond intimated that he could not seriously consider this proposal, any more than the proposal for the total EXclusion of Ulster.

It became apparent that a deadlock had arisen, and the question was raised as to whether it was of any value to continue the Conference . . .

Gwynn, The History of Partition, pp. 117–31

*The Conference did meet for one more day, but failed to produce any compromise on the area of Ulster to be excluded. The time limit was not even discussed.*

## SOURCE 12   Leo Amery Letter to Neville Chamberlain, 25 July, 1914

*Amery was a pronounced opponent of Home Rule and a strong believer in the Empire. Both he and Chamberlain were Conservative MPs at the time.*

I have never seen a scene of such anger in our Lobby as there was when the Conference was first announced, and it was only when assurances spread around that there was no likelihood of anything coming of it that feeling was in the least mollified. As it is we are now in a splendid position to say that for the sake of peace we have explored a certain path to the utmost and found it led nowhere . . .

The Leo Amery Diaries, vol. I, 1896–1929 (Hutchinson, 1980) p. 101

## 1D  The Outbreak of War in Europe and its Effects on the Ulster Crisis

## SOURCE 13   John Redmond's Speech to the House of Commons, 4 August, 1914

*This speech was delivered during the debate which took place following Grey's announcement to the House of Commons that England had declared war on Germany.*

I hope the House will not consider it improper on my part, in the grave circumstances in which we assemble, if I intervene for a very few moments. I was moved a great deal by that sentence in the speech of the Secretary of State for Foreign Affairs [Grey] in which he said that the one bright spot in the situation was the change of feeling in Ireland. In past times, when this Empire has been engaged in these terrible enterprises, it is true – it would be the utmost affectation to deny it – the sympathy of the Nationalists of Ireland, for reasons to be found deep down in centuries of history, has been estranged from this country.

Allow me to say, sir, that what has occurred in recent years has altered the situation completely. I must not touch, and I may be trusted not to touch on any controversial topic; but this I may be allowed to say, that a wider knowledge of the real facts of Irish history has, I think, altered the views of the democracy of this country towards the Irish question, and today I honestly believe that the democracy of Ireland will turn with the utmost anxiety and sympathy to this country in every trial and danger that may overtake it . . .

I say to the Government that they may tomorrow withdraw every one of their troops from Ireland. I say that the coast of Ireland will be defended from invasion by her armed sons, and for this purpose armed Nationalist Catholics in the South will be only too glad to join with armed Protestant Ulstermen in the North. Is it too much to hope that out of this situation there may spring a situation which will be good not merely for the Empire but good for the future welfare and integrity of the Irish nation?

Gwynn, *The History of Partition,* pp. 137–9

## QUESTIONS ON SOURCES 1–13

1.  On what grounds did Bonar Law feel justified in offering unconditional support to Ulster's resistance to Home Rule (Source 1)? (C)

2.  Would he have condoned the use of force (Source 1)? (C)

3.  Why was the Conservative party so willing to support Ulster Unionism (Sources 1, 2)? (S)

4.  What can you infer, from Source 3, about (a) *Punch's* attitude to John Redmond and (b) *Punch's* attitude to the strength of Ulster Unionism? (C)

5.  What, according to Redmond, was Asquith's motive in making concessions to the Ulster Unionists (Source 5)? How does this conform with the correspondence referred to in Source 4? (E)

6.  How reliable an indicator of Carson's real views on the future of Ulster was the speech he made on 4 February, 1914 (Sources 4, 6, 9)? (E)

7.  What motives inspired Lloyd George's Memorandum on Ulster (Source 7)? (E)

8.  Why did Lloyd George remark that 'this House of Commons cannot last beyond December 1915', and why was he mistaken in that prediction (Source 7)? (S)

9.  What were the essential points of difference between Redmond and Carson, as revealed in Sources 9 and 11? (S)

10. To what extent can the Conservative party be blamed for the failure to reach agreement on Ulster between 1912 and 1914 (Sources 1, 9, 10, 12)? (S)

11. How consistent was the attitude of the Irish Nationalist party to the exclusion of Ulster in the negotiations that took place in 1914 (Sources 5, 8, 11)? (S)

12. Would you agree that both the Liberals and the Irish Nationalists seriously underestimated the strength of *Ulster* nationalism (Sources 1, 2, 4–8, 11)? (S)

13. Is it your impression from Sources 10–13 that it was only the outbreak of war in Europe that prevented the outbreak of civil war in Ireland in 1914? (S)

# SOURCE MATERIAL 2
# The Easter Rising, 1916

*Sources 14–28, on the Easter Rising, have been divided into three groups: A. the origins of the Rising (Sources 14–17); B. the Rising itself (Sources 18–21); and C. the consequences of the Rising (Sources 22–8).*

## 2A   Nationalist Attitudes to Rebellion

### SOURCE 14   A Speech by Padraic Pearse at the Funeral of O'Donovan Rossa, 1 August, 1915

*O'Donovan Rossa was a Fenian hero who had participated in Irish revolutionary activities throughout his life. He died in New York in July 1915, and his body was brought home for public burial in Dublin. The funeral was attended by thousands of nationalist sympathisers.*

Life springs from death, and from the graves of patriot men and women spring living nations. The Defenders of this Realm have worked well in secret and in the open. They think that they have pacified Ireland. They think that they have purchased half of us and intimidated the other half. They think that they have foreseen everything, think that they have provided against everything; but the fools, the fools, the fools! They have left us our Fenian dead, and while Ireland holds these graves, Ireland unfree shall never be at peace.

T. Coffey, *Agony at Easter* (Penguin, 1969) p. 14

### SOURCE 15   Padraic Pearse, *Peace and the Gael*

*This passage was written in December 1915.*

The last sixteen months have been the most glorious in the history of Europe. Heroism has come to earth. On whichever side, the men who rule the peoples have marshalled them, whether England to uphold the tyranny of the seas, or with Germany to break that tyranny, the people themselves have gone into battle because the old voice that speaks out of the soil of a nation has spoken anew . . . It is good for the world that such things should be done. The old heart of the earth needed to be warmed with the red wine of the battlefields. Such august homage was never before offered to God, the homage of millions of lives given gladly for love of country. What peace Ireland has known these latter days has been the devil's peace, peace with dishonour.

G. Dangerfield, *The Damnable Question* (Constable, 1977) p. 182

## SOURCE 16   James Connolly, Article in the
*Workers' Republic,* 30 October, 1915

*Connolly played a leading part in organising the Dublin Transport Workers' Strike in 1913. It was after the police brutality experienced during this strike that Connolly decided to found the Citizen Army, an exclusively working-class organisation, designed to protect workers' interests. Publication of the* Workers' Republic *began in May 1915 at Liberty Hall, headquarters of the Citizen Army.*

An armed organisation of the Irish working class is a phenomenon in Ireland. Hitherto the workers of Ireland have fought as part of the armies led by their masters, never as members of an army officered, trained and inspired by members of their own class. Now, with arms in their hands, they propose to steer their own course, to carve their own future. Neither Home Rule, nor the lack of Home Rule, will make them lay down their arms. However it may be for others, for us of the Citizen Army there is but one ideal – an Ireland ruled and owned by Irish men and women, sovereign and independent from the centre to the sea . . . We cannot be swerved from our course by honeyed words . . . nor betrayed by high sounding phrases. The Irish Citizen Army will only co-operate in a forward movement. The moment that forward movement ceases it reserves for itself the right to step out of alignment, and advance by itself if need be, in an effort to plant the banner of freedom one reach further towards its goal.

Owen D. Edwards and Fergus Pyle (eds.), *1916: The Easter Rising*
(MacGibbon & Kee, 1968) p. 127

## SOURCE 17   Eoin MacNeill's View of Revolutionary
Action

*MacNeill was a Professor of Early and Medieval Irish History at University College, Dublin. He played an active part in founding the Irish Volunteers in 1913, and became their Chief of Staff when the movement split in 1914 and Redmond's supporters left to form the National Volunteers. He was strongly opposed to Irish participation on the British side in the First World War.*

I do not know at this moment whether the time and circumstances will yet justify military acts, but of one thing I am certain, that the only possible basis for successful revolutionary action is deep and widespread popular discontent. We have only to look around us to realise that no such condition exists in Ireland. A few of us, a small proportion who think about the evils of English government in Ireland are always discontented. We should be downright fools, if we were to measure many others by the standard of our own thoughts.

F.W. Martin, 'Eoin MacNeill and the 1916 Rising', *Irish Historical Studies,* XII, p. 240

# 2B  The Easter Rebellion and its Portrayal

## SOURCE 18  Proclamation of the Republic

*This document, the joint work of Pearse and Connolly, was read out by Pearse on the steps of the General Post Office at 12.45 p.m. on Monday, 24 April, 1916. It evidently met with an indifferent reception.*

POBLACHT NA h–EIREANN

THE PROVISIONAL GOVERNMENT
of the
IRISH REPUBLIC

TO THE PEOPLE OF IRELAND
Irishmen and Irishwomen: in the name of God and of the dead generations from which she receives her old tradition of nationhood, Ireland, through us, summons her children to her flag and strikes for her freedom.

Having organised and trained her manhood through her secret revolutionary organisation, the Irish Republican Brotherhood and the Irish Citizen Army, having patiently perfected her discipline, having resolutely waited for the right moment to reveal itself, she now seizes that moment, and supported by her exiled children in America and by gallant allies in Europe, but relying in the first upon her own strength, she strikes in the full confidence of victory.

We declare the right of the people of Ireland to the ownership of Ireland and to the unfettered control of Irish destinies, to be sovereign and indefeasible. The long usurpation of that right by a foreign people has not extinguished that right, nor can it ever be extinguished except by the destruction of the Irish people. In every generation the Irish people have asserted their right to national freedom and national sovereignty; six times during the past three hundred years they have asserted it in arms. Standing on that fundamental right and again asserting it in arms in face of the world, we hereby proclaim the Irish Republic as a Sovereign Independent State and we pledge our lives and the lives of our comrades-in-arms to the cause of its freedom, of its welfare and of its exaltation among the nations.

The Irish Republic is entitled to and hereby claims, the allegiance of every Irishman and every Irishwoman. The Republic guarantees religious and civil liberty, equal rights and equal opportunities to all its citizens and declares its resolve to pursue the happiness and prosperity of the whole nation and all of its parts, cherishing all the children of the nation equally, and oblivious of the differences, carefully fostered by the government, which have divided a minority from the majority in the past.

Until our arms have brought the opportune moment for the establishment of a permanent National Government, representative of the whole people of Ireland and elected by the suffrage of all her men and women, the Provisional Government, hereby constituted, will administer the civil and military affairs of the Republic in trust for the whole people.

We place the cause of the Irish Republic under the protection of the Most High God, Whose blessings we invoke upon our arms, and we pray that no one who serves that cause will dishonour it by cowardice, inhumanity or rapine. In this supreme hour the Irish nation must, by its valour and discipline and by the readiness of its children to sacrifice themselves for the common good, prove itself worthy of the august destiny to which it is called.

THOMAS J. CLARKE

SEAN MacDIARMID                                 THOMAS MacDONAGH

P.H. PEARSE                                           EAMONN CEANNT

JAMES CONNOLLY                                   JOSEPH PLUNKETT

Curtis and MacDowell (eds.), *Irish Historical Documents,* pp. 317–18

*On Monday, 24 April detachments of rebels occupied the following places: the General Post Office, the Four Courts, Jacob's Biscuit Factory, Boland's Bakery, the Mendicity Institution, and St Stephen's Green. After a week of street fighting, the Post Office was surrounded and set alight. Pearse then ordered an unconditional surrender, and by Sunday, 30 April all the outposts still in rebel hands had given in.*

## SOURCE 19    A Speech by Pearse to his Fellow-Rebels, Thursday, 27 April

I desire now, lest I may not have an opportunity later, to pay homage to the gallantry of the soldiers of Irish freedom who have during the past four days been writing with fire and steel the most glorious chapter in the later history of Ireland. Justice can never be done to their heroism, to their discipline, to their gay and unconquerable spirit in the midst of peril and death . . .

If they do not win this fight, they will at least deserve to win it. But win it they will although they may win it in death. Already they have done a great thing. They have redeemed Dublin from many shames, and made her name splendid among the names of cities. They have held out for four days against the might of the British Empire. They have established Ireland's right to be a Republic, and they have established this government's right to sit at the peace table at the end of the European War.

Coffey, *Agony at Easter,* p. 172

## SOURCE 20    A Message from Connolly to the Defenders of the General Post Office, Friday, 28 April

Let us remind you of what you have done. For the first time in seven hundred years the flag of a free Ireland floats triumphantly in Dublin city. The British army, whose exploits we are forever having dinned into our ears, which boasts of having stormed the Dardanelles and the German lines on the Marne, behind their artillery and machine guns are afraid to advance to the attack or storm our forces. The slaughter they suffered in the first few days has totally unnerved them, and they dare not attempt an infantry attack upon our positions.

Coffey, *Agony at Easter,* p. 196

# SOURCE 21    Press Reports of the Easter Rising

### (a) J.E. Healey's Report of Events in Dublin, *The Times*, 1 May

*J.E. Healey was editor of the* Irish Times *and Irish Correspondent of* The Times. *The* Irish Times *was a conservative Unionist newspaper, but had built up a reputation for good, detailed reporting.*

From Tuesday morning onwards in every suburb the soldiers kept pushing in towards the city, doing their best to clear the streets as they came along. The rebels had occupied three or four houses in every street. As one house was taken they escaped along the roof to another. The sniping was continuous and unfortunately accurate. Officers told me that this was far more dangerous and trying fighting than they had seen in France . . .

When I got out of Dublin this [Saturday] afternoon with extreme difficulty in the hope of being able to transmit this message to the *Times* street fighting was still active, and the road where I live was filled with the crackle of rifle shots. As I write these lines, however, I am informed by telephone that the rebels have made an unconditional surrender. It is good news if true, and the defeat of the latest German effort has been effected at a heavy cost of valuable lives. There is no doubt that the troops have suffered heavily and that many harmless civilians have been killed. The casualties among the Sinn Feiners will probably rise to many hundreds. The fighting was stark and grim.

### (b) From our Belfast Correspondent, *The Times*, 1 May

At 4 o'clock yesterday afternoon the Irish rebellion – an episode in Irish history which all practical and sensible people in this country regard as the most inglorious and disgraceful outbreak of organised rowdyism which ever sullied the annals of this country – came to a sudden end.

### (c) Editorial in the *Daily News*, 1 May

*The* Daily News *was an English newspaper of Liberal views.*

. . . But there is at least one aspect of this lamentable affair from which we may extract satisfaction. It has shown very strikingly the divorce of this wild movement from the general body of the Irish people. The outstanding fact of the whole episode is its political isolation from the spirit of the nation . . .

In Dublin itself the whole population was as much outraged as it was alarmed by the whole affair, and it is probable that the British soldier has never had such a cordial welcome in the Irish capital as he has had during the past few days . . .

In a very real sense we may say that the rising, deplorable as it is in the sacrifice of life that it has entailed, is not wholly without a gratifying side. It has revealed as nothing else could reveal the loyalty of the Irish people and the happy change that a wiser policy and a larger liberty have brought in their train.

# 2C   The Aftermath of the Rebellion

*On Friday, 28 April Lieutenant-General Sir John Maxwell arrived to take command in Ireland. On him rested the main responsibility for handling the rebels who had surrendered. Those considered suitable for trial were tried secretly by General Field Court Martial under the Defence of the Realm Act. The following were executed by firing squad (dates refer to the date of execution):*

3 May    *Padraic Pearse, Thomas MacDonagh, Thomas J. Clarke*
4 May    *William Pearse, Joseph Plunkett, Edward Daly, Michael O'Hanrahan*
5 May    *John MacBride*
8 May    *Cornelius Colbert, Eamonn Ceannt, Michael Mallin, Sean Heuston*
12 May   *James Connolly, Sean MacDiarmid*

*These men had all taken part in the Dublin Rising. On 9 May Thomas Kent was also executed for killing a policeman in Cork.*

## SOURCE 22   Healey's Report for *The Times*, 2 and 3 May

### (a) 2 May

From J.E. Healey [in Dublin]: Everywhere, among Unionist and Nationalist alike one hears stern expression of the hope that the lesson of the insurrection will not be spoiled by untimely weakness. There must be no mistake about the nature of this rising. It was a brutal, savage and bloody business . . . The nation must see that in return for the heavy cost it receives at least a sure guarantee of righteous punishment for the offenders and of firm, just and powerful government for Ireland.

### (b) 3 May

With the end of the insurrection the public begin to fear that the Government may relapse into its old policy of leniency and weakness. I shall only say that Irish public opinion is absolutely unanimous in its demand that the rebellion shall be crushed and its authors and agents punished with relentless severity.

## SOURCE 23   Debate in the House of Commons, 3 May

*John Redmond:* Let me say in concluding one sentence. This outbreak happily seems to be over. It has been dealt with firmly. That was not only right, it was the duty of government. But as the rebellion, or outbreak – call it what you like – has been put down with firmness, I do beg of the government, and I speak from the bottom of my heart – with all my earnestness of feeling – I do beg of them not to show undue hardship or severity to the great mass of those who are implicated and on whose shoulders lies a guilt far different from that which lies on the instigators and promoters of this outbreak. (Hear, hear) Let them in the name of God not add this to the miserable memories of the Irish people to be started up for generations.

*Sir Edward Carson:* With reference to the speech of the Hon. member for Waterford [Redmond] and what he has said about these unfortunate dupes in Ireland, let me say that, while I think it is in the best interests of this country that this conspiracy of Sinn Feiners, which has nothing to do with either of the two political parties in Ireland (Hear, hear) ought to be put down with courage and determination and with an example which would prevent a revival, it would be a mistake to suppose that any Irishman calls for vengeance. (Hear, hear) It will be a matter requiring the greatest wisdom, the greatest coolness, may I say, in dealing with these men, and all I say to the Executive is, whatever is done, let it not be done in a moment of temporary excitement, but with due deliberation in regard both to the present and to the future. (Cheers)

*The Times,* 4 May, 1916

## SOURCE 24   Questions in the House of Commons, 9 May

Mr J. Redmond (Nationalist, Waterford) asked the Prime Minister whether he was aware that the continuance of military executions in Ireland had caused rapidly increasing bitterness and exasperation among large sections of the public who had not the slightest sympathy with the insurrection, and whether, following the precedent set by General Botha in South Africa* he would cause an immediate stop to be put to these executions?

*Mr Asquith:* Before I answer this question let me say that from the very first, my honourable and learned friend has strongly urged on the Government – and his arguments have not fallen on deaf and unwilling ears – the importance of clemency to the rank and file of the persons engaged in the insurrection. In answer to the question, and to another of which I have received private notice . . . I have to say that General Sir John Maxwell has been in direct, personal communication with the Cabinet on this subject. We have great confidence in the exercise of his discretion in particular cases, and his general instructions, which conform to his own judgment in the matter, are to sanction the infliction of the extreme penalty as sparingly as possible, and only in cases of responsible persons who were guilty in the first degree. No one is more anxious than the Government and Sir John Maxwell himself that this case should be confined within the narrowest limits and cease at the earliest possible moment.

*Mr Lynd:* Has Sir John Maxwell acted entirely on his own judgment, or has he been in consultation with the Cabinet?

*Mr Asquith:* I said so.

*Sir W. Byles:* Were the first executions at any rate decided by the Cabinet or by the military authorities?

*Mr Asquith:* They were decided by the military authorities.

*The Times,* 10 May

*In 1914 10 000 Boers not reconciled to British rule took part in a pro-German rebellion against the South African government. Only one rebel was put to death, in his case because he had previously taken an oath of loyalty to the king. Botha was the South African Prime Minister at the time.*

## SOURCE 25   Communiqué from Sir John Maxwell, Dublin, 12 May

In view of the severity of the rebellion, its connection with German intrigues and propaganda, and in view of the great loss of life and destruction of property arising therefrom, the General Officer Commanding in Chief has found it imperative to inflict most severe sentences on the known organisers of this detestable rising, and on those commanders who took an active part in the actual fighting which occurred.

*The Times,* 13 May

## SOURCE 26   A Speech given by John Dillon to the House of Commons, 11 May

*Dillon was Redmond's second-in-command in the Irish Nationalist party, and had experienced the Easter Rebellion at first hand; for two days that part of the city in which he lived was in the hands of the rebels. He made this speech in support of the following motion: 'That, in the interests of peace and good government in Ireland, it is vitally necessary that the Government should make immediately a full statement of their intentions as to the continuance of executions in that country carried out as a result of secret military trials, and as to the continuance of martial law, military rule, and the searches and wholesale arrests now going on in various districts of the country.' Dillon drew attention to the shooting in cold blood of a Mr Sheehy-Skeffington, an innocent bystander (the officer concerned was subsequently court martialled); the searching of loyal districts; and the indiscriminate arrests that had taken place. By their actions, Dillon said, the government was in danger of forfeiting all the support which they had come to enjoy.*

. . . It is the first rebellion that ever took place where you had a majority on your side. It is the fruit of our life work . . . We have risked our lives a hundred times to bring about this result. We are held up to odium as traitors by those men who made this rebellion, and our lives have been in danger a hundred times during the last thirty years because we have tried to reconcile the two things, and you are now washing our whole life work in a sea of blood . . .

There is no disguising the fact – and – remember that the insurrection was confined to an infinitesimal part of Ireland – out of the whole of Ireland there were only four or five spots where there was any insurrection at all, and yet you have placed the whole of Ireland under martial law, and you have swept away every trace of civil administration in the country . . .

Compare the conduct of the Government in dealing with this rebellion with the conduct of General Botha. I say deliberately that in the whole of modern history, taking all circumstances into account, there has been no rebellion or insurrection put down with so much blood and so much savagery as the recent insurrection in Ireland. Go back to the history of any insurrection in any modern civilised country. Take the great rebellion in America, which lasted for three years, and which had not one tithe of the excuse which these Sinn Feiners could advance. A million men lost their lives and a vast amount of property was destroyed. When the insurrection was over I do not think Abraham Lincoln executed one single man, and by that act of clemency he did an enormous good for the whole of the country . . .

Although I could not see anything, because you had to keep to your own house unless you wanted a bullet in your head, and I had no fancy for that, I have had a good deal of opportunity of collecting information as to what actually took place, and, according to the information that has reached me, there were isolated and very few acts of savagery and murder on the side of the insurgents, as there were also on the side of the soldiers, very few. As I say, there were some very bad actions, but as regards the main body of the insurgents, their conduct was beyond reproach as fighting men. I admit they were wrong; I know they were wrong; but they fought a clean fight, and they fought with superb bravery and skill, and no action of savagery against the normal customs of war that I know of has been brought home to any leader or organised body of insurgents. I have not heard of a single act. I may be wrong, but that is my impression . . .

We, I think, have a right, we who speak for the vast majority of the Irish people, and we do; who have risked a great deal to win to your side in this great crisis of your Empire's history; we who have endeavoured, and successfully endeavoured, to secure that the Irish in America shall not go into alliance with the Germans in that country – we, I think, were entitled to be consulted before this bloody course of executions was entered upon in Ireland . . .

I do most earnestly ask the Prime Minister to stop these executions now, absolutely and finally. With every fresh man killed it becomes no longer a question of malice or individual sentence; it has gone beyond that. This series of executions is doing more harm than any Englishman in this House can possibly fathom . . .

Edwards and Pyle (eds.), 1916: The Easter Rising, pp. 62–78

## SOURCE 27  *The Times,* 12 May

Thirteen rebels have been shot and sentence is to be executed on two others. It is idle to represent this punishment as excessive or revengeful or to pretend, with the Nationalist Manifesto, that this 'shocks and horrifies' Ireland.

Everybody will learn with relief that the necessity for further executions of this kind is now over, but a certain number of these executions were absolutely necessary to teach the traitors who take German money that they cannot cover Dublin with blood and ashes without forfeiting their lives. We think, however, that the Government have been foolish in not stating plainly the reasons why those men were shot and we welcome Mr Asquith's promise that any further trials for murder shall be held with open doors . . .

## SOURCE 28  Letter from Mr George Bernard Shaw to the *Daily News,* 10 May, 'The Irish Executions'

*Shaw, the famous dramatist, was born in Dublin, and took a close interest in Irish affairs. One of his best plays,* John Bull's Other Island, *deals with the Anglo-Irish relationship.*

Sir,
In your article under the above heading on the 6th inst. you say that 'so far as the leaders are concerned no voice has been raised in this country against the

infliction of the punishment which has so speedily overtaken them'. As the Government shot the prisoners first and told the public about it afterwards, there was no opportunity for effective protest.

But it must not be assumed that those who merely shrugged their shoulders when it was useless to remonstrate accept for one moment the view that what happened was the execution of a gang of criminals. My own view – which I should not obtrude on you had you not concluded that it does not exist – is that the men who were shot in cold blood after their capture or surrender were prisoners of war, and therefore it was entirely incorrect to slaughter them. The relation of Ireland to Dublin Castle is in this respect precisely that of the Balkans to Turkey, of Belgium or the city of Lille to the Kaiser, and of the United States to Great Britain . . .

---

# QUESTIONS ON SOURCES 14–28

1. Explain the final sentence of Pearse's speech, 'They have left us our Fenian dead . . .' (Source 14). (S)

2. Compare the views of Redmond and Pearse on Britain's reasons for fighting in the First World War (Sources 13, 15). Whose was nearer the truth? (E)

3. What similarities can you detect between Ulster nationalism and Irish nationalism as reflected in Sources 2 and 18? (S)

4. How well-timed was the Easter Rebellion (Sources 17, 18)? (S)

5. What indications can you find of Connolly's influence in the Proclamation of the Irish Republic (Sources 16, 18)? (S)

6. What did Pearse and Connolly claim that the Easter Rising had achieved (Sources 19, 20)? (C)

7. Compare the views of the Rising as seen by *The Times* correspondents in Dublin and Belfast (Sources 21(a), (b)) with that of John Dillon (Source 26). Whose account strikes you as the most reliable, and why? (E)

8. How accurate in your view is the *Daily News'* assessment of public attitudes to the Rising in Ireland (Source 21(c))? (E)

9. Who bears the main responsibility for executing the leaders of the Rising (Sources 22–25)? (S)

10. Do you see any difference in the attitudes of John Redmond and John Dillon to the Rising (Sources 23, 26)? (S)

11. On what grounds did (a) Dillon and (b) Shaw condemn the executions (Sources 26, 28)? (C)

12. How justifiable are the historical parallels invoked by Dillon and Shaw to support their viewpoints (Sources 26, 28)? (S)

13. What ought the British government, in your view, to have done with the leaders of the Rising (Sources 21–8)? (S)

14. 'The Irish public opinion that, as Pearse saw so clearly, measures everything for itself, soon saw the Rising as something to be proud of.' (M. Wall) How do you account for this outcome (Sources 14–28)? (S)

# SOURCE MATERIAL 3
# Ireland, 1916–22

*Sources 29–37 cover: A. the Government of Ireland Act, 1920 (Sources 29, 30); and B. the negotiations for, terms of, and reactions to the Irish Treaty, 1921 (Sources 31–7).*

## 3A   The Enactment of Partition

**SOURCE 29**   Letter from Walter Long to Lloyd George, 3 February, 1920

*Walter Long was now First Lord of the Admiralty in Lloyd George's National Coalition Government, formed in 1919. Long continued to take an active interest in Irish affairs.*

Most of the people with whom I discussed this question were of the opinion that the whole of the province [of Ulster] should be excluded; but on the other hand, the people in the inner circle hold the view that the new province should consist of the six counties, the idea being that the inclusion of Donegal, Cavan and Monaghan would provide such an access of strength to the Roman Catholic party, that the Supremacy of the Unionists would be severely threatened.

D.G. Boyce, 'British Conservative Opinion, the Ulster Question and the Partition of Ireland', *Irish Historical Studies*, 1970–1, p. 99

**SOURCE 30**   The Terms of the Government of Ireland Act, December 1920

An Act for the better government of Ireland.
Be it enacted . . .
    1. (1)  On and after the appointed day there shall be established for Southern Ireland a parliament to be called the parliament of Southern Ireland consisting of his majesty, the Senate of Southern Ireland and the house of commons of Southern Ireland, and there shall be established for Northern Ireland a parliament to be called the parliament of Northern Ireland consisting of his majesty, the Senate of Northern Ireland, and the house of commons of Northern Ireland.
    (2)  For the purpose of this act, Northern Ireland shall consist of the parliamentary counties of Antrim, Armagh, Down, Fermanagh, Londonderry and Tyrone, and the parliamentary boroughs of Belfast and Londonderry, and Southern Ireland shall consist of so much of Ireland as is not comprised within the said parliamentary counties and boroughs.
    2. (1)  With a view to the eventual establishment of a parliament for the whole of Ireland and to bringing about harmonious action between the parliaments and

governments of Southern Ireland and Northern Ireland, and to the promotion of mutual intercourse and uniformity to matters affecting the whole of Ireland and to providing for the administration of services which the two parliaments mutually agree should be administered uniformly throughout the whole of Ireland, or which by virtue of this act are to be so administered, there shall be constituted as soon as may be, after the appointed day a Council to be called the Council of Ireland.

(2) Subject as herein after provided, the Council of Ireland shall consist of a person nominated by the Lord Lieutenant acting in accordance with instructions from his majesty who shall be president, and forty other persons, of whom seven shall be members of the Senate of Southern Ireland, thirteen shall be members of the house of commons of Southern Ireland, seven shall be members of the Senate of Northern Ireland, and thirteen shall be members of the house of commons of Northern Ireland.

3. (1) The parliaments of Southern Ireland and Northern Ireland may, by identical acts, agreed to by an absolute majority of the house of commons of each parliament at the third reading (hereinafter referred to as constitutional acts), establish in lieu of the Council of Ireland a parliament for the whole of Ireland.

(2) On the date of the Irish Union the Council of Ireland shall cease to exist and there shall be transferred to the Parliament and government of Ireland all powers then exercisable by the Council of Ireland.

Curtis and MacDowell (eds.), *Irish Historical Documents*, pp. 297–303

# 3B  The Irish Treaty

## SOURCE 31  Memorandum drawn up by Tom Jones, 13 November, 1921

*Tom Jones was at this time assistant secretary to the Cabinet. This document is a memorandum of a proposal which Lloyd George had put to Arthur Griffith the previous day, 12 November. Lloyd George needed to know in advance that this proposal would not be repudiated when it was raised at the forthcoming Conservative party conference, due to assemble on 17 November. Griffith assented to the document as a correct record of what had been discussed, and when Lloyd George produced it on 5 December, Griffith acknowledged that he had agreed to it.*

If Ulster did not see her way to accept immediately the principle of a Parliament of all Ireland, she would continue to exercise through her own Parliament all her present rights; she would continue to be represented in the British Parliament, and she would continue subject to British taxation, except in so far as already modified in the Act of Union of 1920. In this case, however, it would be necessary to revise the boundary of Northern Ireland. This might be done by a Boundary Commission which would be directed to adjust the line by inclusion and exclusion so as to make the boundary conform as closely as possible to the wishes of the population.

F. Pakenham, *Peace by Ordeal* (Jonathan Cape, 1935) p. 218

**SOURCE 32**   Account of an Interview between Lloyd George and Michael Collins, 5 December, 1921

*Collins had been Chief of Staff in the IRA during the guerilla war against Britain, and his acquiescence to the treaty terms was essential. No exact record of what was said at this meeting has survived. The following account is taken from a secondary source, F.S.L. Lyons, Ireland since the Famine.*

On 5 December he [Lloyd George] saw a reluctant Collins and found him anxious about the form of the Oath and still more about the question of Ulster. There was little common ground between them on the former question, but on the latter it seems that Collins was only too ready to let himself believe that after the Boundary Commission had done its work economic pressures would bring about 'the essential unity' of Ireland.

F.S.L. Lyons, *Ireland since the Famine* (Weidenfeld & Nicolson, 1971) p. 437

**SOURCE 33**   The Final Negotiation, 5 December, 1921

Griffith was prepared to sign an agreement on these lines. But what, asked Lloyd George, of the rest of the Irish delegation? 'The Irish delegates' he said at last, 'must settle now. They must sign the agreement for a Treaty or else . . . quit and both sides would be free to resume whatever warfare they could against each other.' Brandishing two letters in their faces he reminded them that he had to send one of them to Sir James Craig [premier of Northern Ireland] that night. Would it be the letter confirming that agreement had been reached or would it be the other saying that Sinn Fein representatives refused to come within the empire? 'If I send this letter it is war and war within three days. Which letter am I to send?'

*The footnote reference reads:* 'These crucial exchanges are set out in F. Pakenham, *Peace by Ordeal*, pp. 206–302, and in R. Taylor, *Michael Collins*, Appendix D, pp. 247–52.'

Lyons, *Ireland since the Famine*, pp. 437–8, 806

**SOURCE 34**   The Irish Treaty, 6 December, 1921

*The terms of the Treaty were signed by the Irish delegation in the early hours of 6 December, 1921, but they were only finally approved by the Dáil, by 64 votes to 57, on 7 January, 1922. The following excerpts relate only to the controversial issues of the constitutional status of the new state, the Oath of Allegiance and the position of Ulster.*

1. Ireland shall have the same constitutional status in the Community of Nations known as the British Empire as the Dominion of Canada, the Commonwealth of Australia, the Dominion of New Zealand, and the Union of South Africa, with a parliament having powers to make laws for the peace and good government of Ireland and an executive responsible to that Parliament, and shall be styled and known as the Irish Free State.

2. Subject to the provision hereafter set out the position of the Irish Free State in relation to the Imperial Parliament and government and otherwise shall be that of the Dominion of Canada.

*The form of the Oath of Allegiance to be taken by all ministers and civil servants was as follows:*

I . . . do solemnly swear true faith and allegiance to the Constitution of the Irish Free State as by law established and that I will be faithful to HM King George V, his heirs and successors at law in virtue of the common citizenship of Ireland with Great Britain and her adherence to and membership of the group of nations known as the British Commonwealth.

11.  Until the expiration of one month from the passing of the act of parliament for ratification of this instrument, the powers of the parliament and government of the Irish Free State shall not be exercisable as respects Northern Ireland, and the provisions of the Government of Ireland Act, 1920 shall so far as they relate to Northern Ireland, remain in full force and effect, and no election shall be held for the returning of members to serve in the Irish Free State for constituencies in Northern Ireland.

12.  If before the expiration of the said month, an address is presented to his majesty by both houses of parliament of Northern Ireland to that effect, the powers of the parliament and government of the Irish Free State shall no longer extend to Northern Ireland, and the provisions of the Government of Ireland Act, 1920 (including those relating to the Council of Ireland) shall so far as they relate to Northern Ireland continue to be of full force and effect . . .

Providing that if such an address is so presented a commission consisting of three persons, one to be appointed by the government of the Irish Free State, one to be appointed by the government of Northern Ireland, and one who shall be chairman to be appointed by the British government shall determine in accordance with the wishes of the inhabitants, so far as may be compatible with economic and geographic conditions the boundaries between Northern Ireland and the rest of Ireland for the purpose of the Government of Ireland Act, 1920 and of this instrument, the boundary of Northern Ireland shall be such as may be determined by such commission . . .

Signed

| | |
|---|---|
| D. Lloyd George | Art O. Griobtha (Arthur Griffith) |
| Austen Chamberlain | Michael O. Coileain (Michael Collins) |
| Birkenhead | Riobard Barton (Robert Barton) |
| Winston S. Churchill | Endhmean S.O. Dugain (Eamon Dugan) |
| L. Worthington-Evans | Seoign Ghabhain Dhubhthaigh (George Gavan Duffy) |
| Hamar Greenwood | |
| Gordon Hewart | |

Curtis and MacDowell (eds.), *Irish Historical Documents*, pp. 322–6

# SOURCE 35   Lloyd George's View of the Irish Treaty

*This excerpt is taken from a speech made by Lloyd George during a House of Commons debate on the Treaty.*

The youngest Dominion [South Africa] marched into the war under its own flag. As for the flag of Ireland, it was torn from the hands of men who had volunteered to die for the cause which the British empire was championing. The result was a rebellion, and at the worst moment of the war, we had to divert our minds to methods of dealing with the crisis in Ireland. Henceforth that chair will be filled by a willing Ireland, radiant because the long quarrel with England will have been settled by the concession of liberty to her own people, and she can now take part in the partnership of empire, not merely without loss of self-respect, but with accession of honour to herself and of glory in her own nationhood.

Curtis and MacDowell (eds.), *Irish Historical Documents,* p. 327

## SOURCE 36    The Debate in the Dáil, 14 December, 1921–7 January, 1922

*De Valera:* I am against the treaty because it will not end the centuries of conflict between the two nations of Great Britain and Ireland . . . A war-weary people will take things which are not in accordance with their aspirations. You may have a scratch election now and you may get a vote of the people, but I tell you this treaty will renew the contest that is going to begin the same history that the union began, and Lloyd George is going to have the same fruit for his labours that Pitt had. When in Downing Street the proposals to which we could unanimously assent in the cabinet were practically turned down at point of pistol and immediate war was threatened upon our people. It was only then that this document has been signed by plenipotentiaries not perhaps individually under duress, but it has been signed, and would only affect this nation as a nation signed under duress, and this nation would not respect it.

I wanted, and the cabinet wanted, to get a document that would enable Irishmen to meet Englishmen and shake hands with them as fellow-citizens of the world. That document makes British authority our master in Ireland. It was said that they only had an oath to the British king in virtue of common citizenship, but you have an oath to the Irish constitution, and that constitution which will have the king of Great Britain as head of Ireland. You will swear allegiance to that constitution and to that king; and if the representatives of the people of Ireland should ask the people of Ireland to do that which is inconsistent with the republic, I say they are subverting the republic. It would be a surrender which was never heard of since the days of Henry II . . .

*A. Griffith:* We went then to London, not as republican doctrinaires, but looking for the substance of freedom and independence. If you think that what we brought back is not the substance of independence, that is legitimate ground for attack upon us, but to attack us on the ground that we went there to get a republic is to attack us on false and lying grounds . . .

This treaty is not an ideal thing; it has faults. I could draw up a treaty – many of us could draw up a treaty which would be more satisfactory to the Irish people. We could 'call spirits from the vasty deep', but will they come when you call them? We have a treaty signed by the heads of the British government; we have nothing signed against it. I could draw up a much better treaty myself, and one that would suit myself; but it is not going to be passed. We are, therefore, face to face with a practical situation. Does the treaty give away the interests and honour of Ireland? I say it does not. I say it serves the interests and honour of Ireland. It is not dishonourable to Ireland. It is not an ideal thing; it could be better. It has no more finality than we are the final generation on earth (applause). No man is going – as was quoted here – No man can set bounds to the march of a nation. But we here accept the treaty, and deal with it in good faith, with the English people, and through the files of events, reach, if we desire it, any further status that we desire or require after.

Curtis and MacDowell (eds.), *Irish Historical Documents*, pp. 328–30

# SOURCE 37 Changes to the Border Proposed by the Boundary Commission in 1925

*These were the changes recommended by the Boundary Commission that was eventually set up under Article 12 of the Irish Treaty.*

The Border as it is  ⸺

Line proposed by the Boundary Commission, 1925  ----

Arrows indicate direction of transfer

Based on A.T.Q. Stewart, *The Narrow Ground, Aspects of Ulster* (Faber & Faber, 1977) p. 171

# QUESTIONS ON SOURCES 29–37

1.  What can you infer from Source 29 about Conservative intentions for Ulster? (S)

2.  Why might Southern Ireland feel that its interests would be inadequately represented in the Council of Ireland (Source 30)? (C)

3.  What indications are there in the Government of Ireland Act, 1920 that it was intended as a temporary measure (Source 30)? (C)

4.  'Revision of the boundaries was interpreted by Griffith as meaning all areas with Nationalist majorities would be detached from Northern Ireland. Nearly all of two of the six counties, Tyrone and Fermanagh, he was assured, would be transferred from Northern Ireland to the new Dominion; besides large parts of counties Down and Armagh. It would be scarcely conceivable that a "Northern Ireland" consisting of less than four counties could continue a separate existence for long.' (Gwynn, *The History of Partition*) Is there any evidence that Griffith did make these assumptions (Source 31)? (E)

5.  It has been said that Lloyd George 'resorted to trickery, threats and eventually an ultimatum of renewed and annihilating war in order to extort the Irish signatures'. (P. O'Farrell, *Ireland's English Question*) From Sources 31–3, would you agree? (S)

6.  What differences in relation to Ulster's boundaries can you detect between the Memorandum drawn up by Tom Jones and Article 12 of the Irish Treaty (Sources 31, 34)? How important are they? (S)

7.  Was Lloyd George guilty of deliberate misrepresentation in his defence of the Irish Treaty (Source 35)? (E)

8.  Did De Valera exaggerate the sacrifices made by the Irish delegates in signing the Irish Treaty (Source 36)? (S)

9.  In the debate on the Treaty in the Dáil, Ulster and Partition took up nine out of 338 pages. Griffith made no mention of Article 12 in his speech (Source 36). How do you account for this? (S)

10. Was the Irish government entitled to feel that the Boundary Commission had misinterpreted the intentions behind the Treaty of 1921 (Sources 34, 37)? (S)

11. 'Of course the Protestants of Ulster were not the invention of British conservatives. But the problems of Ulster would not have assumed such serious dimensions had not the determination of Unionist Ulster to resist incorporation in a unitary state been given the support, however equivocal, of British conservatives.' (D.G. Boyce, 'British Conservative Opinion, the Ulster Question and the Partition of Ireland', *Irish Historical Studies*, 1970–1) Do you agree, and if so, why? (S)

# LOCATION OF SOURCES

1    R. Blake, *The Unknown Prime Minister: The Life and Times of Andrew Bonar Law* (Eyre & Spottiswoode, 1955) p. 130

2    E. Curtis and R.B. MacDowell (eds.), *Irish Historical Documents* (Methuen, 1943) p. 304

3    *Punch,* 8 October, 1913

4    D. Gwynn, *The History of Partition, 1912–25* (Brown & Nolan, 1950) p. 76

5    *Ibid,* pp. 79–80

6    Curtis and MacDowell (eds.), *op. cit.,* pp. 306–7

7    Gwynn, *op. cit.,* pp. 85–6

8    Gwynn, *op. cit.,* pp. 93–5

9    I. Colvin, *The Life of Lord Carson,* vol. II (Gollancz, 1934) pp. 297–8

10   R. Murphy, 'Faction and the Home Rule Crisis, 1912–14', *History,* June 1986, p. 231

11   Gwynn, *op. cit.,* pp. 117–31

12   *The Leo Amery Diaries,* vol. I, 1896–1929 (Hutchinson, 1980) p. 101

13   Gwynn, *op. cit.,* pp. 137–9

14   T. Coffey, *Agony at Easter* (Penguin, 1969) p. 14

15   G. Dangerfield, *The Damnable Question* (Constable, 1977) p. 182

16   Owen D. Edwards and Fergus Pyle (eds.), *1916: The Easter Rising* (MacGibbon & Kee, 1968) p. 127

17   F.W. Martin, 'Eoin MacNeill and the 1916 Rising', *Irish Historical Studies,* XII, p. 240

18   Curtis and MacDowell (eds.), *op. cit.,* pp. 317–18

19   Coffey, *op. cit.,* p. 172

20   Coffey, *op. cit.,* p. 196

21–5 Microfilm copies of *The Times* and the *Daily News,* May 1916, Bodleian Library, Oxford

26   Edwards and Pyle (eds.), *op. cit.,* pp. 62–78

27   *The Times,* May 1916

28   *Daily News,* May 1916

29   D.G. Boyce, 'British Conservative Opinion, the Ulster Question and the Partition of Ireland', *Irish Historical Studies,* 1970–1, p. 99

30   Curtis and MacDowell (eds.), *op. cit.,* pp. 297–303

31   F. Pakenham, *Peace by Ordeal* (Jonathan Cape, 1935) p. 218

32    F.S.L. Lyons, *Ireland since the Famine* (Weidenfeld & Nicolson, 1971) p. 437

33    *Ibid.,* pp. 437–8, 806

34    Curtis and MacDowell (eds.), *op. cit.,* pp. 322–6

35    Curtis and MacDowell (eds.), *op. cit.,* p. 327

36    Curtis and MacDowell (eds.), *op. cit.,* pp. 328–30

37    A.T.Q. Stewart, *The Narrow Ground, Aspects of Ulster* (Faber & Faber, 1977) p. 171

# Case Study 4

# THE GENERAL STRIKE, 1926

The General Strike of 1926 was the most serious industrial dispute ever to occur in Britain, even though it lasted for only nine days. The lock-out in the coal industry which precipitated the General Strike endured for seven months, and was ultimately much more damaging in its effects. Both episodes raise a number of contentious and important issues. In the first place, why was the coal industry so bedevilled by conflict in the inter-war period? Was it simply because of the obstinacy of the leaders on both sides, as Lord Birkenhead averred? After a meeting with the miners' representatives he wrote: 'It would be possible to say without exaggeration of the miners' leaders that they were the stupidest men in England, if we had not had frequent occasion to meet the owners.' (L.S. Amery, *My Political Life*) Or were there more fundamental problems? Why did the dispute in the coal industry lead to a General Strike when the General Council of the TUC were so clearly opposed to such a venture? How revolutionary, both in intent and in practice was the General Strike? Was its failure a betrayal of the working class or a triumph for the cause of constitutional legality and social peace?

The answers to these and related questions are still in dispute, and depend to a great extent on the political standpoint of the observer. The accounts of those who participated in the strike are equally at variance in some cases. Members of the government were naturally anxious to stress the unconstitutional nature of the strike, and the real threat which it posed to the authority of Parliament. The TUC, on the other hand, maintained that the strike was an industrial dispute, pure and simple. When the strike failed, perceptions differed over the reasons, and whether, indeed, it had failed. Thus the events of 1926 provide a good exercise in disentangling truth from bias, and myth from reality.

# 1. THE CAUSES OF THE STRIKE

### The Problems of the Coal Industry

After the First World War the British coal industry was in a vulnerable situation. In 1913 British coal production reached a peak of 287 million tons, of which 98 million tons were exported. British exports accounted for over half the international trade in coal. But after 1918, while domestic consumption held up reasonably well, British coal exports now faced severe foreign competition. They fell to 36 million tons in 1921, and only recovered temporarily in 1923–4, when French occupation of the Ruhr brought German coal production to a standstill (Source 1). The industry was ill adapted to meet the challenge of foreign competition. Ownership was very fragmented with 1500 colliery companies operating over 2500 separate coal mines. The coal seams themselves were owned by 4000 different landowners who expected a royalty on every ton of coal produced, adding to its selling cost. Variations in the geological strata of the different pits and in the level of mechanisation meant wide differences in productivity, ranging from 280 tons per worker per year in some pits in South Yorkshire to 177 tons per worker in North Wales. Mining had always been a hard and dangerous occupation. Between 1922 and 1924 3603 miners were killed and over 500 000 injured. Such conditions produced an intransigent and united labour force, willing to respond to militant leadership. There had been serious coal strikes in the years before the First World War when the industry was reasonably prosperous. Faced with a declining market, and the consequent pressure to reduce wages, the industry was bound to become an arena for conflict between the forces of capital and labour.

The struggle between the owners and the miners between the wars centred on three main issues: control of the industry, wage levels and hours of work. The owners wanted a free hand to run the industry as they pleased, and an end to the system of control that had operated during the war when all profits had been pooled to enable standard wages to be paid throughout the industry. The owners' only recipe in the face of reduced demand for coal was either to reduce wages or to lengthen hours. They also wanted an end to the national minimum wage, established in 1912, so that wages could be more closely related to productivity. The miners saw nationalisation as the only long-term solution to the problems of the coal industry. They were determined not to sacrifice the principle of national wage agreements; and they wanted to ensure that their wages at least kept pace with the rise in living costs.

## The Growth of Conflict

These issues all came to a head in 1919. An impending strike was averted by the appointment of the Sankey Commission to look into all the problems of the industry. The commission was headed by Mr Justice Sankey, and included four members of the Miners' Federation of Great Britain (the MFGB). Others were appointed by the government and the Mining Association, representing the owners. Not surprisingly, the Commission could not agree on its recommendations and it produced four separate reports. The Chairman's report, supported by seven of the thirteen members, came down in favour of nationalisation, a majority of one. But in August 1919 Lloyd George made it clear that he was not prepared to accept this solution. The miners were left with a sense of grievance and a feeling that government promises were not to be trusted. The one positive outcome of the Commission was the Seven Hours Act, passed in 1920, which reduced the working day (excluding winding time) to seven hours.

There was relative peace in the coal industry until 1921 when the post-war boom collapsed. The government advanced the date under which the mines were due to pass out of government control from 31 August to 31 March. The mine owners immediately abandoned the national wage agreements that had been in force since 1912. The return to district agreements was bound to lead to huge wage cuts, by as much as 50 per cent in some cases, and the MFGB refused to accept the owners' terms. In consequence the miners were locked out from 31 March onwards. The Executive of the MFGB sought the aid of the other unions in the Triple Alliance that had been forged in 1914, namely the National Union of Railwaymen and the unions represented in the Transport Workers' Federation. On 8 April a conference of these unions assembled and voted to strike as from 12 April, on behalf of the miners. Strike notices were withdrawn when negotiations were opened with the government on 11 April. On 15 April Lloyd George hinted that the government might consider a return to the principle of a national pool of mining profits, and this olive branch was enough to persuade J.H. Thomas of the National Union of Railwaymen that the miners should be prepared to meet the Prime Minister again. Their refusal to do so, according to Thomas, released the other unions from their obligations to the miners, and the Triple Alliance strike never took place. This retreat came to be known in Labour mythology as 'Black Friday', and memories of it continue to haunt the trade union movement. The miners were left to strike on their own, and were forced back to work some three months later with wage cuts averaging 30 per cent.

These cuts were briefly restored in 1924 (Source 2), thanks to the brief period of prosperity enjoyed by the industry during the French occupation of the Ruhr, which lasted from January 1923 until August 1924. This brought an increase in British coal exports in 1923 to 98 million tons. The Dawes Plan, negotiated in August 1924, brought French occupation to an end and reparations payments in coal were resumed. Britain's return to the gold standard in April 1925 also had the effect of raising British export prices, by as much as 10 per cent according to some economists. The combined effect of these events was once again to depress British coal exports, and according to the Samuel Commission 73 per cent of the coal produced in the final quarter of 1925 was sold at a loss. In November 1924 the Mining Association invited the MFGB to a meeting 'in view of the extremely serious condition of the coal industry at the present time'. Each side then proceeded to conduct its own investigations, but concentrated on different aspects of the problem and produced its own remedies. To the miners the problem was one of under-consumption which would be solved only by 'a general policy of the world working class' (R. Page Arnot, *The Miners, Years of Struggle*). In the short term, they recommended the halting of reparations payments by Germany. If economies had to be made they should be sought in the reorganisation of the industry, rather than at the expense of wages. The owners' solutions were longer hours, lower wages, or some combination of the two.

On 1 July, 1925 the owners published their terms (Source 3). The 1924 wage agreement was to be ended, as was the principle of a national minimum wage. But profits of £13 out of every £100 of the proceeds remaining after all costs of production (excluding wages) had been met were to be guaranteed. Wages, instead of being the first charge on the industry, would henceforth be paid out of what was left after the 13 per cent profit had been deducted. The return to local district wage agreements would have varying effects, but it was anticipated that wages would fall by anything between 13.4 and 47.9 per cent in consequence. The MFGB reacted with predictable bitterness. A delegate conference on 3 July unanimously rejected the terms (Source 4). The government, anxious at this stage to avert a breakdown, appointed a mediator, W.G. Bridgeman, the First Lord of the Admiralty, and set up a Court of Enquiry under H.P. Macmillan, another High Court Judge. The MFGB refused to cooperate with either of these initiatives until the owners had withdrawn what were considered to be outrageous proposals. In the meantime on 10 July the MFGB laid its own case before the General Council of the TUC.

A special committee of the TUC was set up to maintain links between the two bodies, and it was this committee which on 23 July agreed that as a first step an embargo should be placed on the movement of coal. On Thursday, 30 July the decision was taken to put the embargo into effect, and this was approved by a Special Conference of Union Executives. The government climbed down. On Friday, 31 July Baldwin announced that the government would provide financial assistance to maintain existing wage rates in the coal industry until 1 May, 1926 and that another Royal Commission would be set up to make recommendations for the industry. The TUC's show of solidarity had worked, and the date of the government's surrender became known, appropriately, as 'Red Friday'.

The promised Royal Commission was set up in September 1925. It was headed by Sir Herbert Samuel, leader of the Liberal party, assisted by Sir William Beveridge (a civil servant). General Sir Herbert Lawrence (a retired army officer and managing partner of Glyn Mills, a merchant bank) and Kenneth Lee (a businessman and banker). No representative of the mining industry, either from the owners' or the workers' side was included. The Commission took evidence for the next six months and its Report was published on 6 March, 1926. On every issue but wages its recommendations favoured the miners rather than the owners (Source 5). The Report rejected the owners' suggestion of a longer working day on the grounds that this could only lead to an increase in the existing surplus of coal. But on the issue of wages the Report was uncompromising. The only short-term solution to the financial problems of the industry was a reduction in wages, though no specific figures were mentioned. Neither the Mining Association nor the MFGB could take much comfort from the Report, but the government pledged itself to implement its recommendations if both sides could be induced to accept them. The next two months were taken up with protracted negotiations involving the Mining Association, the MFGB, the General Council of the TUC and the government. It is unnecessary to pursue all the false hares put up and the dead ends that were reached, for in the final analysis the central issue was always whether the miners could be induced to accept some reduction in pay.

On 30 April, 1926 the Mining Association produced their final terms. These involved a return to an eight-hour day, and a 13½ per cent reduction to the national standing wage of 1924. The terms were clearly unacceptable to the MFGB and were rejected unanimously (Sources 6 and 7). There followed a hectic weekend of negotiations, conducted at various levels. The story is a complex one and has been told by many of the participants (Sources 12–17). The only way out of the impasse was to secure the consent of the miners to temporary wage cuts, pending the reorganisation of the industry on a more profitable basis. How close the MFGB came to making such a concession is hard to determine (Source 15).

While the negotiations were proceeding, two conferences were also in session: the Delegates Conference of the MFGB, and the Special Conference of Union Executives representing the 141 unions affiliated to the TUC. After the MFGB rejected the owners' terms a lock-out was declared (the owners refused to employ any miners except on their newly announced terms), and the General Council took up the miners' case. On Saturday, 1 May they put two resolutions to the Special Conference of Union Executives, the first proposing a national stoppage in support of the miners' current terms of employment, the second empowering the General Council to take over the conduct of the dispute. Each was carried decisively. Only the Seamen's Union cast its 49 911 votes against strike action, while 3 653 527 votes were cast in favour. Strike orders were to be sent out by executives of the unions concerned, and the strike was timed to begin at midnight on Monday, 3 May (Source 11).

Hardly had the votes been counted than Walter Citrine, Acting General Secretary of the TUC, sent two letters to Baldwin, one offering cooperation in the distribution of essential foodstuffs, the other indicating the General Council's willingness to discuss the matter further. Baldwin took up the offer, and two sub-committees were set up to conduct further negotiations. The General Council's team consisted of Arthur Pugh (Chairman of the TUC), J.H. Thomas (General Secretary of the NUR) and A.B. Swales (General Secretary of the Amalgamated Engineering Union). The Cabinet was represented by Baldwin (Prime Minister), Arthur Steel-Maitland (Minister of Labour) and Lord Birkenhead (Secretary of State for India). The two groups met at 8.30 on the evening of Saturday, 1 May, and after five hours of talks had agreed on a procedural formula (Source 12). At 1.15 a.m. on Sunday, 2 May the meeting adjourned, on the understanding that the formula would be put both to the Miners' Executive and to the full Cabinet.

The Cabinet duly met at noon on Sunday, 2 May. Unfortunately most of the members of the Miners' Executive had gone back to their districts on the Saturday evening and could not be recalled to London until the Sunday evening. The two sub-committees met at 9.00 p.m., and were joined at 10 Downing Street by other members of the Cabinet and the Miners' Executive in the course of the evening. At 11.30 a new formula was devised by Lord Birkenhead (Source 13) to which the members of the TUC's sub-committee may have assented (Source 15). It was while this document was being considered by the full Cabinet that a telephone message came through from the editor of the *Daily Mail* to the effect that printers had refused to print an editorial condemning the strike (Source 14). This gave a decisive advantage to the hawks in the Cabinet – Churchill, Amery and Joynson-Hicks in particular. Baldwin was persuaded to call an end to the negotiations. A document, prepared beforehand, was speedily amended to take account of the *Daily Mail* incident and presented to the General Council's negotiators. They retired to draft their reply, but when Pugh and Citrine returned to the Cabinet Room it was to find that Baldwin had retired to bed and the rest of the Cabinet had gone home. Nothing now stood in the way of the General Strike.

# 2. THE COURSE OF THE STRIKE

The General Strike lasted for nine days. In accordance with instructions from the General Council the first-line unions ceased working at midnight on Monday, 3 May. Nine days later representatives of the General Council called at No. 10 Downing Street to announce that the strike was over. In addition to the million or so miners who had been locked out, the strike initially involved about 1.5 million workers in the transport industries, the printing trade, the iron and steel trades, heavy chemicals, the building trades and the electricity and gas industries. These were joined at midnight on Tuesday, 11 May by workers in the shipbuilding and engineering industries. Altogether the greatest number of workers engaged in the stoppage at any one time was therefore about 3 million.

The government was well prepared. Under the Emergency Powers Act of 1920 it had authority to deal with 'any activity calculated to deprive a substantial proportion of the community of the essentials of life'. Such powers were invoked by a royal proclamation declaring a state of emergency on Saturday, 1 May. The country was placed under the control of ten Civil Commissioners who had already drawn up plans with local authorities for the maintenance of supplies. During the course of the strike, 226 000 Special Constables were enrolled; volunteers were recruited to assist in various ways through the Organisation for the Maintenance of Supplies, a body set up in September 1925 with the threat of a general strike in mind. The armed forces were available wherever they were needed. The navy manned power stations and ships were moored in potential trouble spots such as the Clyde and Tyneside. Troops were used to escort food convoys in London and to guard possible targets.

By comparison the TUC was caught badly unprepared. Bevin subsequently admitted that preparations for a general strike only began in earnest on 27 April, 1926. The General Council directed operations from its headquarters in Eccleston Square (Source 18), but because of the fragmented nature of the trade union movement there was no clear chain of command. Control of the strike in the localities supposedly rested with individual unions. In most big cities unions were also grouped into trades councils on which they would be represented. These could have provided an obvious mechanism through which the General Council might have coordinated the strike. Unfortunately the General Council, Bevin in particular, refused to adopt this course on the grounds that individual unions would have resented their loss of independence. It was also feared that left-wing elements might use the trades councils to radicalise the strike. Thus trades councils were not used as a channel of communication, and their functions were confined to the maintenance of law and order. In practice, strike committees were set up in every area, many of them deriving their membership from the trades councils, and it was these committees that effectively took charge of the strike. In some areas, notably in the North-east and the Fife coalfield, the strike committees operated almost as an alternative government, taking responsibility for the distribution of all essential supplies (Source 25). In others they did their best to cooperate with the local police force and saw their main role as assisting in keeping the peace.

This variety of response to the strike reflects its ambivalent character. On the one hand, the General Council continued to maintain that the General Strike was an industrial dispute whose sole purpose was to defend the living standards of the miners. On the other, the government was equally persistent in its view that it was a threat to the authority of Parliament and consequently to the constitution (Sources 18–22).

The experience of the strike left equally contrasting impressions. No one was killed directly as a result of the strike, if one excludes the four killed in train accidents caused by operator inexperience. But violence flared up on various occasions (Sources 26, 27). Over 3000 people were arrested for offences connected with the strike, and of these 1041 received prison sentences. The government took the threat to law and order very seriously and an inflammatory speech could result in arrest and detention (Source 28). While some observers saw the peaceful conduct of most strikers as a tribute to the fundamental good sense and moderation of the British people, others feared (or in a few cases hoped for) an outbreak of class warfare (Sources 22, 25).

# 3. THE ENDING OF THE STRIKE AND ITS CONSEQUENCES

The General Strike had barely begun before attempts were being made to halt it. As soon as Herbert Samuel heard that the strike had begun, he returned from holiday in Italy, arriving at Dover on Thursday, 6 May. On Friday, 7 May, he met members of the TUC's negotiating committee at a private house belonging to a South African millionaire, Abe Bailey, who was a friend of J.H. Thomas. The following morning, Saturday, 8 May, he visited Baldwin with a set of draft proposals for ending the strike, which came to be known as the Samuel Memorandum (Source 29). Although Baldwin made it quite clear that Samuel could not commit the government in any way, the TUC's negotiators were still willing to regard Samuel as a reliable intermediary (Source 30).

On Sunday, 9 May, the Miners' Executive insisted on being brought into the discussions, and made their objections to the Samuel Memorandum quite clear, as Samuel indicated in a letter, written to Baldwin (but not posted) on Tuesday, 11 May (Source 31). But by this time members of the General Council were coming to feel that the intransigence of the miners was no longer justified. Although instructions had been sent to workers in the engineering and shipbuilding industries to join the strike from midnight on Tuesday, 11 May, that very evening the negotiating committee telephoned Baldwin to ask for a meeting at Downing Street on the following day. Whether the General Council had already decided to call off the strike is still a moot point. A final attempt was made to secure the approval of the MFGB to the Samuel Memorandum on the morning of 12 May, without success. At 12.20 p.m. a deputation from the General Council, headed by Arthur Pugh, its Chairman, met a group of

Cabinet ministers at 10 Downing Street. Pugh announced that the General Strike was 'to be terminated forthwith' and unconditionally, though hopes were expressed that negotiations with the miners would be resumed immediately, and that employers would cooperate in the reinstatement of workers who had been on strike (Source 32).

Instructions were sent out to individual unions calling for members to resume work as soon as the necessary arrangements could be made. Despite Baldwin's plea, made in the House of Commons that evening that 'we should resume our work in a spirit of co-operation, putting behind us all malice and vindictiveness', many employers took the opportunity to impose new working conditions. Where this happened, it strengthened the resistance of those who were reluctant to abandon the miners, and there were actually more men on strike on Thursday, 13 May, than at any other time. Baldwin felt it necessary to give additional reassurances to those who had been on strike. In a speech to the House of Commons on the Thursday evening, he said: 'I will not countenance any attack on the part of any employers to use this present occasion for trying in any way to get reductions in wages below those in force before the strike or any increase in hours.' By the end of the weekend of 15/16 May agreements had been reached in most industries, and the General Strike was effectively over.

The miners' lock-out continued. Baldwin offered fresh terms on 14 May, involving a promise to implement part of the Samuel Commission's recommendations, a national wages board on which the miners would be represented and a temporary subsidy of £3m while new wage levels were being worked out. But some wage reductions would be inevitable, and an increase in working hours likely. The miners refused pointblank to consider the terms, as did the employers. The government's only further contribution to the dispute was the repeal in July of the Seven Hours Act, thus enabling employers to increase working hours rather than reduce wages. Despite various initiatives by Churchill and the Bishops of the Church of England, among others, the owners refused to moderate their terms. By the end of November the miners could hold out no longer, and drifted back to work. District agreements replaced national agreements. Hours were generally increased to 7½ or 8 hours and wage reductions averaged 15 per cent.

It is hard to quantify the results of the General Strike. Its immediate effects were seen in the loss of 162 million working days. Coal production fell from 243 million tons in 1925 to 126 million tons in 1926. Trade union membership, already declining, fell from 5.3 million in 1926 to 4.3 million in 1933. For the miners the strike was an unmitigated defeat. Memories of it continued to fuel the demand for nationalisation of the mining industry, eventually achieved in 1947. The legacy of bitterness in the coal industry has lasted until the present day. The prosperous coalfields of Leicestershire and Nottinghamshire that were first to return to work in 1926 were also those which refused to support the miners' strike of 1984–5. The breakaway Miners' Industrial Union was founded by George Spencer, a right-wing Labour MP, in the autumn of 1926 to enable miners in the relatively prosperous Nottinghamshire coalfield to break ranks, and return to work. In 1984 the pattern was repeated when Nottinghamshire miners refused to support another national stoppage, and formed another breakaway union, the Union of Democratic Mineworkers.

For the trade union movement as a whole the General Strike was also a defeat, underlined by the passage in 1927 of the Trades Disputes Act (Source 36). In March 1926, Baldwin had opposed the Macquisten Bill, designed to reduce trade union immunities, on the grounds that it would increase class bitterness. After the General Strike he supported the Trades Disputes Act. It stayed on the statute book for nineteen years.

Opinions are more divided over whether the working class as a whole suffered as a result of the General Strike. To some observers, the mood of working-class solidarity which the strike evoked was a success of a kind (Source 41). For others, the strike provided a necessary lesson in tactics, underlining the need to take a parliamentary road to socialism. But to those on the left of the Labour party, as to members of the Communist party, the General Strike was a wasted opportunity, which might have succeeded had its leaders not betrayed their supporters. Members of the government, not unnaturally, took a different view.

# 4. VERDICTS ON THE GENERAL STRIKE

The General Strike was twice pronounced illegal during its course. On 6 May, 1926 Sir John Simon, a leading Liberal MP and former Attorney-General (1913–15) delivered a powerful condemnation of the General Strike in the House of Commons, and he returned to the attack on 11 May (Source 33). On 11 May Mr Justice Astbury condemned the strike in a judgment delivered in the Chancery Division of the High Court (Source 34). The case arose out of an action brought by the National Sailors' and Firemen's Union, one of the very few to oppose the call for a General Strike on 1 May. The General President of the Union, Mr Havelock Wilson sought an injunction to restrain London officials from calling London members out on strike without the authority of the Executive Council of the union. He gained his injunction, and Mr Justice Astbury used the opportunity to declare the General Strike wholly illegal. The Simon view of the strike was opposed on 10 May by Sir Henry Slesser, who had been Solicitor-General in MacDonald's 1924 Labour government, but it received its most effective rebuttal in an article written for the *Yale Law Journal* by A.L. Goodhart, the editor of the English *Law Quarterly Review* in 1927 (Source 35). It was at least partly to affirm the illegality of the General Strike that the Trades Disputes Act of 1927 was passed (Source 36).

Verdicts on the political justification for the strike have been equally marked. George V, not unnaturally, recorded his sense of relief that the strike was over, and attributed its failure to the good sense of the British people (Source 37). The Communist party saw the end of the General Strike as a betrayal of the working class (Source 39). To moderate trade unionists like Citrine, the Strike did not fail, but taught important lessons for the future (Source 38), while to others it left the bitter taste of defeat

(Source 40). Alternatively, the General Strike was seen as a triumph of working-class solidarity (Source 41). Different explanations for the failure of the strike are given by Tom Jones (Source 42), Beatrice Webb (Source 43) and A.J. Cook (Source 44).

# FURTHER READING

## Background

Wilfred Harris Crook, *The General Strike* (University of North Carolina Press, USA, 1931)
C. Farman, *May 1926, The General Strike, Britain's Aborted Revolution* (Panther Books, 1974)
M. Morris, *The General Strike* (Historical Association, 1975)
M. Morris, *The General Strike* (Penguin, 1976)
Gerard Noel, *The Great Lockout, 1926* (Constable, 1976)
P. Renshaw, *The General Strike* (Eyre Methuen, 1975)

## Contemporary Accounts and Memoirs

L.S. Amery, *My Political Life*, vol. II (Hutchinson, 1953)
Walter Citrine, *Men at Work* (Hutchinson, 1964)
A.J. Cook, *The Nine Days* (The London Co-operative Printing Society, 1926)
Thomas Jones, *Whitehall Diary*, vol. II. ed. K. Middlemas (OUP, 1969)
Beatrice Webb, *Diaries*, ed. Margaret Cole (Longman, 1956)

## Biographies

A. Bullock, *The Life and Times of Ernest Bevin* (Heinemann, 1960)
D. Dilks, *Neville Chamberlain*, vol. I, 1869–1929 (CUP, 1984)
M. Gilbert, *Winston Churchill*, vol. V (Heinemann, 1975)
K. Middlemas and J. Barnes, *Baldwin* (Weidenfeld & Nicolson, 1964)
H. Nicolson, *George V* (Constable, 1952)

## Documentary Sources

R. Page Arnot, *The General Strike, May 1926: Its Origin and History* (Labour Research
      Department, 1926)
R. Page Arnot, *The Miners, Years of Struggle* (Allen & Unwin, 1953)
Emile Burns, *The General Strike, May 1926: Trades Councils in Action* (Labour Research
      Department, 1926)
Scott Nearing, *The British General Strike* (Vanguard Press, USA, 1926)
*The British Gazette, The British Worker* (David & Charles, 1971)

# SOURCE MATERIAL 1
# The Causes of the Strike

*Sources 1–17 cover the causes of the General Strike and are divided into three groups: A. the problems of the coal industry after the First World War (Sources 1–7); B. the support received by the miners from the trade union movement (Sources 8–11); and C. the events culminating in the final breakdown of relations between the government and the TUC (Sources 12–17).*

## 1A  Problems of the Coal Industry

**SOURCE 1**  Employment and Output (Selected Years)

| Year | Number employed (thousands) | Output (millions of tons) | Exports (millions of tons) |
|------|------|------|------|
| 1913 | 1107 | 287 | 94 |
| 1918 | 990 | 228 | 41 |
| 1920 | 1227 | 230 | 39 |
| 1921 | 1132 | 163 | 36 |
| 1922 | 1094 | 250 | 82 |
| 1923 | 1160 | 276 | 98 |
| 1924 | 1172 | 267 | 79 |
| 1925 | 1086 | 243 | 67 |
| 1926 | * | 126 | 28 |
| 1927 | 998 | 251 | 68 |
| 1933 | 772 | 207 | 53 |
| 1936 | 756 | 228 | 46 |
| 1938 | 782 | 227 | 46 |

*National dispute, lasting approximately seven months from 1 May.

R. Page Arnot, *The Miners, Years of Struggle* (Allen & Unwin, 1953) pp. 524–5

## SOURCE 2  The 1924 Wage Agreement

*This embodied the proposals of the Buckmaster Enquiry, and represented the best terms achieved by the miners during the inter-war period.*

1. Standard profits shall consist of a sum equal to 15 per cent of standard wages instead of 17 per cent as at present.

2. The surplus remaining after the deduction from proceeds of the cost of standard wages, costs other than wages, and standard profits, shall be divided between wages and profits in the proportion of 88 per cent to wages and 12 per

cent to profits instead of the present proposal of 83 per cent to wages and 17 per cent to profits.

3. The general minimum percentage on standard wages shall be increased from 20 to 33.

4. In no district shall the wages of any adult able-bodied day-wage workman fall below a figure 40 per cent above the standard wage (as defined in clause 7 of the wages agreement dated July 1, 1921) of the lowest-paid class of day-wage workmen in the district.

Page Arnot, *The Miners, Years of Struggle* p. 348

# SOURCE 3   The Owners' Offer, 30 June, 1925

*By the middle of 1925 the coal industry was losing £1 million a month and 400 collieries had been forced to close. This was the background to the terms offered on 1 July, 1925, due to come into effect on 31 July.*

On June 30, 1925 the owners gave formal notice of termination of the agreement on July 31, and presented a statement of the new terms on which they were prepared to make a new agreement. These terms involved a total change in the existing method of wage fixing. Local wage agreements covering each area were to be substituted for the national wage agreement. More serious even than this reversion to pre-war methods was the suggested complete reversal of the relative importance of wages and profits as a first charge on the industry. Whereas hitherto, in the 1921 and 1924 agreements, a minimum wage had been guaranteed even if profits were entirely absorbed in the payment, the proposed arrangement involved the surrender of the minimum wage and the possibility that wages might sink to any figure the workers of any given locality might be forced to accept. The actual wage rates offered in the new terms would have entailed a reduction, varying in the districts, from 13 to almost 48 per cent on the standard rates.

Wilfred Harris Crook, *The General Strike* (University of North Carolina Press, USA, 1931) pp. 285–6

# SOURCE 4   The Miners' Reaction to the Owners' Offer

*This statement was submitted by the MFGB to a special conference of the TUC which met on 24 July, 1925.*

These proposals, if put into operation, would, in effect, transfer all the economic ills of the industry to the already overburdened shoulders of the mineworkers, and the mine-owners would assure to themselves a good profit under all conceivable circumstances. There would be very little incentive to efficiency on their part, and they would be able automatically to rid themselves of all their troubles by progressive reductions in wages.

Experience teaches us that the awful state to which the mine-workers would eventually be reduced if these proposals were operated, is too terrible to contemplate. It must be borne in mind that the mine-owners have consistently refused to allow us to have any share of the control of the industry, yet we are asked to allow our wages to be entirely at their mercy, and the burden of bad management, inefficient methods of production, administration and distribution could all be automatically transferred to our shoulders without any let or hindrance whatsoever.

Page Arnot, *The Miners, Years of Struggle,* pp. 365–6

# SOURCE 5  The Samuel Commission Recommendations

*The recommendations were divided into two. The first group was addressed to the permanent aspect of the problems of the coal industry, the second group dealt with the temporary aspect. In the first part there were proposals for the nationalisation of coal royalties, the reorganisation of the industry to eliminate inefficient pits, more provision for research, improvements in the system of distribution, and suggestions to improve relations between employers and employed. Included here are the sections on 'Labour' and 'The Immediate Problem'.*

6. LABOUR.– The relations between employers and employed are of fundamental importance, and here also we are convinced that a number of changes are necessary.

(1) The principle on which the recent wage agreements have been based is, in our opinion sound, but amendments are needed in the methods of ascertaining the proceeds of the industry for the fixing of wages. A large proportion of the coal is sold by the mines to associated industries, and the most important of these amendments relates to the prices at which these transfers are made.

(2) The standard length of the working day, which is now on the average 7½ hours underground, should remain unaltered. The optional re-distribution of hours within the present weekly total, over a week of five days instead of six, should be considered. The multiple shift system should be extended.

(3) Joint pit committees should be established generally.

(4) The methods of payment of men not employed at the face should be revised where possible so as to give them a direct interest in output.

(5) The introduction of a family allowance system, either nationally or by districts is desirable. Pooling schemes should be adopted to prevent married men with families being prejudiced in obtaining employment.

(6) Profit-sharing schemes providing for the distribution to the workmen of shares in the undertakings, should be generally adopted in the industry, and should be made obligatory by statute.

(7) For all new collieries, a proper provision of houses for the workers should be a condition of the lease.

(8) The general establishment of pit-head baths is necessary. This should be undertaken by the existing Miners' Welfare Fund, which should be increased by a substantial contribution from royalties.

(9) When prosperity returns to the industry, we consider that annual holidays with pay should be established.

*The Immediate Problem*

To bring any of these measures of re-organisation into effect must need a period of months; to bring them all into full operation must need years. The Miners' Federation fully recognise that, even if nationalisation were to be accepted, much time must elapse before the great changes it involves could be put into force and the effects be seen. Meantime, the hard economic conditions of the moment remain to be faced.

The dominant fact is that, in the last quarter of 1925, if the subsidy be excluded, 73 per cent of the coal was produced at a loss.

We express no opinion whether the grant of a subsidy last July was unavoidable or not, but we think its continuance indefensible. The subsidy should stop at the end of its unauthorised term, and should never be repeated.

We cannot approve the proposal of the Mining Association, that the gap between costs and proceeds should be bridged by an increase in the working day, reductions in the miners' wages, some economies in other costs, and a large diminution in railway rates, to be effected by lowering the wages of railwaymen. In any case, these proposals go beyond the need, for we do not concur in the low estimate of future coal prices on which they are based.

While the mine owners present a plan which is unacceptable, the Miners' Federation abstained from making any suggestion as to the means for meeting the immediate situation. The duty therefore devolves upon the Commission to formulate its own proposals.

If the present hours are retained, we think a revision of 'the minimum percentage addition to standard rates of wages', fixed in 1924 at a time of temporary prosperity, is indispensable. A disaster is impending over the industry, and the immediate reduction of working costs that can be effected in this way, and in this way alone, is essential to save it. The minimum percentage is not a 'minimum wage' in the usual sense of that term. The wages of the lowest paid men will be safeguarded by a continuance of the system of subsistence allowances. The reductions that we contemplate will still leave the mine-owners without adequate profits in any of the wage-agreement districts, and without profits in most districts. If trade improves and prices rise a profit will be earned. If prices do not rise, an adequate profit must be sought in the improved methods which in any case should be adopted. Should the miners freely prefer some extension of hours with a less reduction of wages, Parliament would no doubt be prepared to authorise it. We trust however that this will not occur.

We consider that it is essential that there should be, as there has always been hitherto, considerable variations in the rates of wages in the several districts. But we are strongly of the opinion that national wage agreements should continue. Such agreements are entered into in all other British industries of importance.

We recommend that the representatives of the employers and the employed should meet together, first nationally and then in the districts, in order to arrive at a settlement by the procedure that we have previously suggested.

By a revision of the minimum percentage coal mining would be saved from an immediate collapse, but it seems inevitable that a number of collieries would still have to be closed. This may give rise to the necessity for a transfer of labour on a considerable scale. We recommend that the Government should be prepared in advance with such plans to assist it as are practicable, and should provide funds for the purpose.

R. Page Arnot, *The General Strike, May 1926: Its Origin and History* (Labour Research Department, 1926) pp. 96–100

## SOURCE 6   Letter from Stanley Baldwin to Herbert Smith, President of the MFGB

*This letter conveyed the mine owners' final terms to the MFGB following two months of negotiation in relation to the Samuel Commission Report.*

10 Downing Street, SW1,
30 April, 1926

Dear Mr Smith,

I am communicating with you by letter because it is important to save time.

I have now received from the coal-owners the offer which, as I told you last night, they have been considering in conjunction with their district representatives. The offer is as follows, namely:

A uniform national minimum of 20% over 1914 standard on a uniform 8-hour basis, with corresponding hours for surface men. (The representatives of North Wales do not wish to stand out of the national agreement, but feel that the pits in the area would be unable to work on this minimum.)

In putting before you this proposal from the coal-owners, I would remind you that, as I explained to you yesterday, it is contemplated that the 1919 (Seven Hours') Act should remain on the Statute Book, and that there should be legislation providing temporarily for the working of the additional hours.

The Government would set up a Commission not later than December 31st, 1929, to advise whether as a result of reorganisation or better trade or both, the condition of the coal industry has improved to an extent that makes a reversion to the standard hours justifiable . . .

There would, of course, be the national agreement as already indicated. The Government has already intimated its general acceptance of the report of the Royal Commission, provided it was also accepted by the mine-owners and the miners, and although unfortunately there has not been on the part of the mine-owners and the miners the same unqualified acceptance, the Government desire, nevertheless to reaffirm their willingness to give effect to such of the proposals in the Report as we believe will be of benefit to the industry.

In particular, the Government propose in any case at once to arrange an authoritative inquiry into the best method of following up the recommendations of the Commission with regard to selling organisations and amalgamations.

If the proposals before you are not acceptable, I should be glad to receive from you any counter-proposals and I am holding myself available to meet you again as soon as you let me know that you are available for further discussion.

I am sending a copy of this letter to Mr Pugh.

Yours very truly, STANLEY BALDWIN

Page Arnot, *The Miners, Years of Struggle*, pp. 413–14

## SOURCE 7  The Reply of the MFGB to Baldwin's Offer

30 April

Dear Prime Minister,

The proposals of the coal-owners, delivered by messenger this afternoon (April 30th), have been considered by our Executive Committee, and also by the Conference, which as you are aware has been in London since Wednesday, to which we are empowered to send the following reply:

The miners note with regret that, although the report of the Coal Commission was issued on 6th March, 1926, the mine-owners have only submitted a proposal for a national wage agreement and a national uniform percentage so late as April 30th, at 1.15 p.m., when at least two-thirds of the mine-workers in the coalfields are already locked out by the coal owners . . .

The reply of the miners, after considering the proposals in the light of the present situation, is therefore as follows:- They are unanimously of the opinion that the proposals cannot be accepted, but on the other hand, feel that the statement of proposals submitted (as enclosed) of the Trades Union Congress afford a reasonable basis of negotiation and settlement.

Our views on the question of extended hours are well known to you, and it is only necessary to say that the present hours

(a) Are long enough to supply all the coal for which a market can be found;

(b) Are as long as men should be expected to pursue such a dangerous calling and

(c) That to extend the hours in present circumstances is simply to swell the ranks of the unemployed;

(d) That to increase hours is to invite similar measures on the part of our foreign competitors;

(e) That such a proposal is contrary to the findings of the Royal Commission;

As to counter-proposals, we can only say that we will co-operate to the fullest extent with the Government and the owners in instituting such reorganisation as is recommended by the Commission. Until such reorganisation brings greater prosperity to the industry, the miners should not be called upon to surrender any of their present inadequate wages and conditions.

On behalf of the Miners' Federation. Your faithfully,

HERBERT SMITH (President); T. RICHARDS (Vice-President);

W.P. RICHARDSON (Treasurer); A.J. COOK (Secretary)

Page Arnot, *The Miners, Years of Struggle*, p. 415

## QUESTIONS ON SOURCES 1–7

1. Explain the fall in coal output in 1921 and 1925 (Source 1). (C)

2. What light do the employment and output figures in Source 1 shed on the changes in productivity in the coal industry between the wars? (C)

3. Were the miners' objections to the owners' wage proposals of 1 July, 1925 exaggerated (Sources 3, 4)? (E)

4. What can you infer about working conditions in the coal industry from Section 6 of the Samuel Commission's recommendations (Source 5)? (S)

5. What were the main differences between the owners' proposals of 1 July, 1925, the Samuel Commission proposals, and the owners' proposals of 30 April, 1926, with respect to hours and wages in the coal industry (Sources 3, 5, 6)? (S)

6. How much, in your view, did the composition of the Samuel Commission influence its findings (Source 5)? (E)

7. From the evidence presented here, would you conclude that the government's sympathies lay with the mine owners rather than with the miners? (S)

8. How convincing a case did the MFGB make in its opposition to longer hours as a solution to the problems of the coal industry (Source 7)? (S)

## 1B  Trade Union Support for the Miners

**SOURCE 8**  Statement Issued to the Press, 11 July, 1925 by the General Council of the TUC

*The MFGB had placed the owners' offer of 1 July, 1925 before the General Council. This document indicates the reaction of the official leadership.*

The General Council appreciates to the full the fact that no self-respecting body of organised workers could negotiate on such terms, and they completely endorse the refusal of the Miners' Federation to meet the owners until the proposals have been withdrawn . . .

　　The General Council are confident they will have the backing of the whole organised Trade Union movement in placing themselves without qualification and unreservedly at the disposal of the Miners' Federation to assist the Federation in any way possible.

Page Arnot, *The General Strike, May 1926: Its Origin and History*, p. 30

## SOURCE 9   Letter from Walter Citrine to A.J. Cook, 8 April, 1926

*Walter Citrine was at the time Acting General Secretary of the TUC; A.J. Cook was General Secretary of the MFGB. This letter was written after publication of the Samuel Report, in answer to a request from the MFGB for a reaffirmation of support from the TUC.*

Dear Mr Cook,

The Industrial Committee of the General Council have carefully considered the statements placed before them by your representatives at their meeting today, during which you asked for a declaration from the Committee as to the support they would accord your Federation in respect of any attempts by the Coal owners to enforce –

(a)  A reversion to District Agreements

(b)  A lengthening of Hours

(c)  A reduction in Wages

The Committee fully realise the seriousness of the present position, but they are of the opinion that matters have not yet reached the stage when any final declaration of the General Council's policy can be made.

It appears to them that negotiations are yet in a very early stage, and that efforts should be made to explore to the fullest extent the possibility of reducing the points of difference between your Federation and the Coal owners, and for that purpose they advise the immediate continuance of negotiations as suggested in the accompanying resolution . . .

The Committee wish to assure you that they are extremely desirous of doing anything they possibly can to facilitate settlement, and they will hold themselves in readiness in case your Federation should desire to utilise their services.

Yours sincerely,

(signed) WALTER M. CITRINE (Acting Secretary)

Page Arnot, *The General Strike, May 1926: Its Origin and History*, pp. 107–8

## SOURCE 10   Resolution Passed at a Conference Held by the National Minority Movement, 21 March, 1926

*The National Minority Movement had developed after 1924, when Communists were officially excluded from the Labour party. Its Secretary was Harry Pollitt, a member of the Communist party, and the 1926 Conference was chaired by Tom Mann, who had been associated with the syndicalist movement before the war, and who was a founder-member of the British Communist party. The NMM appealed to left-wing groups within the Labour party and the trade union movement, and the March conference was attended by 883 delegates, representing 547 different organisations, including 52 trades councils.*

The preparations for the capitalist offensive assume even larger dimensions. The present industrial position is full of menace and the attack threatens to be the most colossal in the history of the working class movement.

Ever since the temporary check given to the capitalist offensive at the end of July by the united action of the Trade Union movement, under the leadership of the General Council of the Trades Union Congress, the capitalist class has missed no opportunity to renew the attack.

They have made separate attacks upon the seamen, miners, railwaymen, building workers, textile workers, engineers and many others, in order to divide and conquer them sectionally.

The engineering crisis, the findings of the Coal Commission, the government support of the employers' attack upon the Fair Wage Clause, as applicable to building workers, all lead up to a general capitalist attack in mass.

Just as last July, so today, it is imperative that all the forces of the working class movement should be mobilised under one central leadership to repel the attack and to secure the demands of every section of the workers.

Once again the General Council must take the lead; once again the entire movement must be gathered together for the fight . . .

Page Arnot, *The General Strike, May 1926: Its Origin and History*, pp. 112–16

*The Resolution went on to urge trades councils to form themselves into Councils of Action and to urge the General Council to convene a National Council of Action to prepare for 'the complete scientific utilisation of the whole Trade Union Movement in the struggle'.*

## SOURCE 11   The TUC's Memorandum on the General Strike

*This Memorandum was drawn up by the General Council and approved by 3 653 529 votes to 49 911 at the Conference of Executives of unions affiliated to the TUC on Saturday, 1 May. Workers were to be called out by individual unions as from midnight on Monday, 3 May.*

SCOPE.– The Trade Union Congress General Council and the Miners' Federation of Great Britain, having been unable to obtain a satisfactory settlement of the matters in dispute in the coal-mining industry and the Government and the mineowners having forced a lock-out, the General Council, in view of the need for co-ordinated action on the part of the affiliated Unions, in defence of the policy laid down by the General Council of the Trades Union Congress directs as follows:-

1. TRADES AND UNDERTAKINGS TO CEASE WORK
Except as herein after provided, the following trades and undertakings shall cease work, as and when required by the General Council
    Transport . . .
    Printing trades, including the Press
    Productive industries
    Building Trades . . .
    Electricity and Gas.– The General Council recommend that the Trade Unions connected with the supply of electricity and gas shall co-operate with the object of ceasing to supply power . . .

Sanitary Services.– The General Council direct that sanitary services be continued.

Health and Food Services.– The General Council recommend that there should be no interference in regard to these, and that the Trade Unions concerned should do everything in their power to organise the distribution of food and milk to the whole population.

2. TRADE UNION DISCIPLINE.– (a) The General Council direct that, in the event of Trade Unionists being called upon to cease work, the Trade Unions shall take steps to keep a daily register to account for every one of their members. It should be made known that any workers called upon to cease work should not leave their own district, and by following another occupation, or the same occupation in another district, blackleg their fellow-workers.

(b) The General Council recommend that the actual calling out of the workers should be left to the Unions . . .

3. TRADES COUNCILS.– The work of the Trades Councils, in conjunction with the local officers of the Trade Unions actually participating in the dispute shall be to assist in carrying out the foregoing provisions, and they shall be charged with the responsibility of organising the Trade Unionists in dispute in the most effective manner for the preservation of peace and order.

4. INCITEMENT TO DISORDER AND SPIES.– A strong warning must be issued to all localities that any person found inciting the workers to attack property or inciting the workers to riot must be dealt with immediately. It should be pointed out that the opponents will in all probability employ persons to act as spies and others to use violent language in order to incite the workers to disorder.

5. TRADE UNION AGREEMENTS.– The General Council further direct that the Executives of the Unions concerned shall definitely declare that in the event of any action being taken and Trade Union agreements being placed in jeopardy, it be definitely agreed that there will be no general resumption of work until those agreements are fully recognised.

6. PROCEDURE . . .

(Signed)  A. PUGH, Chairman

WALTER M. CITRINE, Acting Secretary

Page Arnot, *The General Strike, May 1926: Its Origin and History,* pp. 160–3

## QUESTIONS ON SOURCES 8–11

1. Compare the strength of the TUC's commitment to the miners' case in Sources 8 and 9. How do you account for this difference? (S)

2. What view did the National Minority Movement take of the Samuel Commission Report (Source 10)? (C)

3. Was this view justified? (E)

4. Does the TUC Memorandum on the General Strike (Source 11) support the view that the strike was called solely for the purpose of helping the miners? (C)

5. How effective did the General Council intend the General Strike to be (Source 11)? (C)

6. Compare the approaches of the National Minority Movement and of the General Council of the TUC to the organising of a General Strike (Sources 10, 11). (S)

---

# 1C  The Final Breakdown in Negotiations

*The events which led to the final breakdown in relations between the government and the TUC occurred over the weekend of Saturday, 1 May–Sunday, 2 May.*

## SOURCE 12  The Formula Agreed at 1.15 a.m. on Sunday, 2 May

*This formula was accepted by the two sub-committees representing the Cabinet and the General Council which met at No. 10 Downing Street at 8.30 p.m. on Saturday, 1 May. After five hours of talks this was the final outcome.*

The Prime Minister has satisfied himself as a result of the conversations he has had with the representatives of the Trades Union Congress, that if negotiations are continued (it being understood that the notices cease to be operative) the representatives of the Trades Union Congress are confident that a settlement could be reached on the lines of the Report within a fortnight.

Page Arnot, *The General Strike, May 1926: Its Origin and History*, p. 145

## SOURCE 13  The Birkenhead Formula, Produced during the Evening of Sunday, 2 May

*This document was drafted by Birkenhead during the course of the negotiations on the Sunday evening. Whether it was ever accepted by the trade union representatives on the negotiating committee is open to dispute – see Source 15.*

We will urge the miners to authorise us to enter upon a discussion with the understanding that they and we accept the Report as a basis of settlement, and we approach it in the knowledge that it may involve some reduction in wages.

Page Arnot, *The General Strike, May 1926: Its Origin and History*, p. 147

## SOURCE 14  The *Daily Mail* Editorial for Monday, 3 May

*This was the editorial which the chapel of the National Society of Operative Printers and Associates (Natsopa) at the London printing works of the Daily Mail refused to print on the night of Sunday, 2 May, an action which supposedly provoked the Cabinet into calling off negotiations. The Natsopa chapel had no official backing and 750 000 copies with the offending editorial were printed in the Manchester Office and duly circulated throughout the country.*

### FOR KING AND COUNTRY

The miners, after weeks of negotiation, have declined the proposals made to them, and the coal mines of Britain are idle.

The Council of the Trades Union Congress, which represents all the other Trades Unions, has determined to support the miners by going to the extreme of ordering a general strike.

This determination alters the whole position. The coal industry, which might have been reorganised with goodwill on both sides, seeing that some give and take is plainly needed to restore it to prosperity, has now become the subject of a great political struggle, which the nation has no choice but to face with the utmost coolness and the utmost firmness.

We do not wish to say anything hard about the miners themselves. As to their leaders, all we need say at this moment is that some of them are (and have openly declared themselves) under the influence of people who mean no good to this country.

The General Strike is not an industrial dispute; it is a revolutionary movement, intended to inflict suffering upon the great mass of innocent persons in the community and thereby put forcible constraints upon the Government. It is a movement that can only succeed by destroying the Government and subverting the rights and liberties of the people. This being the case it cannot be tolerated by any civilised government and it must be dealt with by every resource at the disposal of the community. A state of emergency and national danger has been proclaimed to resist attack. We call upon all law-abiding men and women to hold themselves at the service of King and Country.

Scott Nearing, *The British General Strike* (Vanguard Press, USA, 1926),
p. 141

## SOURCE 15   Accounts of the Final Breakdown on Sunday, 2 May

### (a) Tom Jones

*Jones was Deputy Secretary to the Cabinet and in No. 10 Downing Street on the evening of 2 May.*

*2 May*
4.45 (p.m.) Saw the PM and Steel-Maitland [Minister of Labour]. Both very worried as to the result of the Cabinet meeting, and the result of the vanishing of the Miners' Executive into the country, and the inability of the TUC to report to the Government by 1.00 p.m. as they promised to do. A letter was said to be on its way from the TUC. Steel-Maitland said that going home last night he had felt extremely nervous about the formula, so had Wilson [Sir Horace Wilson, Permanent Secretary at the Mines Department].

Neither had slept and both were much less satisfied with it today. He thought we ought not to try to force the TUC to send out telegrams cancelling the orders for a general strike. With this I agreed. The PM said nothing. He arranged to postpone the Cabinet to a later hour to await the TUC letter. His own view was that the TUC were still bluffing, and are really afraid of the consequences of the strike action which they had taken . . .

Dined alone at the 'Ship' and on my way back ran into Hankey [Secretary to the Cabinet]. He told me what had happened at the 6.45 p.m. Cabinet. Just after the Cabinet assembled a message came that the TUC would be glad to see the PM and that they had not been able to get into touch with the miners. The Cabinet discussed several drafts of a communication which could be handed to the TUC at, or after the interview with them according as the discussion developed. It was arranged that the PM should see the TUC at 9.00 p.m. with Steel-Maitland, and that the rest of the Cabinet should gather at No. 11 at 9.30 for consultation. The Cabinet approved a draft to be handed to the TUC if, after consultation, it was thought wiser to do so [Source 16]. The Cabinet also authorised the sending out of telegrams to set in motion the necessary steps for dealing with the General Strike.

11.30 Herbert Smith [President of the Miners' Federation] and Cook [General Secretary] arrived with the recalled Miners' Executive . . . Cook asked me, could he have a wash as he was very tired. I took him into the lavatory and plunged at once into a discussion of how far he was prepared to go in the matter of wages. He said the word revision would ease matters if he used it instead of reduction. Next, he did not want to depart from the 33%, the present national minimum, but we could get the reduction in another way by knocking off the 14.2% compensation for the loss of an hour by hewers. This would hit only the better paid piece workers. We could also use some formula about the revision of wages above a specified figure, e.g. 8/- a day. He felt he could not stay longer away from his executive . . .

At 12.15 Lee [a member of the Samuel Commission] rang up to ask did we want to see the owners, as they were still waiting for a summons and they would find themselves locked out of their hotels if they did not get home to bed. It was about midnight, I think, when messages came through to say that the 'Daily Mail' staff had refused to print an editorial 'For King and Country' and that the paper would not appear next day . . . Gower [Private Secretary to Baldwin] went to No. 11 with a message about the 'Daily Mail'. He told the Home Secretary to announce to the Cabinet 'The "Daily Mail" has ceased to function.' 'Hear, hear!' said F.E. [Birkenhead]. 'Not a time for flippancy' said some other Minister. This news had a marked effect on the Draft of the Note . . .

Thomas Jones, *Whitehall Diary*, vol. II, ed. K. Middlemass (OUP, 1969) pp. 29–33

## (b) Lord Birkenhead

*Birkenhead was a key member of the negotiating sub-committee on the government side. This Memorandum was recorded in Jones's diary on 6 May.*

It has occurred to me that it may be useful if I place on record for confidential purposes my recollection of what took place during the private negotiations on

Saturday and Sunday between three Ministers and three representatives of the Trade Unions.

My recollection is precise and will, I believe, not be disputed.

We never were on Saturday in reach of any agreement or even of a formula upon which agreement might appear to rest. But the talk was frank and friendly and in view of the gravity of the issues, we were all unwilling to part with an absolute admission of failure.

In these circumstances the document was produced which was circulated to the Cabinet on Sunday morning [Source 12].

The Sunday conversation began by a statement made by Mr Pugh to the effect that on principle his friends accepted the impressions upon the mind of the Prime Minister recorded in the document already referred to. But they could not assent to the statement that they were confident a conclusion would be reached. It would be more accurate to say that they had not formed such an opinion. In the second place, they were unable to make the expression 'on the lines of the Report' more definite. They were still unable to accept the phrase 'accept the Report'. And if the fortnight provisionally allotted to the discussions proved inadequate (and no one seriously argued on its adequacy) Mr Thomas frankly stated that they would expect the Government to provide a subsidy for whatever period was in fact occupied by the negotiations on reorganisation. I told him that further negotiations seemed to me to be useless unless the Trade Unionist leaders were prepared to take the responsibility of advising the Miners that either in the matter of hours or wages there must be a concession while the matter of reorganisation was under adjustment. In the conversation that followed he used expressions which indicated that he was going as far as was in any way possible, then or thereafter, for him to go. I said, 'Well, if that is as far as you feel able to go, it would at least be useful that I should take down your exact words for the consideration of the Cabinet. I make it plain that in my judgment there is no chance whatever that an assurance so vague and limited will be accepted by them; but you are at least entitled that the words used by you should be placed before them for consideration.' I then took down the words which were recorded in the second document [Source 13] which was explained by me to the Cabinet on our return. Neither in the Saturday discussion nor in the Sunday discussion was any encouragement given either by myself or by my colleagues to the view that we were in reach of a settlement . . .

Jones, *Whitehall Diary*, vol. II, pp. 34–5

### (c) **Walter Citrine**

*Citrine, as Acting General Secretary, was present at the negotiating committee meeting that took place on the Sunday evening. The following excerpt is taken from his autobiography,* Men at Work, *published in 1964.*

Birkenhead then read out some words he had jotted down in the course of the discussion. I had not got the Prime Minister's formula in front of me when I spoke, but as far as I can recall, the words were identical, but he wished to add a most important sentence to the effect that negotiations would be carried on with the knowledge that they might involve some reduction in wages.

We said we could not possibly put this formula to our people as they would be certain to reject it, and if we did so, it might look as though we had some sympathy with it. We argued that the mere insertion of these words implied the negotiations would begin on the assumption that they would end in a reduction in wages. In other words they completely prejudged the negotiations.

Birkenhead seemed fed up, but he soon recovered his equanimity. The discussions were continued, consistently revolving round this point. We could all see that we were not getting anywhere.

Walter Citrine, *Men at Work* (Hutchinson, 1964) p. 169

## (d) Leopold Amery

*Amery was Colonial Secretary at the time, and though not a member of the negotiating committee was present at the full meetings of the Cabinet that took place on Sunday, 2 May. His memoirs were first published in 1953.*

Presently, after 11 p.m. an exhausted Baldwin came and collapsed into an armchair, leaving it to Birkenhead to state the very inconclusive result, which was to the effect that the Trade Union delegates had gone back to consult the miners on a formula urging the latter to agree to enter a discussion which might involve some reduction in wages. Some of us would have been prepared to continue negotiations so long as there was the faintest chance of an agreement. But opinion hardened very much in view of the fact that notices ordering the General Strike to begin next day had been sent out, regardless of the negotiations the night before. While we were still discussing the news arrived that the *Daily Mail* had been suppressed by the printers who disliked the leading article. This tipped the scale. It was clear that the only issue that now mattered, for the government or the public, was whether Government and Parliament were to surrender to coercion. A note previously drawn up by the Cabinet was now stiffened to make it quite clear to the Trade Union leaders that negotiations could not be continued unless the interference with the press was repudiated and the General Strike called off. We dispersed about 12.30, leaving Baldwin to hand the note to the Trade Union leaders, and go to bed.

L.S. Amery, *My Political Life*, vol. II (Hutchinson, 1953) pp. 483–4

## (e) *New Statesman*, 22 May, 1926

*The* New Statesman *was at this time under the editorship of Kingsley Martin, and was generally sympathetic to left-wing causes.*

The Prime Minister, Lord Birkenhead and Sir Arthur Steel-Maitland were fighting desperately for peace, while a section of the Cabinet, led by Winston Churchill, Mr Neville Chamberlain, and Mr Bridgeman, were itching for a fight. The peace party succeeded in arranging terms based on the Royal Commission Report, upon which the strike would be called off and the miners left, if they would not agree, to fight alone. With these terms they returned in triumph to the Cabinet room, only to find Messrs Churchill and Chamberlain in charge, and a clear majority in favour of war at all costs. The Birkenhead–Baldwin terms were accordingly turned down, and when the Prime Minister proposed, nevertheless, to go forward with the negotiations and avert the strike, he was faced with the immediate resignation of seven of his colleagues – Churchill, Neville Chamberlain, Bridgeman, Amery, Jix [Joynson-Hicks], Cunliffe-Lister, and one other of whose identity we are not sure . . . Mr Churchill was the villain of the piece. He is reported to have remarked that he thought 'a little bloodletting would be all to the good'. . .

Nearing, *The British General Strike*, pp. 38–9

### (f) A.J. Cook

*Cook's account of the General Strike,* The Nine Days, *was published in 1926.*

Meanwhile the negotiating committee of the TUC had twice seen the Government in secret, in spite of their pledge to the miners only to negotiate with them; they had twice tried to get the miners to accept formulae which would have meant reductions in wages, in spite of their declared opposition to reductions. No other facts are needed to show the state of mind in which some members of the General Council faced the test of real action . . .

A.J. Cook, *The Nine Days* (The London Co-operative Printing Society, 1926) p. 16

## SOURCE 16   The Government's Final Communiqué

*This was the document prepared in the Cabinet on the afternoon of Sunday, 2 May and amended in the evening to take account of the printers' refusal to print the offending editorial in the* Daily Mail.

HM Government believe that no solution of the difficulties in the coal industry which is both practicable and honourable to all concerned can be reached except by a sincere acceptance of the report of the Commission.

In the expression 'acceptance of the report' is included both the reorganisation of the industry, which should be put in hand immediately, and, pending the results of the reorganisation such interim adjustments of wages or hours of work as will make it economically possible to carry on the industry . . . but since the discussions which have taken place between the miners and the members of the Trade Union Committee it has come to the knowledge of the Government, not only that specific instructions have been sent under the authority of the Executives of Trade Unions represented at the Conference, convened by the General Council of the TUC, directing their members in several of the most vital industries to carry out a general strike on Tuesday next, but that overt acts have already taken place, including gross interference with freedom of the press.

Such action involves a challenge to the constitutional rights and freedom of the nation. His Majesty's Government, therefore, before it can continue negotiations must require from the Trade Union Committee both a repudiation of the actions referred to that have already taken place, and an immediate and unconditional withdrawal of the instructions for a general strike.

Page Arnot, *The General Strike, May 1926: Its Origin and History*, pp. 147–8

# SOURCE 17   The Reply of the General Council

*The trade union representatives, now in No. 11 Downing Street, were taken aback by the government's ultimatum. A quick reply, repudiating the action of the* Daily Mail *printers was drafted and delivered to No. 10 Downing Street at 1.15 a.m., but by this time Baldwin had retired to bed and other members of the Cabinet had gone home. A more considered reply was drawn up in the early hours of Monday, 3 May and delivered by hand to 10 Downing Street at 3.30 a.m. This is the version reproduced here.*

Your letter of the 3rd inst. announcing the Government's decision to terminate the discussion which was resumed on Saturday night, was received by the General Council with surprise and regret . . .

The first reason given was that specific instructions have been sent under the authority of the trade unions represented at the conference, convened by the General Council of the TUC, directing their members in several industries and services to cease work.

I am directed to remind you that there is nothing unusual for workmen to cease work in defence of their interests as wage-earners, and that the specific reason for the decision in this case is to secure for the mine workers the same right from the employers as is insisted upon by employers from workers, namely that negotiations shall be conducted free from the atmosphere of strike or lock-out. This is the principle which Governments have held to be cardinal in the conduct of industrial negotiations.

With regard to the second reason, that 'overt acts have already taken place, including gross interference with the freedom of the press', it is regretted that no information is contained in your letter. The General Council had no knowledge of such acts having occurred, and the decision taken by them definitely forbade any such independent and unauthorised action . . .

Page Arnot, *The General Strike, May 1926: Its Origins and History*, pp. 148–9

# QUESTIONS ON SOURCES 12–17

1.  What significant difference do you notice between the formula agreed on at 1.15 a.m. on Sunday, 2 May and the Birkenhead formula (Sources 12, 13)? (C)

2.  Did the *Daily Mail* editorial of Monday, 3 May misrepresent the position of the TUC (Sources 11, 14)? (C)

3.  How much weight would you attach to the conversation between A.J. Cook and Tom Jones recorded in Source 15(a)? (E)

4.  What difference do you detect between Birkenhead's and Citrine's accounts of the origins of the Birkenhead formula (Sources 15(b), (c))? Whose do you regard as the more reliable? (E)

5.  What discrepancies do you detect in the accounts of the Cabinet's reception of the Birkenhead formula as given by Amery, the *New Statesman* and A.J. Cook (Sources 15(d)–(f))? How do you account for these differences? (E)

6.  What was the 'gross interference with freedom of the press' referred to in Source 16, and what implications would you draw from the language used to describe it? (E)

7.  From your reading of Sources 12–17, would you conclude that the negotiations that took place over the weekend of 1/2 May were doomed to fail? (S)

# SOURCE MATERIAL 2
# The Course of the Strike

*Sources 18–28 relate to the course of the strike, and show: A. the attitude of the TUC, who sought to direct the strike, and that of the government, who had to deal with it (Sources 18–22); and B. the varying responses to the strike call at the local level, and public perceptions of these events (Sources 23–8).*

## 2A  The Strike at the Centre

### SOURCE 18   Walter Citrine's View of the General Council at Work

Then there is myself, the acting secretary, making copious notes, peeping from behind a pile of papers, and pouring a steady flow of advice into the unheeding ears of the chairman, bobbing up and down like a jack-in-the-box in a futile endeavour to get the floor to say nothing in particular. The rest of the members sit about looking tired, somewhat bored, worried but far from rattled; almost in a state of coma. Some improve the shining hour by reading the *British Worker*, unheeding the peroration of the orator holding the floor. Not much sign here of alleged revolutionaries who are plotting to overthrow the Constitution and the Government.

And so Labour's General Staff goes on, directing the fighting units, and by a general mixture of sound sense and huggermugger, somehow and in some way guide the strike movement.

Citrine, *Men at Work*, pp. 191–2

### SOURCE 19   *British Gazette,* 5 May

*The* British Gazette *was the government-sponsored newspaper, edited by Winston Churchill and printed on presses belonging to the* Morning Post. *Churchill was violently opposed to the General Strike, as was the* Morning Post's *proprietor, the Duke of Northumberland. J.C.C. Davidson, Baldwin's private secretary did his best to temper Churchill's more pugnacious views, but as the government's own newspaper, the* British Gazette's *editorials were assumed to reflect the views of the Cabinet, even where they may not have done.*

The general strike is in operation, expressing in no uncertain terms a direct challenge to ordered government. It would be futile to attempt to minimise the seriousness of such a challenge, constituting as it does an effort to force upon 47 000 000 British citizens the will of less than 4 000 000 others engaged in the vital services of the country.

The strike is intended as a direct hold up of the nation to ransom. It is for the nation to stand firm in its determination not to flinch. 'This moment', as the Prime Minister pointed out in the House of Commons, 'has been chosen to challenge the existing Constitution of the country and to substitute the reign of force for that which now exists . . . I do not believe there has been anything like a thoroughgoing consultation with the rank and file before this despotic power was put into the hand of a small executive in London . . . I do not think all the leaders who assented to order a general strike fully realised that they are threatening the basis of ordered government and coming nearer to proclaiming a civil war than we have been for centuries past.'

# SOURCE 20   *British Worker,* 5 and 6 May

*The* British Worker *was edited by Hamilton Fyfe, normally editor of the* Daily Herald, *which supported the Labour party. Eleven issues were produced between 5 and 17 May. The* British Worker *reflected the view of the General Council of the TUC. The 'Message to All Workers' that appeared on 5 May was repeated in two subsequent issues.*

5 May Message to All Workers
The General Council of the TUC wishes to emphasise the fact that this is an industrial dispute. It expects every member taking part to be exemplary in his conduct and not to give any opportunity for police interference. The outbreak of any disturbance would be very damaging to the prospect of a successful termination of the dispute.

The Council asks pickets especially to avoid obstruction and to confine themselves strictly to their legitimate duties.

The workers' response has exceeded all expectations. The first day of the great General Strike is now over. They have manifested their determination and unity to the whole world. They have resolved that the attempt of the mineowners to starve three million men, women and children shall not succeed.

6 May
NO ATTACK ON THE CONSTITUTION
*Confusing the Issues*
Those who support Mr Baldwin and his Cabinet in their declaration of war upon organised labour are making great efforts to confuse the issue and to prevent the nation from understanding what is at stake. They talk and write wildly about an attempt to upset the constitution, to usurp the authority of ministers, to set up a rival to the House of Commons.

Mr Baldwin, who urged everyone to 'keep steady', has so entirely lost his balance that he declared in yesterday's issue of the newspaper which he is issuing from the 'Morning Post' office:- 'The General Strike is a challenge to Parliament . . . Constitutional Government is being attacked.'

That is untrue. No one should know that it is untrue better than Mr Baldwin, who has followed from the beginning the dispute between Miners and Mineowners, and who is aware that it has been an industrial dispute throughout.

No political issue has ever been mentioned or thought of in connection with it. It began over wages and conditions of working. It has never been concerned with anything else.

When the Mineowners, backed by Mr Baldwin, expected the mineworkers to go on negotiating under threat of losing their livelihoods, the other Trade Unions were moved to intervene.

They were compelled to intervene. Menacing workers with a lock-out during negotiations eats at the root of the methods which Trade Unions have built up for settling disputes in a reasonable and peaceful way.

Only when the very proper request for the withdrawal of the notices had been refused did the Trade Unions decide upon a General Strike. At the special Trade Union Congress it was perfectly clear that nothing was in anybody's mind save the fundamental issue. Had any speaker mentioned Revolution he would have been told to shut up.

The General Strike is not a 'Menace to Parliament'. No attack is being made on the Constitution. We beg Mr Baldwin to believe that.

# SOURCE 21

### (a) *British Gazette*, 7 May

Message from the Prime Minister
Constitutional Government is being attacked. Let all good citizens, whose livelihood and labour have thus been put in peril bear with fortitude and patience the hardships with which they have been so suddenly confronted . . . The laws of England are in your keeping. The General Strike is a challenge to Parliament and the road to anarchy and ruin.

### (b) *British Worker*, 7 May

The General Council struggled hard for peace . . . They are anxious that an honourable peace shall be secured as soon as possible. They are not attacking the Constitution. They are not fighting the Community. They are defending the mine workers against the mine owners.

### (c) *British Gazette*, 8 May

An organised attempt is being made to starve the people and to wreck the state, and the legal constitutional aspects are entering a new phase.

### (d) *British Worker*, 13 May

The General Council congratulates strikers on their conduct.

Every observer of the situation, both British and foreign, is impressed by the good order everywhere maintained.

It constitutes a record for a dispute of this kind.

It shows how thoroughly the workers accept the insistence of the General Council that this is a purely industrial dispute. The General Council congratulates trade unionists on their magnificent response to its appeal for discipline.

# SOURCE 22   Instructions from the Communist Party (Undated)

*The British Communist party had fewer than 5000 active members in 1926. Communist party members were disallowed from standing as Labour candidates in both local and national elections at the 1924 Labour party conference. But Communists had more influence in certain trade unions, and also through the National Minority Movement. A.J. Cook had at one time been a member of the Communist party and continued to use Marxist rhetoric in his speeches.*

FIGHT TO WIN!

THE POLITICAL MEANING OF THE GENERAL STRIKE

WORKERS OF BRITAIN!

You have begun a General Strike of vast extent in defence of the miners' standard of living, knowing full well that further degradation for the miners means immediate attacks on the wages and hours of other workers. The General Strike is not only a magnificent act of brotherly support for the miners, it is an act of self-defence on the part of the working class, who with their families constitute the best majority of the people.

The first watchwords of the General Strike, therefore, have been and remain:- 'All together behind the Miners – Not a Penny off the Pay. Not a Second on the Day!'

But now that the struggle has begun, the workers have it in their power to put an end once for all to this continual menace to their living and working conditions. Simply to beat off the employers' present offensive means that they will return to the attack later on, just as they did after Red Friday last year. The only guarantee against the ravenous and soulless greed of the coal-owners is to break their economic power.

THEREFORE LET THE WORKERS ANSWER THE BOSSES' CHALLENGE WITH A CHALLENGE OF THEIR OWN:- 'NATIONALI-SATION OF THE MINES WITHOUT COMPENSATION FOR THE COAL OWNERS UNDER WORKERS' CONTROL THROUGH PIT COMMITTEES! . . .'

The Communist Party continues to instruct its members and to urge the workers to take every practical step necessary to consolidate our positions against the capitalist attack. Such essential steps are:- to form a Council of Action immediately; to organise able-bodied Trade Unionists in a Workers' Defence Corps against the OMS and the Fascisti; to set up feeding arrangements with the Co-operative Societies; to hold mass meetings and issue strike bulletins, and to make their case known to the soldiers.

But the Communist Party warns the workers against the attempt being made to limit the struggle to its previous character of self-defence against the capitalist offensive. Once the battle has been joined, the only way to victory is to push ahead and hit hard. And the way to hit the capitalist hardest is for Councils of Action to throw out the clear watchwords:-

NOT A PENNY OFF THE PAY. NOT A SECOND ON THE DAY! NATIONALISE THE MINES WITHOUT COMPENSATION, UNDER WORKERS' CONTROL! FORMATION OF A LABOUR GOVERNMENT – The Central Committee of the Communist Party of Great Britain.

Page Arnot, *The General Strike, May 1926: Its Origin and History,* pp. 179–81

# 2B | The Strike at Grass Roots

## SOURCE 23  Beatrice Webb's Diary, 3 May, 1926

*Beatrice Webb was married to Sydney Webb, a leading member of the Labour party. Together they formed a formidable partnership, and produced a series of works on trade union history, socialism and policy. Beatrice Webb came from a wealthy, middle-class background, and while this did not affect her socialist convictions it coloured her views of fellow members of the Labour party and trade union movement.*

The net impression left on my mind is that the General Strike will turn out not to be a revolution of any sort but a batch of compulsory Bank Holidays without any opportunity for recreation and a lot of dreary walking to and fro. When the million or so strikers have spent their money they will drift back to work and no one will be any better and many will be a great deal poorer and everybody will be cross.

C. Farman, *May 1926, The General Strike, Britain's Aborted Revolution*
(Panther, 1974) p. 147

## SOURCE 24  Cooperation between Strikers and Local Authorities

The incredulous comment of one French observer when he learned of the football match between strikers and police in Plymouth was 'The British are not a nation, they are a circus.' Dozens of similar diversions must have been as infuriatingly inexplicable to continental observers. The Mayor of Lewes put up the prize in a public billiard match between strikers and police. At Banbury joint concerts were arranged and both sides competed in a tug-of-war. At Norwich strikers and police organised a series of athletic matches under the auspices of the Chief Constable. In all the eastern counties between London and the Humber strike committees worked with the police and civic leaders 'to keep the peace and organize recreations'. At Lincoln, where the Chief Constable was 'a consistent friend of Labour and absolutely refused the assistance of either military or mounted police', the strike committee provided all of the special constables recruited during the emergency . . . Bath Council of Action was 'complimented and thanked by the Mayor and Chief Constable for maintaining perfect order; advised Mayor first day of strike to disband local specials as superfluosities'.

Farman, *May 1926, The General Strike, Britain's Aborted Revolution*, p. 229

# SOURCE 25  Plan of Campaign, Blaydon-on-Tyne Labour and Trades Council

*This Plan of Campaign was drawn up by Robin Page Arnot and others at the Durham mining village of Chopwell on Saturday, 1 May. Page Arnot was then Secretary of the Labour Research Department. On Sunday, 2 May it was unanimously adopted by about 50 delegates to the Blaydon-on-Tyne Labour and Trades Council. They included trade union officials, Labour councillors and members of the local branches of the Communist party and Plebs League. On 4 May a Joint Strike Committee was formed to coordinate all strike activities in Durham and Nothumberland, and efforts were made to implement the Plan, with some success.*

## PLAN OF CAMPAIGN

*Preamble.–*No time to be spent tonight on discussion of purpose of strike (to aid the mines) or origin or possible ending or national aspect or international aspect. Not concerned for next few days with any wider horizons; concerned only with concentrating on our limited objective.

*Objective.–*To defeat the Civil Commissioner appointed for this region. The Civil Commissioner is appointed by the Government and is armed with the Emergency Powers Act in order to break the strike. Our immediate aim is to prevent him doing that in this town. But in order to do that effectually we must offer a resistance through-out the whole region over which he has been given plenary powers. That is, we must defeat the Civil Commissioner and all his strike-breaking apparatus.

*The document goes on to list the government's powers under the Emergency Powers Act and the resources available to it to break the strike.*

*Working Class Machinery.–*To meet all this we must improvise. The improvised machinery must be simple, easy to throw up, all inclusive. All activities in each locality should be centralised in a single body to be called Council of Action, Strike Committee, Trades Council or what you will; all such bodies should be linked up and centralised in the county capital town under a body responsible for the whole region. . .

*Tasks of Councils of Action.–*The Council of Action will have a number of tasks for which Sub-Committees should be set up. These will include: Communications (Despatch Riders etc.); Feeding Centres; Food and Transport; Co-operative Societies; Local Government; Sports (to serve a double purpose); Defence Corps; Picketing; Permits; Organisation of Women; Publicity (a) local stencils; (b) other publicity; Information . . .

*Food and Transport.–*The TUC instructions for the general strike, if and when it should come off, include the provision of Food Transport and Health Services. Whatever the intention of the General Council in laying down this instruction, it is clear that on this point depends the success of the general strike. Whoever handles and transports food, the same person controls food: whoever controls food will find the 'neutral' part of the population rallying to their side. Who feeds the people wins the strike! The problem of the general strike can be focused down to one thing – the struggle for food control.

*Morale.*–All these activities and all this machinery needed for these activities are designed for the purpose of defeating the Civil Commissioner's attempt to break the general strike. But they have another objective. That is the building up of our own morale both locally and nationally. Every officer who reports that picketing has stopped his transport, every military officer who reports that he cannot trust his men to act against the strikers because of effective fraternisation is a means by which when the report has filtered through to Whitehall the morale of the Chief Civil Commissioner and thence of the Cabinet, is impaired and weakened.

Page Arnot, The Miners, Years of Struggle, pp. 436–9

## SOURCE 26   The Derailing of the *Flying Scotsman*

On the morning of 10 May 1926, there was a meeting of miners at West Colliery near the pit village of Cramlington, about twelve miles north of Newcastle. There was a discussion about such trains as were being manned by blacklegs. About fifteen miners left the meeting determined to do something about it on their own initiative. Later in the day the Flying Scotsman, travelling south on what was then the LNER main line from Edinburgh to King's Cross, was derailed near Cramlington. Four weeks later nine miners were arrested and charged with maliciously displacing a rail on the said line. Eight of them were quickly brought to trial in Newcastle when several local miners gave evidence for the prosecution that the defendants had been in the group who removed the rail. All were found guilty, and one of the three sentenced to eight years' imprisonment, Mr Arthur Wilson, now lives in Dudley, just south of Cramlington. His house overlooks a section of the very line from which he helped to remove that famous rail fifty years ago. Would he do it again if he had the chance? His answer is 'yes' in the sense that he has no regrets over his action. So miserable and desperate had life become for him and his kind that nothing was to be lost by a possibly murderous act of this nature. What if someone had been killed? 'We'd have been hanged of course', is his immediate and stoical reply.

Conversation with author, May 1975, Gerard Noel, The Great Lockout, 1926<br>(Constable, 1976) pp. 96–7

## SOURCE 27   The Strike in London : Movement of Food from London Docks

*The most striking example of the use of force on the government's side occurred on Friday and Saturday, 9 and 10 May, when 1000 volunteers were moved by water to ships lying idle in the Thames estuary. Grain was unloaded and transported in armed convoys of lorries to flour mills in the city. The following accounts are taken from* The Times, *which continued to print a restricted edition throughout the strike, and from the* New York World, *whose reporter, Alfred Murray, covered the strike.*

### (a) *The Times*

The authorities, reluctant as they have been to use the services of the troops, had no alternative if London was to get the flour it needed. Ever since the first day of the strike the strikers have concentrated their efforts upon preventing access to the docks. Officials and volunteer workers have been intimidated by a formidable array of pickets; the police themselves have suffered many fierce attacks, and lorries have been stopped by obstinate crowds that have stood across the roadway and made progress impossible . . . The result has been that, although there was an ample supply of flour lying at the docks and any number of willing volunteers ready to move it, to all intents it was locked up as far as London was concerned.

### (b) The New York *World*

At the zero hour these volunteers debarked and marched to the Rankes and Vernon mills through streets lined with soldiers. Machine guns had been placed in position, and armored cars stationed at strategic points, but the sullen masses of strikers who congregated after dawn were awed by the military and permitted most of the 'moving on' to be done by the mounted police, unarmed as always, but backed by enough artillery to kill every living thing in every street in the neighborhood of the mills.

*Author's footnote*: The officers in command of the convoy had received orders to get through at any cost, according to a Ministry of Trade official's statement to the writer, so that the American reporter was not too imaginative. Luckily no force had to be used.

Crook, The General Strike, pp. 417–19

### (c) Food Convoys in the East India Dock Road, London

BBC Hulton Picture Library

# SOURCE 28   The Control of Public Opinion

*The government did not interfere directly with freedom of the press or broadcasting during the General Strike. The* British Worker *was allowed to appear and humorous criticism of government policies was evidently tolerated (Sources 28 (a) and (d)). But Randall Davidson, Archbishop of Canterbury, was not allowed to broadcast an appeal for a simultaneous return to work and a resumption of negotiations when he tried to do so on 7 May. Attempts were made to prevent the circulation of Communist-inspired publications such as the* Workers' Bulletin. *Any encouragement to the armed forces to show their sympathy for the workers was treated as sedition.*

### (a)  *Paisley Strike Bulletin*, 10 May, 1926

PUFF, PUFF, PUFF, GOES THE ENGINE .

### (b)  Speech by Sharpurti Saklatvala, MP for Battersea, Hyde Park, 1 May, 1926.

We tell the Government that young men in the Forces whether Joynson-Hicks likes it or not; whether he calls it sedition or not to soothe the financiers and his rich friends, we have a duty towards those men to say to them that they must lay down their arms.

*Saklatvala was arrested for this utterance on Tuesday, 4 May and subsequently sentenced to two months' imprisonment.*

M. Morris, *The General Strike* (Penguin, 1976) p. 384

### (c)  The Case of Edward Wilson

Wilson was arrested for distributing copies of *Northern Light* and charged with contravening Section 21 of the Emergency Regulations by doing a certain act likely to cause disaffection among the civil population. He was sentenced to three months imprisonment with hard labour, and one of the presiding magistrates remarked: 'Why you and those who are associated with you don't go off to Russia I don't know . . . We don't want you . . . you are just a source of danger to the community and the sooner you make up your minds to either reform or get away, the better for all concerned.'

Farman, *May 1926, The General Strike, Britain's Aborted Revolution*, p. 227

**(d)** *Star*, **15 May, 1926**

Impressions of the Great Strike.          By LOW.

# QUESTIONS ON SOURCES 18–28

1.  How do you account for the very different perceptions of the nature of the General Strike, as conveyed by Walter Citrine and Stanley Baldwin (Sources 18, 19)? (S)

2.  What arguments were used by the *British Gazette* to support its view that the General Strike was 'a direct challenge to ordered government' (Source 19)? (C)

3.  How did the *British Worker* refute these allegations (Sources 20, 21)? (C)

4.  Compare the objectives of the General Strike as seen by the General Council of the TUC and by the Communist party (Sources 20, 22). (S)

5.  On the basis of Sources 24–7, in which parts of the country was violence least likely to occur during the General Strike? (S)

6.  How revolutionary was the programme laid down by the Blaydon-on-Tyne Labour and Trades Council (Source 25)? (C)

7.  How reliable a guide to the sentiments of the mining community as a whole do you regard the testimony of Arthur Wilson (Source 26)? (E)

8.  Compare the accounts given in *The Times* and in the New York *World* of the events that took place in London during the weekend of 9/10 May with the photograph of the food convoys (Source 27). Would you regard the *World* report as unduly sensational? (E)

9.  How extensive was government interference with the free expression of opinion during the General Strike? Was it excessive in the circumstances (Source 28)? (S)

10. What can you infer from Source 28 about public attitudes to law and order? (E)

11. From the evidence presented in Sources 18–28, did the government exaggerate the danger of revolutionary violence in its handling of the General Strike? (S)

# SOURCE MATERIAL 3
# The Ending of the Strike and its Consequences

## SOURCE 29   The Samuel Memorandum

*This is the final version that was accepted by the negotiating committee of the General Council and recommended to the Miners' Executive on the night of Tuesday, 11 May and again on the morning of Wednesday, 12 May.*

(1)  The negotiations upon the condition of the coal industry should be resumed, the subsidy being renewed for such reasonable period as may be required for that purpose.

(2)  Any negotiations are unlikely to be successful unless they provide for means of settling disputes in the industry other than conferences between the mineowners and the miners alone. A National Wages Board should therefore be established, which would include representatives of those two parties, with a neutral element and an independent chairman . . . The proposals in this direction tentatively made in the report of the Royal Commission should be pressed, and the powers of the proposed Board enlarged.

(3)  The parties to the Board should be entitled to raise before it any points they consider relevant to the issue under discussion, and the Board should be required to take such points into consideration.

(4)  There should be no revision of previous wage rates unless there are sufficient assurances that the measures of reorganisation proposed by the Commission will effectively be adopted . . .

(5)  After these points have been agreed and the Mines National Wages Board has considered every practicable means of meeting such immediate financial difficulties as exist, it may if that course is found to be absolutely necessary, proceed to the preparation of a wage agreement.

(6)  Any such agreement should
    (i)   If practicable, be on simpler lines than those hitherto followed.
    (ii)  Not adversely affect in any way the wages of the lowest-paid men.
    (iii) Fix reasonable figures below which the wage of no class of labour, for a normal customary week's work should be reduced in any circumstances.
    (iv) In the event of new adjustments being made, should provide for the revision of such adjustments by the Wages Board from time to time if the facts warrant that course.

(7)  Measures should be adopted to prevent the recruitment of new workers over the age of 18 years into the industry, if unemployed miners are available.

(8) Workers who are displaced as a consequence of the closing of uneconomic collieries should be provided for by –

    (a) The transfer of such men as may be mobile, with the Government assistance that may be required, as recommended in the report of the Royal Commission.

    (b) The maintenance, for such period as may be fixed, of those who cannot be so transferred, and for whom alternative employment cannot be found; . . .

    (c) The rapid construction of new houses to accommodate transferred workers . . .

Page Arnot, *The General Strike, May 1926: Its Origin and History*, pp. 225–6

## SOURCE 30  The Pugh–Samuel Correspondence

*These letters were exchanged between Arthur Pugh and Herbert Samuel on Wednesday, 12 May, prior to the visit of the TUC's delegation to Downing Street later that morning.*

12 May, 1926

DEAR MR PUGH,

    As the outcome of the conversations which I had with your Committee, I attach a memorandum embodying the conclusions that have been reached. I have made it entirely clear to your Committee that I have been acting entirely upon my own initiative, have received no authority from the Government, and can give no assurances on their behalf. I am of opinion that the proposals embodied in the memorandum are suitable for adoption, and are likely to promote a settlement of the differences in the coal industry. I shall strongly recommend their acceptance by the Government when the negotiations are renewed.

Your sincerely, HERBERT SAMUEL

London, 12 May, 1926

SIR HERBERT SAMUEL

DEAR SIR,

    The General Council having carefully considered your letter of to-day, and the memorandum attached to it, concurred in your opinion that if offers a basis on which the negotiations upon the conditions in the coal industry can be renewed.

    They are taking the necessary measures to terminate the General Strike, relying upon the public assurance of the Prime Minister as to the steps that would follow. They assume that during the resumed negotiations the subsidy will be renewed and that the lock-out notices to the Miners will be immediately withdrawn.

        Yours faithfully,

            ARTHUR PUGH, Chairman

            WALTER M. CITRINE, Acting Secretary

Page Arnot, *The General Strike, May 1926: Its Origin and History*, pp. 224–5

## SOURCE 31   The Response of the MFGB to the Samuel Memorandum

*The following account is taken from the statement that was produced by the MFGB for the Conference of Executives of all unions affiliated to the TUC that was held on 20 and 21 January, 1927.*

### XXIII–THE SAMUEL NEGOTIATIONS

. . . On Monday, the 10th May, the officials of the Miners' Federation were invited to meet Sir Herbert [Samuel] by, and in company with, the officials of the General Council. Sir Herbert then made certain proposals which were not committed to paper, but which represented a departure from the settled policy of the movement. The Miners' officials re-affirmed the position of their own constituents, and made it perfectly clear to Sir Herbert that they could not accept any proposals which involved reductions in wages. Nevertheless, on Tuesday evening, the 11th May, the Miners' Executive were sent for by the General Council, and were informed that they (the Council) had agreed upon and accepted proposals as the outcome of conversations between their officials and Sir Herbert Samuel that day. The proposals were handed to us by the General Council, and we were asked to consider them and let the Council have our decision upon them that evening. It must be clearly pointed out that the proposals, when handed to the Miners' representatives, had already been accepted by the Council, were not open to amendment in any way, and constituted a departure from the policy of the movement. Further, the General Council had already decided to call off the strike and had arranged a meeting with the Prime Minister to inform him of this decision.

The action of the General Council in accepting proposals in advance of any decision by the miners was, in fact, an ultimatum by the Council to the miners; they were obviously determined to compel us to a decision which would mean a breaking of pledges to our own constituents.

### XXIV

The miners' representatives felt that whatever the consequences might be they must not break faith with their own people but must keep their hands perfectly clean. They also felt very strongly and their fears were afterwards amply justified, that there was no real guarantee behind the terms and no warrant that they would be accepted by the Government and the mine-owners.

The following resolution was therefore passed, which was at once handed over to the General Council:

'The Miners' Executive have given careful and patient consideration to the draft proposals prepared by the TUC Negotiating Committee and endorsed by the General Council as representing the best terms which can be obtained to settle the present dispute in the coal industry.

'They regret the fact that no opportunity for consideration was afforded the accredited representatives of the Miners' Federation in the preparation of the draft or in the discussions of May 11th leading thereto.

'At best the proposals imply a reduction of the wages rates of a large number of workers, which is contrary to the repeated declarations of the Miners'

Federation, and which they believe their fellow Unionists are assisting them to resist.

'They regret therefore, whilst having regard to the grave issues involved, that they must reject the proposals. Moreover, if such proposals are submitted as a means to call off the general strike such a step must be taken on the sole responsibility of the General Council.'

Page Arnot, *The Miners, Years of Struggle,* pp. 514-15

# SOURCE 32 Negotiations at 10 Downing Street between Members of the General Council and Members of the Cabinet at 12.20 p.m. on Wednesday, 12 May

*This account has been reconstructed from stenographers' notes taken at the time. Those present included on the government side: Baldwin, Birkenhead, Neville Chamberlain, Steel-Maitland and Mr T. Jones, Deputy Secretary of the Cabinet. The General Council were represented by Pugh, Citrine, Thomas and Bevin among others.*

THE PRIME MINISTER: Mr Pugh, will you be good enough to make a statement?

MR PUGH: Well, sir, when we separated over a week ago it was of course recognised and expressed on both sides that the ultimate end would be a settlement of this matter by negotiations, and although the conflict has been very much extended and developments have taken place since then, clearly both sides and all sides and all parties have had in view, they must have had, the ultimate arrangements that would have to be made to bring this trouble to a successful end ... Well, as a result of developments in that direction and the possibilities that we see in getting back to negotiations and your assurance, speaking for the general community of citizens as a whole, that no steps should be left unturned to get back to negotiations, we are today, sir, to say that this general strike is to be terminated forthwith in order that negotiations may proceed, and we can only hope may proceed in a manner which will bring about a satisfactory settlement. That is the announcement which my General Council is impowered to make.

THE PRIME MINISTER: That is, the general strike is to be called off forthwith?

MR PUGH: Forthwith, that means immediately. There is just a point about the actual arrangement, but that is in effect what it means. It is merely a matter of the best way to get it done with the least confusion.

THE PRIME MINISTER: I mean there would be a great deal for both of us to do. All I would say in answer is I thank God for your decision and I would only say now, I do not think it is a moment for lengthy discussion; I only say now I accept fully and confirm fully all I have said in the last two paragraphs of my broadcast message.*

I shall call my Cabinet together forthwith, report to them what you have said, and I shall lose no time in using every endeavour to get the two contending parties together and do all I can to ensure a just and lasting settlement ...

*J.H. Thomas and Ernest Bevin then raised the two questions of re-instatement of workers who had been on strike, and on the need for immediate resumption of negotiations with the miners.*

THE PRIME MINISTER: Well, Mr Bevin, I cannot say more here at this meeting. I did not know what points you were going to raise, or that anything would be said beyond the statements of Mr Pugh. The point you have put is one I must consider, and I will consider it at once. I would only say in my view the best thing to do is to get as quickly as possible into touch with the employers. I think that the quicker this is done the less friction there will be. You know my record. You know the object of my policy and I think you may trust me to consider what has been said with a view to seeing how best we can get the country quickly back into the condition in which we all want to see it . . .

In regard to the second point there again I cannot say at this moment what will happen because I shall have to see the parties. My object, of course, is to get the mines started the first moment possible and get an agreement reached . . . I cannot say until I have seen them exactly what the lines will be upon which my object can best be attained, but you may rely on me and rely on the Cabinet that they will see no stone is left unturned to accomplish that end. Now, Mr Pugh, as I said before, we have both of us a great deal to do and a great deal of anxious and difficult work, and I think that the sooner you get to your work and the sooner I get to mine the better.

Crook, *The General Strike*, pp. 604–8

*\* The final two paragraphs of Baldwin's broadcast message, delivered on Saturday, 10 May were as follows:*

Meanwhile, notwithstanding the dislocation of transport and of fuel supplies, I hope employers will do all in their power to keep their works running in order to mitigate the hardships which must necessarily fall upon the people in an emergency such as this. This is the Government position – The General Strike must be called off without reserve. The mining industry dispute can then be settled. This is a fair arrangement, and it would be a thousand times better to accept it than continue a struggle which can only increase misery and disaster the longer it lasts. A solution is within the grasp of the nation the instant that the Trade Union leaders are willing to abandon the General Strike.

I am a man of peace. I am longing and working and praying for peace, but I will not surrender the safety and security of the British Constitution. You placed me in power 18 months ago by the largest majority accorded to any Party for many years. Have I done anything to forfeit that confidence? Cannot you trust me to ensure a square deal, to secure even justice between man and man?

Page Arnot, *The General Strike, May 1926: Its Origin and History*, p. 196

# SOURCE MATERIAL 4
# Verdicts on the General Strike

## SOURCE 33   The Speeches of Sir John Simon

### (a) 6 May

Every workman who was bound to give notice before he left work, and who, in view of that decision, has either chosen of his own free will or has felt impelled to come out by leaving his employment without proper notice, has broken the law . . . it would be lamentable if the working classes of this country go on with this business without understanding that they are taking part in a novel and entirely illegal proceeding. It is this feature of the General Strike that constitutes its novelty.

*Simon continued to argue that any trade union leader who advised strike action was liable for damages 'to the uttermost farthing of his personal possessions'.*

### (b) 11 May

Once you proclaim a General Strike, you are as a matter of fact starting a movement of a perfectly different and of a wholly unconstitutional and unlawful character . . . Once you get the proclamation of a General Strike such as this, it is not, properly understood, a strike at all because a strike is a strike against employers to do something, but a General Strike is a strike against the general public to make the public, Parliament and the Government do something.

Crook, *The General Strike*, pp. 470–1

## SOURCE 34   The Astbury Judgment

The so-called general strike called by the Trades Union Congress is illegal and contrary to the law, and those persons inciting or taking part in it are not protected by the Trades Disputes Act of 1906. No trade dispute has been alleged or shown to exist in any of the Unions affected, except in the miners' case, and no trade dispute does or can exist between the Trades Union Congress on the one hand and the Government and the nation on the other. The orders of the Trades Union Council above referred to are therefore unlawful, and the defendants are at law acting illegally in obeying them and can be restrained by their own Union from doing so.

Crook, *The General Strike*, pp. 472–3

**SOURCE 35**   A.L. Goodhart, 'The Legality of the
                General Strike in England', *Yale Law
                Journal* (Feb. 1927)

Taking part in a strike is not a criminal offence (a) if the act is done in
contemplation or furtherance of a trade dispute as defined by the Trade
Disputes Act, 1906, and (b) if such act committed by one person would not be
punishable as a crime, with particular reference to the exceptions set out in the
Conspiracy, and Protection of Property Act, 1875 (riot, sedition, any offence
against the State or sovereign etc.).

*Goodhart then examined whether the General Strike was in furtherance of a trade dispute,
and whether such a strike was an offence against the State.*

Sympathetic strikes have been in practice for over fifty years, and to hold them
illegal at the present time would be to constitute a revolution in what has been
universally held to be the law ... The important point to remember is that the
sympathetic striker is protected even though he himself has no quarrel with the
employer originally struck against or with his immediate employer ...

*In answer to Sir John Simon's contention that the strike was illegal in that it brought
unconstitutional pressure to bear upon the Government and Parliament, Mr Goodhart held
that: 'the purpose of a sympathetic strike must always be to bring pressure upon a third party.
Can a distinction be drawn because the third party is the government? Such pressure may,
perhaps, be an offense against the State, but it is nevertheless in furtherance of a trade
dispute.' For an offence against the State to have been committed, a specific crime is required.
There were three possibilities: treason, seditious conspiracy or criminal conspiracy. Goodhart
concluded that none of the actions that had taken place during the General Strike could be
construed to have fallen into any of these categories.*

The General Strike, therefore, does not come under any of the various kinds of
seditious intention. It is only because there is a mistaken idea that all acts which
are harmful to the State must be seditious, that it is possible to suggest that the
leaders of the General Strike were guilty of this crime.

Crook, The General Strike, pp. 474–6

**SOURCE 36**   The Trades Disputes Act, 1927

*Legislation to curb the power of the trade unions had been contemplated in March 1926 (the
Macquisten Bill), and again during the General Strike, when Baldwin was dissuaded by
George V and Tom Jones from introducing an emergency measure. When the strike was over,
employers' organisations such as the National Confederation of Employers' Organisations
and the National Union of Manufacturers urged the government to act. The Cabinet refused
to go as far as the employers would have liked in removing trade union immunities, but the
act as finally passed banned general and sympathetic strikes, imposed new limits on*

*picketing, reduced the rights of civil servants and altered the terms on which trade unionists were allowed to contribute to the financial support of the Labour party through the political levy.*

1. (I) It is hereby declared–
   (a) that any strike is illegal if it
   (i) has any object other than or in addition to the furtherance of a trade dispute within the trade industry in which the strikers are engaged; and
   (ii) is a strike designed or calculated to coerce the Government either directly or by inflicting hardship upon the community; ...

2. [This section deals with the rights of trade unionists refusing to take part in illegal strikes.]

3. (I) It is hereby declared that it is unlawful for one or more persons (whether acting on their own behalf or on behalf of a trade union or of an individual employer or firm, and notwithstanding that they may be acting in contemplation or furtherance of a trade dispute) to attend at or near a house or place where a person resides or works ... for the purpose of obtaining or communicating information or of persuading or inducing any person to work or from working, if they so attend in such numbers as to be calculated to intimidate any person in that house or place ...

4. (I) It shall not be lawful to require any member of a trade union to make any contribution to the political fund of a trade union unless he has at some time after the commencement of this Act and before he is first after the thirty-first day of December, 1927, requested to make such a contribution delivered at the head office or some branch office of the trade union, notice in writing in the form set out in the First Schedule to this Act of his willingness to contribute to that fund ...

5. (I) Amongst the regulations as to the conditions of service in His Majesty's civil establishments there shall be included regulations prohibiting established civil servants from being members, delegates, or representatives of any organisation of which the primary object is to influence or affect the remuneration and conditions of employment of its members, unless the organisation is an organisation of which the membership is confined to persons employed by or under the Crown and is an organisation which complies with such provisions as may be contained in the regulations for securing, that it is in all respects independent of, and not affiliated to any such organisation aforesaid the membership of which is not confined to persons employed by or under the Crown or any federation comprising such organisations, that its objects do not include political objects, and that it is not associated directly or indirectly with any political party or organisation ...

Crook, *The General Strike*, pp. 614–22

## SOURCE 37   King George V's Diary, Wednesday, 12 May

At 1.0 p.m. I got the good news that the TUC had been to the Prime Minister and informed him that the General Strike was forthwith called off unconditionally. It is indeed a great relief to me as I have been very anxious about the situation. Our old country can well be proud of itself, as during the last nine days there has been a strike in which 4 million men have been affected; not a shot has been fired and no one killed; it shows what a wonderful people we are . . . The Government have remained firm and backed up by the people have won a great victory . . .

Harold Nicolson, *King George V* (Constable, 1952) p. 420

## SOURCE 38   Walter Citrine's Diary

I do not regard the General Strike as a failure. It is true that it was ill-prepared and that it was called off without any consultation with those who took part in it. The fact is that the theory of the General Strike had never been thought out. The machinery of the trade unions was not adapted for it. Their rules had to be broken for the executives to give power to the General Council to declare the strike. However illogical it may seem for me to say so, it was never aimed against the state as a challenge to the Constitution. It was a protest against the degradation of life of millions of good trade unionists. It was a sympathetic strike on a national scale. It was full of imperfections in concept and method. No General Strike could ever function without adequate local organisation, and the trade unions were not ready to devolve such necessary powers on the only local agents which the TUC has, the Trades Councils.

Morris, *The General Strike*, pp. 279–80

## SOURCE 39   The Communist Party's View of the Ending of the General Strike

STAND BY THE MINERS!
AN APPEAL BY THE COMMUNIST PARTY OF GREAT BRITAIN
The General Council's decision to call off the General Strike is the greatest crime that has ever been permitted, not only against the miners, but against the working class of Great Britain and the whole world. The British workers had aroused the astonishment and admiration of the world by the enthusiasm with which they had entered upon the fight for the miners' standard of living. But instead of responding to this magnificent lead by a call to every section of organised labour to join the fight against the capitalists, the General Council have miserably thrown itself and the miners on the tender mercies of the workers' worst enemies – the Tory Government.

Page Arnot, *The General Strike, May 1926: Its Origin and History*, p. 233

## SOURCE 40   The Recollections of Bill Ballantyne

*Ballantyne was a member of the National Union of Railwaymen, and served on the strike committee at Carstairs, a small railway junction near Glasgow.*

It was a tremendous setback to the trade union and Labour movement: it knocked the bottom out of many men and women who had given their lives to the movement. It began a process of an enforced reduction in all standards of life. The politically active people were stimulated to be more active, but the large bulk of railwaymen and of many other unions were not politically motivated. Though we were demoralized, those of us who had a good socialist grip grew more faithful than ever before. If someone had waved me over the barricades to revolution in 1932, I'd have been ahead of anybody, that's how it affected me.

Morris, *The General Strike*, pp. 284–5

# SOURCE 41   *A Workers' History of the General Strike*

*The book from which this source was taken was written by three left-wing members of the Labour party: R.W. Postgate, Ellen Wilkinson, MP and J.F. Horrabin.*

Lists and names can perhaps speak more strongly than rhetoric or argument. If the facts here set down have not of themselves settled disputes and apportioned guilt or credit, then no words of ours will do better. We prefer to end this story with a salute to the rank and file and their local officials. It is to them that the whole glory of this nine days' wonder belongs. Nothing like this unanimous sacrifice for a largely unselfish end has been seen since August, 1914. The Junkers in those days jeered at the men who rushed into the army as 'mercenaries', and to this the answer was made in a famous poem:-
'These, in the day when heaven was falling
The hour when earth's foundations fled,
Followed their mercenary calling
And took their wages and are dead.'
    But for these others, twelve years later, there was no question of pay, for praise or blame. Many, very many, from boilermakers to builders' labourers, neither received strike pay nor ever expected to draw any. Nevertheless, when the end seemed to have come in despair and disgrace, they held firm and saved faith and honour.
'Their shoulders held the sky suspended
They stood, and earth's foundations stay.'

R.W. Postgate, Ellen Wilkinson and J.F. Horrabin, *A Workers' History of the General Strike* (Plebs League, 1927) p. 96

# SOURCE 42   Tom Jones's Reflections on the Strike

*As Deputy Secretary to the Cabinet, Jones had a ringside view of the General Strike in London. He saw Baldwin every day, and was also confided in by members of the General Council. When the strike was over he compiled his own account of it, from which the following passage is taken.*

Reviewing the whole momentous experience the chief reflections which occur to me at this stage are:
    1. Few competent observers of recent industrial history will regret the General Strike. It, or something like it 'had to come' in view of the temper of the most assertive elements in the trade union world.

2. The General Strike could not succeed because some of those who led it did not wholly believe in it and because few, if any, were prepared to go through with it to its logical conclusion – violence and revolution.

3. It manifested a most impressive trade union loyalty only equalled by the orderly behaviour of all concerned.

4. The rank and file knew little or nothing of the division and jealousies of the central executive and were taken by surprise when the strike was called off. There is widespread anger with TUC fomented by Cook for betraying the Miners, and the tide is turning against the Miners because of their obstinacy in rejecting first the Samuel 'Memorandum' and then the Government's proposals.

5. The motor car, aeroplane and wireless were of immense value to the Government.

6. The TUC made a first class blunder in calling out the printers but it is difficult to run a Government newspaper.

7. The chief asset in keeping the country steadfast during the negotiations was the Prime Minister's reputation for fair dealing enhanced later by his sincere plea against malice and vindictiveness. His seeming weakness has been his strength. Had he yielded to the Die-hard influences he would have prolonged the strike by rallying the whole of Labour in defence of Trade Unionism. He was wise to give them the chance and he was enthusiastically supported in this course by the House of Commons.

Jones, *Whitehall Diary*, vol. II, p. 53

# SOURCE 43  Beatrice Webb, *Diaries*

May 18th 1926. Churchill's announcement in the House today that the General Strike will have cost the Government no more than three quarters of a million – a sum which the death of a couple of millionaires will pay – puts the cap of ridicule on the heroics of the General Strike . . . If anti-Trade Union legislation does not follow it will be due to the utter failure of the movement to carry out its bombastic threat of paralysing the country's life. The Government has gained immense prestige in the world and the British Labour Movement has made itself ridiculous. A strike which opens with a football match between the police and the strikers and ends in unconditional surrender after nine days with densely packed reconciliation services at all the chapels and churches of Great Britain attended by the strikers and their families will make the continental Socialists blaspheme. Without a shot fired or a life lost . . . the General Strike of 1926 has by its absurdity made the Black Friday of 1921 seem to be a red letter day of common sense. Let me add that the failure of the General Strike shows what a sane people the British are. If only our revolutionaries would realise the hopelessness of their attempt to turn the British workman into a Red Russian and the British businessman and the country gentleman into an Italian Fascist! The British are hopelessly good-natured and common-sensical – to which the British workman adds pigheadedness, jealousy and stupidity.

Beatrice Webb, *Diaries*, ed. Margaret Cole (Longman, 1956) pp. 97–8

# SOURCE 44  A.J. Cook, *The Nine Days*

*The pamphlet from which this passage is taken was written by Cook in July 1926 in the heat of the moment, and before the miners' lock-out had run its bitter course.*

This is all we know of the tragic decision, arrived at in our absence, to call off the General Strike. The verbatim report of the interview with the Prime Minister speaks for itself. No statement seemed to have been made by anyone except Bevin regarding the raising of the lock-out and the protection of our men. It seemed that the only desire of some leaders was to call off the strike at any cost, without any guarantees for the workers, miners or others.

By this action of theirs in 'turning off the power', the miners were left alone in their struggle.

A few days longer and the capitalist class, financiers, parasites and exploiters, would have been compelled to make peace with the miners. We should thus have secured in the mining industry a settlement which would have redounded to the honour and credit of the British Labour Movement, and would have been a fitting reward for the solidarity displayed by the workers.

They threw away the chance of a victory greater than any British Labour has ever won . . .

Cook, *The Nine Days*, p. 23

# QUESTIONS ON SOURCES 29–44

1. In what ways, if at all, did the Samuel Memorandum improve upon the Samuel Commission recommendations (Sources 5, 29)? (S)

2. Were the members of the General Council of the TUC unduly optimistic in their assumptions about government policy when terminating the General Strike (Source 30)? (S)

3. Did the account given by the MFGB of the Samuel negotiations fairly represent the actions of the General Council when calling off the strike (Source 31)? (E)

4. What assurances did the General Council seek from Baldwin on Wednesday, 12 May, when calling off the strike (Source 32)? (C)

5. What assurances, if any, did Baldwin give (Source 32)? (C)

6. On what grounds did Sir John Simon and Mr Justice Astbury condemn the General Strike as illegal (Sources 33, 34)? (C)

7. How successfully, in your view, did A.L. Goodhart rebut their arguments (Source 35)? (S)

8. Was the Trades Disputes Act of 1927 simply a partisan political measure (Source 36)? (S)

9. Why, in your view, did Citrine not regard the General Strike as a failure (Source 38)? (S)

10. How justified was the Communist party's indictment of the General Council's decision to call off the General Strike (Source 39)? (S)

11. Did Ballantyne exaggerate the damage done by the General Strike to the trade union movement (Source 40)? (S)

12. 'Nevertheless, when the end seemed to have come in despair and disgrace, they held firm and saved faith and honour' (Source 41). To whom was this tribute paid, and was it deserved? (S)

13. Whose view of the General Strike and the reasons for its failure do you regard as the more reliable, Tom Jones's or Beatrice Webb's (Sources 42, 43)? (E)

14. Would you agree with A.J. Cook's assessment of the trade union leaders who called off the strike (Sources 32, 44)? (S)

15. Was Cook justified in his belief that the General Strike was on the point of success when it was called off (Source 44)? (S)

# LOCATION OF SOURCES

1   R. Page Arnot, *The Miners, Years of Struggle* (Allen & Unwin, 1953) pp. 524–5

2   *Ibid.*, p. 348

3   Wilfred Harris Crook, *The General Strike* (University of North Carolina Press, USA, 1931) pp. 285–6

4   Page Arnot, *op. cit.*, pp. 365–6

5   R. Page Arnot, *The General Strike, May 1926: Its Origin and History* (Labour Research Department, 1926) pp. 96–100

6   Page Arnot, *The Miners, Years of Struggle*, pp. 413–14

7   *Ibid.*, p. 415

8   Page Arnot, *The General Strike, May 1926: Its Origin and History*, p. 30

9   *Ibid.*, pp. 107–8

10  *Ibid.*, pp. 112–16

11  *Ibid.*, pp. 160–3

12  *Ibid.*, p. 145

13  *Ibid.*, p. 147

14  Scott Nearing, *The British General Strike* (Vanguard Press, USA, 1926) p. 141

15  (a) Thomas Jones, *Whitehall Diary*, vol. II, ed. K. Middlemas (OUP, 1969) pp. 29–33
    (b) *Ibid.*, pp. 34–5
    (c) Walter Citrine, *Men at Work* (Hutchinson, 1964) p. 169
    (d) L.S. Amery, *My Political Life*, vol. II (Hutchinson, 1953) pp. 483–4
    (e) Nearing, *op. cit.*, pp. 38–9
    (f) A.J. Cook, *The Nine Days* (The London Co-operative Printing Society, 1926) p. 16

16  Page Arnot, *The General Strike, May 1926: Its Origin and History*, pp. 147–8

17  *Ibid.*, pp. 148–9

18  Citrine, *Men at Work*, pp. 191–2

19–21 *British Gazette, British Worker*, May 1926 (David & Charles, 1971)

22  Page Arnot, *The General Strike, May 1926: Its Origin and History*, pp. 179–81

23  C. Farman, *May 1926, The General Strike, Britain's Aborted Revolution* (Panther, 1974) p. 147

24  *Ibid.*, p. 229

25  Page Arnot, *The Miners, Years of Struggle*, pp. 436–9

26  Gerard Noel, *The Great Lockout, 1926* (Constable, 1976) pp. 96–7

27      (a) Crook, *op. cit.*, pp. 417–19
        (b) *Ibid.*
        (c) BBC Hulton Picture Library

28      (a) *Paisley Strike Bulletin*, 10 May, 1926
        (b) M. Morris, *The General Strike* (Penguin, 1976) p. 384
        (c) Farman, *op. cit.*, p. 227
        (d) *Star,* 15 May, 1926

29      Page Arnot, *The General Strike, May 1926: Its Origin and History*, pp. 225–6

30      *Ibid.*, pp. 224–5

31      Page Arnot, *The Miners, Years of Struggle*, pp. 514–15

32      Crook, *op. cit.*, pp. 604–8; Page Arnot, *The General Strike, May 1926: Its Origin and History,* p. 196

33      Crook, *op. cit.*, pp. 470–1

34      Crook, *op. cit.*, pp. 472–3

35      Crook, *op. cit.*, pp. 474–6

36      Crook, *op. cit.*, pp. 614–22

37      Harold Nicolson, *King George V* (Constable, 1952) p. 420

38      Morris, *op. cit.*, pp. 279–80

39      Page Arnot, *The General Strike, May 1926: Its Origin and History,* p. 233

40      Morris, *op. cit.*, pp. 284–5

41      R.W. Postgate, Ellen Wilkinson and J.F. Horrabin, *A Workers' History of the General Strike* (Plebs League, 1927) p. 96

42      Jones, *op. cit.*, p. 53

43      Beatrice Webb, *Diaries*, ed. Margaret Cole (Longman, 1956) pp. 97–8

44      Cook, *op. cit.*, p. 23

# Case Study 5

# BRITAIN IN THE 1930s: DEPRESSION AND RECOVERY

## 1. THE BRITISH ECONOMY IN THE 1930s

'We are today in the middle of the greatest economic catastrophe – the greatest catastrophe due almost entirely to economic causes – of the modern world . . .' (J.M. Keynes, 1931). The Great Depression, sometimes known as 'the Slump', afflicted nearly every country in the world between 1929 and 1939. It began with the Wall Street Crash in October 1929, which brought the American economy into a serious decline. By 1932 unemployment in the United States had reached 15 million, and industrial output was only 54 per cent of what it had been in 1929.

The collapse of the American economy had two direct consequences for Europe. Firstly, there was a huge reduction in the demand for European exports. Merchandise goods imported into the United States fell from $4439 million in 1929 to $1323 million in 1932, which led in turn to a fall in European industrial output. Secondly, as lenders recalled their loans the flight of American capital from Europe caused a series of currency crises in Austria, Germany and Britain. The consequence of these crises was that first Britain, and then most other European countries, left the gold standard. The world's monetary system entered upon a confused period of floating exchange rates and rising tariffs which caused a serious reduction in world trade.

Britain, as a major exporting country, was inevitably a victim of these events. An economic committee report, produced in 1930, put it succinctly: 'A severe world wide depression has been superimposed on our great national difficulties.'

Since the collapse of the post-war boom in 1920 the level of unemployment in Britain had never fallen below one million. But in 1932, under the impact of the depression, it rose to 2.75 million, over 22.5 per cent of the insured working population (Source 5). It is this figure, above all, that has come to epitomise the 1930s in Britain and has led to it being labelled 'the devil's decade'. The unemployed were largely drawn from the staple industries on which the first industrial revolution was based: coal, iron and steel, shipbuilding and cotton textiles (Sources 6, 7). These industries were concentrated in the lowlands of Scotland, the North-west and the North-east of England, and South Wales, and it was these parts of Britain that were particularly depressed (Source 8). Their plight apparently proved the failure of the capitalist system, especially to left-wing observers (Source 4). But there was another England, not noticed so much at the time, but subsequently explored by economic historians without a political axe to grind. Their view is a rather different one. They point out that many sectors of the economy flourished in the 1930s: electricity supply, housing, chemicals, the motor car and the aircraft industries, for example. It has also been noted that even in the supposedly declining industries, a recovery set in about 1934, and that while unemployment persisted, output in many cases recovered (Source 2).

The first group of sources has been chosen to bring out the apparent contradictions in the behaviour of the British economy during these years. Much of the evidence is statistical, but two sources (3 and 4) have been included which draw inferences from statistical evidence. There is no reason to doubt the reliability of the figures cited, but it should be remembered that statistics, like any other piece of evidence, can be selected to demonstrate whatever the author wishes to prove. What is omitted may be as significant as what is included.

# 2. LIVING STANDARDS

The second group of sources relates to living standards in the 1930s. Just as there are conflicting views about what was happening to the British economy, so there are arguments over living conditions. Popular images of the 1930s – the dole queues, the means test (Source 19), the Jarrow Hunger Marchers – have left the impression of a Britain wracked by poverty, with declining standards of nutrition, health and welfare. On the other hand the 1930s saw the biggest increase in the country's housing stock of any decade in British history. By 1939 car ownership had reached 3 million. Chain stores such as Woolworth, Marks and Spencer and Littlewoods made a huge range of consumer goods available to a new class of customer. During the 1930s real wages (i.e. wages in terms of their purchasing power) increased for the majority of those in employment, if not by very much (Source 15).

Evidence about living standards is drawn from three kinds of source material. The 1930s were fortunately prolific in social investigations of one kind or another. Among them were *The New Survey of London Life and Labour,* edited by H. Llewellyn Smith (1934); H.F. Tout, *The Standard of Living in Bristol* (1938); B. Seebohm Rowntree, *Poverty and Progress* (1941) and John Boyd Orr, *Food, Health and Income* (1937) (Sources 9–12); there is statistical evidence about the distribution of wealth and income (Source 14), and about the behaviour of wages and prices (Sources 15, 16); finally there are the experiences of the unemployed, as recorded for instance in the Pilgrim Trust's *Men Without Work* (Sources 17–22), and the impressions of two contemporary observers, both distinguished authors in their own right, who toured parts of England in 1933 and 1936 respectively, and recorded their experiences in books which have since become minor classics: J.B. Priestley's *English Journey* and George Orwell's *The Road to Wigan Pier* (Sources 23, 24).

Two considerations need to be kept in mind when assessing this evidence. Firstly, poverty is a relative term: one generation's luxuries become another generation's needs. Secondly, it was only in the 1930s that living standards were systematically investigated. Poverty may have been just as widespread in earlier decades, but less noticed because less publicised. This does not make it any more acceptable.

# 3. POLICIES FOR UNEMPLOYMENT

The third area to be investigated concerns government policies towards unemployment. What steps did governments take to lift Britain out of the slump, and what more might they have done? Governments faced two problems in the handling of unemployment. Firstly, they had to provide the unemployed, and their families, with the means of subsistence; secondly, they had to provide, if possible, alternative sources of employment.

The first problem was much more readily solved than the second. By 1930 there was already a well-established, if untidy, network of support for the unemployed. Lloyd George's National Insurance Act of 1911 had established the principle of a self-financing fund to which workers, employers and the state would contribute, and out of which those workers who had contributed (some 3 million) would be entitled to claim benefit when they became unemployed. In 1920 the Act was extended to another 12 million workers, and now its provisions covered most manual occupations, with the exception of agricultural workers, civil servants and domestic service. It was still the intention that the Insurance Fund should be self-financing, with a break-even point when unemployment reached 5.32 per cent. As unemployment rose to over one million in 1921, and to over two million in 1931 that principle had to go by the board.

A further assumption that unemployment would be a short-term phenomenon for the individual worker also had to be abandoned. Under the 1920 Act unemployment benefit was payable for fifteen weeks. That period was extended to 32 weeks in 1921, and provision was made to pay uncovenanted benefit, otherwise known as 'the dole', to those whose statutory entitlement had expired. In 1922 all claimants to the dole had also to prove that they were 'genuinely seeking work', a condition that was not easily fulfilled at times of high unemployment (Source 17).

By 1930 the growing imbalance between the contributions from those in work and the payments to those out of work was threatening to cause a budget deficit, as the Insurance Fund had to be topped up out of general taxation. In March 1931 Ramsay MacDonald appointed the May Commitee (headed by Sir George May) to investigate the problem. In its report, published in July 1931, the Committee forecast a deficit of £120 million, and recommended savings of £67 million on unemployment insurance.

These were to be achieved by tightening up on the rules for eligibility and by reducing the levels of benefit. It was the final recommendation that led to the split in MacDonald's Cabinet on 23 August 1931, and the formation of the National government under MacDonald's leadership the following day, pledged to implement the recommended cuts.

On 11 September Snowden's Budget duly reduced unemployment benefit rates by 10 per cent and introduced a means test at the same time (Source 18). The means test was a household test applied to all those in receipt of uncovenanted benefit, and it took into account the earnings of all members of the household, savings and any other sources of income. Needless to say, it was bitterly unpopular (Source 19).

In 1934 the 10 per cent cut was restored to all those receiving statutory benefits. At the same time an Act was passed to alter the administration of the dole. Previously, this had been in the hands of Public Assistance Committees, responsible to elected local authorities. From 1934 onwards responsibility for all uncovenanted benefit would now be born by an Unemployment Assistance Board (UAB) and its army of officials. The UAB laid down a uniform scale of allowances which were below the standard rate of benefit (24s a week for a married couple as against the standard rate of 26s, for example). Where Public Assistance Committees had been paying the standard rates, the new scale would mean an immediate loss of income to the unemployed. There was such a wave of protest that the government brought in a Standstill Act, maintaining existing rates of benefit for the time being. The new rates were fully implemented only in 1938.

There were no further changes in the mechanism of relief, though the rates of benefit were increased in line with inflation. By 1939 they were 17s for a man, 10s for his wife and 3s for every dependent child. The means test was finally abolished in 1941.

The level of provision for the unemployed has been and remains a matter of controversy. The National Unemployed Workers' Movement staged numerous protests, both at the means test and at the UAB scales introduced in 1934. Labour-controlled councils frequently refused to apply the means test in its full rigour. But equally there were protests from ratepayers at what they considered the extravagance of the dole and at its debilitating effects (Source 21). To other observers it was not the dole that sapped initiative so much as the lack of any prospect of future employment. By the standards of previous generations, and by comparison with other West European countries and the United States, Britain's provision for the unemployed was unprecedented. But this is hardly how it looked to the recipients.

When it came to the second problem, the creation of new jobs, the government's record was less impressive. For a start, conventional economic wisdom, as reflected in the views of most politicians, entrepreneurs, civil servants and economists, held that there was little any government could do to promote employment. Budget deficits were likely to cause inflation; government borrowing would only raise the rate of interest, and so discourage investment; expenditure on public works would pre-empt savings that could be better spent by private industry (Source 26).

Government policies reflected these assumptions. The insistence on balanced budgets led, as we have seen, to cuts in public expenditure (including unemployment benefit) in 1931, and so to a fall in consumption, just as unemployment was rising. In 1932 the Cabinet decided in principle that expenditure on public works was likely to be counterproductive (Source 27). The only direct contributions to employment made by the National governments of 1931–9 were the Special Areas Acts of 1934 and 1937, and the North Atlantic Shipping Act of 1934. Under the Special Areas Act of 1934 two Commissioners were appointed with powers to spend up to £2 million in areas where unemployment was at its highest, that is southern Scotland, the North-east of England, West Cumberland and South Wales. The Special Areas (Amendment) Act of 1937 offered remissions in rates, rents and income tax to firms locating in these areas. The North Atlantic Shipping Act made a loan of £9.5 million to the Cunard Shipping Line to build the liners *Queen Mary* and *Queen Elizabeth*.

So far as other measures to promote employment are concerned, the National government placed its faith in low interest rates, achieved by keeping a tight control over government borrowing, and protection of home industry, secured through the Import Duties Act of 1932. Unemployment certainly fell in the 1930s from a peak of 2 745 000 (registered unemployed) to 1 514 000 in 1939, but this fall owed more to worldwide economic trends than to direct government intervention.

While the politicians and the academic establishment remained firmly convinced that there was little else the government could do, there were some powerful dissentient voices. In 1928 the Liberal party produced a policy document, *Britain's Industrial Future*, which advocated a massive injection of public spending on roads, housing and other public works. These suggestions were incorporated in the Liberal election manifesto, *We Can Conquer Unemployment*, in 1929 (Source 29). In 1930 Oswald Mosley, a member of MacDonald's Cabinet with particular responsibility for dealing with unemployment, produced a Memorandum in which he called for big increases in public expenditure, earlier retirement, a protective tariff and a greatly strengthened government machine to implement these policies (Source 30). The Labour Cabinet rejected his suggestions. In 1936 John Maynard Keynes delivered the strongest theoretical challenge yet mounted to economic orthodoxy in his *General Theory of Employment Interest and Money*. In essence, Keynes argues that full employment was not a natural condition to which all economies tended, and that governments had both the ability and the duty to promote full employment by pursuing appropriate policies (Source 31). In 1938 Harold Macmillan, Conservative MP for Stockton, in the heart of the depressed North-east of England, published *The Middle Way*, in which he accepted the Keynesian diagnosis of unemployment and went some way beyond Keynes in the remedies he recommended (Source 32).

The thinking of Keynes and his supporters became part of the conventional wisdom of the next generation of economists and politicians. In 1944 a White Paper produced by the Treasury in Churchill's Coalition government acknowledged as one of its primary aims 'the maintenance of a high and stable level of employment'. For much of the post-war period that goal was successfully accomplished. But in 1975, or thereabouts, the Keynesian remedies began to fail. As public expenditure mounted, so did unemployment and inflation. In the 1980s unemployment once again reached the 3 million mark, and governments once again found themselves fumbling for solutions.

The sources here have been chosen to indicate policies for the support of the unemployed, and for the promotion of employment. Reaction to those policies is also included. Finally, the critics of government policies, both on the left and on the right, are given a say. This case study should bring out the problems involved in measuring the economic health of a society, and in assessing the welfare of its members. The sources that follow should also be relevant to Britain's present economic situation. There are many affinities between the Britain of the 1930s and that of the 1980s. Unemployment is as much a scourge today as it was then. The gap between the prosperous South-east and the depressed North is just as pronounced. Governments are as baffled in their attempts to find solutions as they were in the 1930s. The inadequacy of government policies for dealing with unemployment in the 1930s has often been remarked. Their failure perhaps looks less culpable today.

# FURTHER READING

## The Economy

D.H. Aldcroft, *The British Economy between the Wars* (Philip Allan, 1983)
D.H. Aldcroft, *The Inter-War Economy, Britain 1919–39* (Batsford, 1970)
S. Glynn and J. Oxborrow, *Inter-War Britain: A Social and Economic History* (Allen & Unwin, 1976)
S.F. Pollard, *The Development of the British Economy, 1914–80* (Arnold, 1983)
W.O. Simpson, *Changing Horizons, Britain 1914–80* (Stanley Thornes, 1986)
R. Skidelsky, *Politicians and the Slump* (Penguin, 1970)
D. Winch, *Economics and Policy* (Fontana, 1972)

## Social Conditions

N. Branson and M. Heinemann, *Britain in the Nineteen Thirties* (Panther, 1973)
S. Constantine, *Social Conditions in Britain, 1918–39* (Methuen, 1983)
S. Constantine, *Unemployment in Britain between the Wars* (Longman, 1980)
J. Stevenson, *Social Conditions in Britain between the Wars* (Penguin, 1977)
J. Stevenson, *British Society, 1914–45* (Penguin, 1984)
J. Stevenson and C. Cook, *The Slump: Society and Politics during the Depression* (Jonathan Cape, 1977)

## Contemporary Observation

George Orwell, *The Road to Wigan Pier* (Penguin, 1962)
J.B. Priestley, *English Journey* (Heinemann, 1984)
Ellen Wilkinson, *The Town that was Murdered* (Gollancz, 1939)
The Pilgrim Trust, *Men Without Work* (CUP, 1938)

# SOURCE MATERIAL 1
# The British Economy in the 1930s

**SOURCE 1** Average Rates of Growth of Selected Economic Indicators in the UK (per cent per annum)

| Date | (1) | (2) | (3) | (4) | (5) | (6) | (7) |
|------|-----|-----|-----|-----|-----|-----|-----|
| 1870–1913 | 1.9 | 1.0 | 1.1 | 2.1 | 0.6 | 2.7 | 0.8 |
| 1870–1938 | 1.6 | 0.9 | 1.2 | 2.1 | – | 0.8 | 0.8 |
| 1900–1913 | 1.5 | 0.9 | 0.9 | 1.7 | 0.2 | 4.2 | 0.6 |
| 1913–1929 | 0.5 | 0.5 | 1.5 | 1.4 | – | −1.3 | 0.4 |
| 1913–1938 | 1.0 | 0.8 | 1.3 | 1.9 | – | −2.3 | 0.7 |
| 1920–1929 | 1.9 | 1.3 | – | 2.8 | 3.8 | 1.6 | 0.7 |
| 1920–1938 | 1.9 | 1.4 | – | 2.8 | 2.8 | −1.2 | 1.0 |
| 1929–1938 | 1.9 | 1.4 | 0.9 | 2.7 | 1.8 | −4.0 | 1.4 |
| 1950–1960 | 2.7 | 2.3 | 2.3 | 3.0 | 2.2 | 1.8 | 2.1 |

(1) Gross Domestic Product (GDP)
(2) GDP per capita
(3) GDP per man hour
(4) Industrial production (including building)
(5) Industrial productivity
(6) Exports
(7) Consumers' expenditure per capita

D.H. Aldcroft, *The British Economy between the Wars* (Philip Allan, 1983) p. 6

**SOURCE 2** Annual Rates of Growth of Output, Employment and Capital in Selected Industries, 1920–38

| | Output | Output per capita | Employment | Capital |
|------|--------|-------------------|------------|---------|
| Vehicles | 6.6 | 3.6 | 3.0 | 5.4 |
| Timber and furniture | 5.2 | 5.0 | 0.2 | n.a. |
| Electricity, gas and water | 5.0 | 2.5 | 2.5 | 3.3 |
| Non-ferrous metal manufacture | 4.8 | 3.6 | 1.2 | 1.4 |
| Electrical engineering | 4.7 | 1.1 | 3.6 | 2.3 |
| Building materials | 3.7 | 1.6 | 2.1 | 0.5 |

*Continued overleaf*

|                                   | Output | Output per capita | Employment | Capital |
|-----------------------------------|--------|-------------------|------------|---------|
| Food                              | 3.6    | 2.1               | 1.5        | 0.6     |
| Clothes                           | 2.7    | 2.9               | −0.2       | 2.3     |
| Mechanical engineering            | 1.7    | 3.7               | −2.0       | 0.3     |
| Iron and steel                    | 1.1    | 3.5               | −2.4       | 0.7     |
| Textiles                          | 0.2    | 1.6               | −1.4       | −0.9    |
| Mines and quarries                | 0.2    | 2.5               | −2.3       | 0.7     |
| Drink                             | −0.2   | −1.0              | 0.8        | 0.4     |
| Shipbuilding                      | −2.7   | 1.9               | −4.6       | −0.8    |
| All industry except agriculture   | 2.8    | 2.9               | −0.1       | 1.4     |

Aldcroft, *The British Economy between the Wars*, p. 43

## SOURCE 3   An Economic Historian's Assessment of the Slump

In comparison with the experience of most other countries, the depression in Britain was mild. For instance the United States suffered declines of 37, 36 and 31 per cent in real income, industrial production and employment respectively, whereas the corresponding figures for Britain were 0.8, 11 and 4.7 per cent. Only in two respects, namely the decline in wholesale prices and the percentage unemployed at the bottom of the depression, did Britain fare as badly as the United States. Few countries suffered as badly as America but then again few could match the relative mildness of the British recession. Real income in Germany fell by 25 per cent, in France by 12 per cent, in Sweden by eight per cent, and in Australia by two per cent. Virtually the only country to emerge unscathed was Japan . . .

Although the main force of the depression had been spent by the end of 1931 it was not until the latter half of 1932 that recovery really began to take hold. Unemployment reached a peak in the third quarter of that year and most economic indicators continued to decline until late in 1932 . . .

By 1934 sustained growth had extended to most sectors of the economy, though it tended to be most vigorous in the new, domestically based industries and least prominent in the old staples. Nevertheless, exports picked up smartly in 1934 and 1935 and this helped to revive the older industries. Investment also increased sharply in 1934 when the largest increase of the inter-war years was recorded. The recovery in employment was more modest and by the end of 1934 there were still over 2 million or nearly 16 per cent of the insured population out of work.

During the course of the next three years the pace of recovery continued practically unchecked . . .

By 1937, therefore, the record of achievement was considerable. Since 1932 real income had increased by 19 per cent, domestic output by over 25 per cent, industrial production by nearly 46 per cent, gross investment by 47 per cent, and even exports by 28.4 per cent. Moreover, in absolute terms the level of economic activity was far higher than it had been in 1929 and 1913. In fact these years witnessed the largest and most sustained growth in the whole of the inter-war period . . .

Aldcroft, *The British Economy between the Wars*, pp. 41–4

# SOURCE 4 A Left-wing View of the Depression

*This source is taken from Wal Hannington's book,* The Problem of the Distressed Areas, *published in 1937. Hannington was a leading member of the Communist party and the main organiser of the National Union of Unemployed Workers.*

The present period of mass unemployment began in 1921. The worst effects of the slump have been felt in four of the basic industries of this country – industries upon which the power of Britain has been built – namely coal, iron and steel, shipbuilding and textiles. It is particularly the industries of coal and iron and steel which are situated in the districts which are today classified as the Special Areas. The unemployment which has affected these industries proves that the crisis within capitalism is deep and fundamental. It is not an unemployment occasioned by seasonal conditions in the whims and fancies of fashion, as might be said of certain of the minor trades. There is, in fact, evidence of the very deep breakdown of the capitalist order of society when the basic industries of the system are plunged into continuous slump; when the mines are sealed up and allowed to become flooded; when steel works are allowed to rust and crumble; when special companies are formed to undertake the task of dismantling and breaking up shipyards; and millions of valuable textile spindles are turned into scrap metal.

What more conclusive proof could be required to show that the condition of the masses of workers rendered idle by the failure of these industries presents not a problem which can work itself out but one which calls for far-reaching and fundamental changes in the system itself?

Wal Hannington, *The Problem of the Distressed Areas* (Gollancz, 1937) p. 31

# SOURCE 5 Unemployment Statistics, 1929–39

*These figures are drawn from the Ministry of Labour* Gazette, *and are based on the numbers of registered unemployed – i.e. that section of the working population that was claiming unemployment benefit.*

| | | | |
|---|---|---|---|
| 1929 | 1 216 000 | 1935 | 2 036 000 |
| 1930 | 1 917 000 | 1936 | 1 755 000 |
| 1931 | 2 630 000 | 1937 | 1 484 000 |
| 1932 | 2 745 000 | 1938 | 1 791 000 |
| 1933 | 2 521 000 | 1939 | 1 514 000 |
| 1934 | 2 159 000 | | |

B.R. Mitchell and P. Deane, *Abstract of British Historical Statistics* (CUP, 1962) p. 66

**SOURCE 6** Percentage of Insured Workers
Unemployed by Industry, 1929–39

| | *1929* | *1930* | *1931* | *1932* | *1933* | *1934* | *1935* | *1936* | *1937* | *1938* | *1939* |
|---|---|---|---|---|---|---|---|---|---|---|---|
| Coal | 19.0 | 20.6 | 28.4 | 34.5 | 33.5 | 29.7 | 27.2 | 22.8 | 16.1 | 16.7 | 12.5 |
| Iron and steel | 20.1 | 28.2 | 43.5 | 47.9 | 41.5 | 27.3 | 23.5 | 17.4 | 11.4 | 19.5 | 15.1 |
| Electrical engineering | 4.6 | 6.6 | 14.1 | 16.8 | 16.5 | 9.6 | 7.0 | 4.8 | 3.1 | 4.7 | 4.4 |
| Shipbuilding | 25.3 | 27.6 | 51.9 | 62.0 | 61.7 | 51.2 | 44.0 | 33.3 | 24.4 | 21.4 | 20.9 |
| Cotton textiles | 12.9 | 32.4 | 43.2 | 30.6 | 25.1 | 23.7 | 22.3 | 16.7 | 10.9 | 23.9 | 16.9 |
| Woollens | 15.5 | 23.3 | 33.8 | 22.4 | 17.0 | 17.8 | 15.5 | 10.3 | 8.8 | 21.3 | 11.0 |
| Boot and shoe manufacturing | 15.5 | 15.2 | 22.2 | 18.0 | 19.5 | 21.4 | 17.1 | 14.6 | 12.1 | 14.3 | 10.4 |
| Distributive trades | 6.2 | 8.1 | 11.6 | 12.6 | 12.4 | 11.3 | 11.3 | 9.8 | 8.9 | 9.2 | 9.0 |
| National government service | 6.9 | 8.2 | 10.3 | 12.4 | 13.3 | 14.5 | 13.8 | 12.9 | 11.7 | 12.1 | 10.0 |
| Local government service | 9.6 | 10.7 | 13.7 | 18.2 | 19.6 | 20.3 | 20.2 | 19.7 | 17.6 | 17.2 | 14.6 |
| TOTAL | 11.0 | 14.6 | 21.5 | 22.5 | 21.3 | 17.7 | 16.4 | 14.3 | 11.3 | 13.3 | 11.7 |

Mitchell and Deane, *Abstract of British Historical Statistics*, p. 67

**SOURCE 7** Employment and Unemployment:
Main Staple Trades, 1920–38

| *Industry* | *1920* | *1924* | *%* | *1929* | *%* | *1938* | *%* | *1938* | *%* |
|---|---|---|---|---|---|---|---|---|---|
| Coal | 1083 | 1056 | 6.8 | 812 | 18.2 | 630 | 41.2 | 674 | 22.0 |
| Cotton | 533 | 564 | 15.8 | 480 | 14.5 | 364 | 31.2 | 301 | 27.7 |
| Woollen | 274 | 295 | 7.0 | 261 | 15.6 | 234 | 26.6 | 220 | 21.4 |
| Ship building | 282 | 155 | 26.4 | 139 | 23.2 | 61 | 59.5 | 129 | 21.4 |
| Iron and steel | 527 | 344 | 19.7 | 342 | 19.9 | 231 | 48.5 | 342 | 24.8 |
| Average % unemployment for all industries | | | 9.9 | | 9.9 | | 22.9 | | 13.3 |

The first column in each year gives the numbers employed in the industry concerned in thousands; the second column gives the percentage unemployed.

D.H. Aldcroft, *The Inter-War Economy, Britain 1919–39* (Batsford, 1970) p. 147

# SOURCE 8 Unemployment Percentages by Regional Divisions (July each year)

| Region | 1912–13 | 1929 | 1932 | 1936 | 1929–36 (average) |
|---|---|---|---|---|---|
| London | 8.7 | 4.7 | 13.1 | 6.5 | 8.8 |
| South-east | 4.7 | 3.8 | 13.1 | 5.6 | 7.8 |
| South-west | 4.6 | 6.8 | 16.4 | 7.8 | 11.1 |
| Midlands | 3.1 | 9.5 | 21.6 | 9.4 | 15.2 |
| North-east | 2.5 | 12.6 | 30.6 | 16.6 | 22.7 |
| North-west | 2.7 | 26.3 | 26.3 | 16.2 | 21.6 |
| Scotland | 1.8 | 11.2 | 29.0 | 18.0 | 21.8 |
| Wales | 3.1 | 18.8 | 38.1 | 28.5 | 30.1 |
| Great Britain | 3.9 | 9.7 | 22.9 | 12.6 | 16.9 |
| Southern Britain | – | 6.4 | 16.2 | 7.4 | 11.0 |
| Northern Britain and Wales | – | 12.9 | 29.5 | 18.0 | 22.8 |

D.H. Aldcroft, *The Inter-War Economy: Britain, 1919–1930*, p. 80

# QUESTIONS ON SOURCES 1–8

1. Explain the terms 'GDP', 'GDP per capita' and 'GDP per man hour' (Source 1). (C)

2. What is the difference between an increase in *production* and an increase in *productivity* (Source 1)? (C)

3. Which is the only economic indicator in Source 1 to register an actual decline between 1919 and 1939? How do you account for this exception? (S)

4. Which were the only industries to experience an overall fall in output between 1920 and 1938 (Source 2)? (C)

5. Which industries registered a fall in employment between 1920 and 1939 (Source 2)? How do you reconcile these figures with the increase in output in some of these industries? (S)

6. Compare Sources 3 and 4. To what extent are the differences in their portrayals of the British economy attributable to the political standpoints of the observers? (E)

7. How reliable are the unemployment figures cited in Source 5? (E)

8. Plot on a graph the unemployment percentages between 1929 and 1939 for the industries with the highest and lowest rates of unemployment (Source 6). (C)

9. To what extent had unemployment in the old staple industries declined by 1939 (Source 6)? (C)

10. Explain, with the aid of examples, the correlation between the unemployment figures in Sources 7 and 8. (S)

# SOURCE MATERIAL 2
# Living Standards

*Sources 9–25 relate to living standards in the 1930s: A. Sources 9–13 are drawn from the work of social investigators such as H. Llewellyn Smith, H.F. Tout and Seebohm Rowntree, who sought to determine the incidence of poverty by measuring income levels against a predetermined standard of needs. Investigations into dietary deficiencies and infant mortality rates are also included. B. Sources 14–16 contain statistical evidence relating to changes in the distribution of wealth and income; the movement of wages and prices in the 1930s; and comparative wage rates. C. Sources 17–25 focus on the plight of the unemployed in both economic and social terms. Evidence is drawn both from those who experienced unemployment, and from those who observed its effects. The final two excerpts are taken from two impressionistic surveys of England in the 1930s, George Orwell's* The Road to Wigan Pier *and J.B. Priestley's* English Journey *and are supplemented by photographic evidence.*

## 2A Social Surveys

### SOURCE 9 H. Llewellyn Smith (ed.), *The New Survey of London Life and Labour*, 1934

*In 1902 Charles Booth published the results of a major investigation into living standards in London,* Life and Labour of the People in London. *In 1929–30, H. Llewellyn Smith and others carried out a similar investigation, from which this source is taken.*

Broadly stated, the effect both of the street survey and of the House Sample Enquiry is to show that the percentage of the population of the Eastern Survey Areas who were below the poverty line at the time of the investigation was only about one third of the percentage found by Charles Booth to be in poverty in East and South East London forty years earlier.

This is an immense reduction, which may be otherwise expressed by saying that if the conditions which prevailed in Charles Booth's time had continued unchanged, the number of persons in the Eastern Survey Area below his 'poverty line' at the date of the investigation in 1929–30 would have numbered at least seven or eight hundred thousand, instead of about one quarter of a million ...

But if in place of concentrating our gaze on the upward changes which have been taking place, we fix our attention on actual present-day conditions in the Eastern Survey Area there is much less ground for complacency. It is disconcerting to learn from the Street Survey that in spite of all the improvements which have taken place, the grim fact remains that one in ten of the human beings who inhabit the Eastern Survey Area, and one in seven of those who live in Charles Booth's 'East London', were found at the time of the investigation to be subject to conditions of privation which if long continued would deny them all but the barest necessities, and cut them off from access to many of the material and cultural benefits of modern progress. Nor is our disquiet diminished by the discovery that not far from half of these persons owed their condition to unemployment or under-employment, which is one of those 'dynamical causes' most likely to be accompanied by conscious unhappiness.

H. Llewellyn Smith (ed.), *The New Survey of London Life and Labour,* vol. III
(P.S. King, 1934) pp. 6–8

# SOURCE 10   H.F. Tout, *The Standard of Living in Bristol,* 1938

*H.F. Tout's investigation into living standards in Bristol was carried out under the auspices of Bristol University. Tout and his fellow researchers took their sample from the 404 000 inhabitants of Bristol in 1937. The following excerpts indicate how the survey was conducted, the standard of 'needs' that was adopted, and the findings of the survey.*

*Methods of the Survey*
The families studied were confined to the working classes and the lower middle classes . . . The families excluded represented about a fifth of all the families in the area. The sample was selected by taking every twentieth address in the Registry of Electors. If more than one family lived in a house, all of them were included in the sample. Quite enough information was available for 92½ per cent of the families approached to enable a judgment to be made as to their position in relation to the standard . . . 4576 families supplied information. It was sufficient to enable the relationship to the needs standard of 4491 of these to be assessed . . .

*Needs Standards*
Every family needs shelter, warmth, light, food, clothes and some cleaning materials. Sometimes expenditure on travel to work is necessary, and nearly all earners are compelled by law to contribute to unemployment and health insurance. These are the only items for which we make allowance on the minimum standard.

The 'needs' of each family are built up by adding to the food and clothes allowances for each person, which depend upon the age, sex and occupation of the person, the scaled family allowances for fuel, light and cleaning. Table 1 gives examples of the effects of the calculations:-

Table 1

|  | *Examples of Standard Needs* | |
| --- | --- | --- |
| *Family consisting of:-* | *Family needs per week exclusive of rent* | |
|  | s | d |
| Man alone | 12 | 9 |
| Woman alone | 11 | 4 |
| Man, wife | 20 | 3 |
| Man, wife, child under 5 | 24 | 3 |
| Man, wife, child 5–9 | 25 | 6 |
| Man, wife, two children 5–9 and 10–13 | 32 | 10 |
| Man, wife, three children, under 4, 5–9, 10–13 | 37 | 8 |
| Man, wife, 65 and over | 14 | 8 |
| Man alone, 65 and over | 9 | 5 |

. . .

*Examples*

*Poverty*

(a) Family of eight consisting of man (aged 40), wife, six children and another expected. Boys aged 12 and 8. Girls age 15, 14, 2 and 1

Income: Man unemployment benefit 38s; two eldest daughters employed as learners in a factory receiving 10s 6d and 7s 6d.

Rent 11s. No travel costs. Gross income 56s.

Standard of living, 21 per cent below needs. Extra income required to reach needs level, 11s 5d.

(b) Family of one, a widow living alone (aged 47).

Income: Widows' Pension 10s; Public Assistance 3s 6d

Rent of house 10s, but she sub-lets all but two rooms for 6s 6d.

Standard of living 11 per cent below needs.

Extra income required to raise to needs level, 1s 4d.

. . .

*Incidence of Poverty*

[Tout demonstrated that 10.7 per cent of families in Bristol fell below his 'needs' line, and that 25 per cent of children suffered from poverty.]

*The Causes of Poverty*

Unemployment is outstandingly the most important reason for family income falling below 'needs', and affects nearly a third of the families. This third is under the standard because benefit and relief scales are below the survey scale of 'needs'. Insufficient wages rank next as a cause of poverty. 'Insufficient' means wages that are not enough to support the family of the worker and not wages that are lower than established rates. The wages called insufficient mostly fall between 42s and 55s. Wages bear no relation to needs, and where the number of children to be supported is large the lower-paid unskilled workers fall below the standard, even if their earnings are regular. If their earnings are not regular their plight is worse.

Wages are based on earning power. In turn unemployment benefit and relief are kept below wages, and so cannot be based entirely upon need. It is not stony heartedness of those responsible for relief that puts unemployment first among the causes of poverty, but their reluctance to upset the delicate balance of the economic system by making relief appear as attractive as work. Thus those who are anxious to find means of combating present distress are faced with a position from which there is no escape so long as the wages of lower paid workers will not support more than a small family . . . This deadlock is responsible for most of the poverty ascribed to unemployment and to insufficient wages, and explains about half of all family poverty. It is responsible for still more child poverty, in fact for about 80 per cent of it . . .

Old age ranks third in importance as a cause of poverty, and rather less than one sixth (15%) of the cases have been ascribed to it . . . Broken families, in which there is no adult male earner are another fairly important cause of poverty, causing 13 per cent of the cases. Sickness ranks next with 9 per cent. The low earnings of some small shop keepers, casual workers, roundsmen, hawkers and the like account for 6 per cent of the poverty found . . .

H.F. Tout, *The Standard of Living in Bristol* (University of Bristol, 1938) pp. 15, 20, 27, 45–6

# SOURCE 11   B. Seebohm Rowntree, *Poverty and Progress,* 1941

*Seebohm Rowntree was born into the prosperous Quaker family whose fortunes were based on the cocoa and chocolate-manufacturing firm of Joseph Rowntree. He worked in the family business but devoted much of his life to social reform. In 1901 he produced* Poverty: A Study of Town Life, *which demonstrated that 27 per cent of the population of York were living 'in poverty'. In 1936 Rowntree repeated his investigations, adopting a slightly more generous definition of poverty than the one he had used in 1901. The results were published in 1941. Rowntree's investigators visited 16 362 families 'comprising practically every working class family in York'. Information about wages was obtained from local employers, and 'in this way I obtained information from their wage books regarding the wages of 60 per cent of the workers covered by my enquiry'. The following excerpts include Rowntree's estimate of the incomes necessary 'to secure the necessaries of a healthy life', his analysis of the incomes received by the families investigated, and his own conclusions.*

While collecting the material for this book, I was also collecting material for a book dealing with the incomes necessary to enable families with different numbers of dependent children to secure the necessaries of a healthy life. I arrived at an estimate of 53s a week for an urban family of man, wife and 3 dependent children. The figure, exclusive of rent, was 43s 6d, made up as follows:

|                      | s   | d  |
|----------------------|-----|----|
| Food                 | 20  | 6  |
| Clothing             | 8   | 0  |
| Fuel and light       | 4   | 4  |
| Household sundries    | 1   | 8  |
| Personal sundries    | 9   | 0* |
|                      | 43  | 6  |

*The amount will, of course, be spent in different ways, but the following illustration of how it might be spent will enable the reader to judge whether or not the allowance is extravagant.

|                                                                           | s | d |
|---------------------------------------------------------------------------|---|---|
| Unemployment insurance                                                    | 1 | 7 |
| Contribution to sick and burial clubs                                      | 1 | 0 |
| Trade Union subscription                                                    | 0 | 6 |
| Travelling to and from work                                                 | 1 | 0 |
| Such necessaries as stamps, writing paper, etc. for the family              | 0 | 6 |
| A daily newspaper                                                           | 0 | 7 |
| Wireless                                                                   | 0 | 6 |
| All else: beer, tobacco, presents, holidays, books, travelling, etc.        | 3 | 4 |
|                                                                           | 9 | 0 |

In this connection I may suitably quote what I wrote in my other book: 'Let me repeat that the standards adopted throughout this book err on the side of stringency rather than that of extravagance. I am convinced that the closest investigation would fail appreciably to lower any of my estimated costs. Indeed, as I have pursued my investigations, I have been increasingly impressed by the fact that to keep a family of five in health on 53s a week, even when the income is guaranteed for 52 weeks in the year, needs constant watchfulness and a high degree of skill on the part of the householder.'

*Rowntree then introduces modifications into his standard to allow for differences in family size. A family of five will clearly need to spend more on fuel for instance, than a family of two.*

Working on the above basis, I have divided the families into the following classes according to their available weekly income, after paying rent and rates:-

*Class*

| 'A' Under 33s 6d          | For man, wife and three children or the |
|---------------------------|------------------------------------------|
| 'B' 33s 6d and under 43s 6d | equivalent of that income in the case of |
| 'C' 43s 6d and under 53s 6d | differently constituted families.        |
| 'D' 53s 6d and under 63s 6d |                                          |
| 'E' 63s 6d and over       |                                          |

From the foregoing it will be seen that a family with an available income of 43s 6d, after paying rent and rates, would be placed in Class 'C' if it consisted of an employed man, wife and three children, in Class 'D' if there were no children, in Class 'B' if there were four children, and in Class 'A' if there were five children.

Classifying upon the basis described above, the following results were obtained:

| Class | | No. of persons | Percentage of working-class population (excluding domestic servants and persons in public institutions) | Percentage of total population |
|---|---|---|---|---|
| 'A' Under 33s 6d | Available income for man, wife and three children, or its equivalent for differently con- stituted families. | 7 837 | 14.2 | 8.1 |
| 'B' 33s 6d to 43s 5d | | 9 348 | 16.9 | 9.6 |
| 'C' 43s 6d to 53s 5d | | 10 433 | 18.9 | 10.8 |
| 'D' 53s 6d to 63s 5d | | 7 684 | 13.9 | 8.0 |
| 'E' 63s 6d and over. | | 19 904 | 36.1 | 20.5 |
| 'F' Domestic Servants | | 4 300 | – | 4.4 |
| 'G' Working class in institutions | | 3 530 | – | 3.6 |
| 'H' Remainder of population (including Acomb) | | 33 944 | – | 35.0 |
| | | 96 980 | 100.0 | 100.0 |

The size of each class may be represented thus:–

Class 'A'

    "  'B'

    "  'C'

    "  'D'

    "  'E'

    "  'F'

    "  'G'

    "  'H'

*Conclusion*

So far this chapter has been concerned with a comparison of economic and social conditions in York today with those at the close of the last century, and we have seen how greatly the workers' standard of living has improved in spite of the fact that the period under review has included four years of devastating warfare in which millions of British citizens were involved.

The economic condition of the workers is better by 30 per cent than in 1899 though working hours are shorter. Housing is immeasurably better, health is better, education is better. Cheap means of transport, the provision of public libraries and cheap books, the wireless, the cinema and other places of entertainment, have placed within the reach of everyone forms of recreation unknown and some unthought of forty years ago.

It is gratifying that so much progress has been achieved, but if instead of looking backward we look forward, then we see how far the standard of living of many workers falls short of any standard which could be regarded, even for the time being, as satisfactory. Great though the progress made during the last forty years has been, there is no cause for satisfaction in the fact that in a country as rich as England, over 30 per cent of the workers in a typical provincial city should have incomes so small that it is beyond their means to live even at the stringently economic level adopted as a minimum in the survey, nor in the fact that almost half the children of working class parents spend the first five years of their lives in poverty and that almost a third of them live below the poverty line for ten years or more . . .

B. Seebohm Rowntree, *Poverty and Progress* (Longman, 1941) pp. v, 28–33, 476

# SOURCE 12    John Boyd Orr, *Food, Health and Income,* 1937

*John Boyd Orr was one of the first investigators of diet. Using an estimate of nutritional needs devised by the American Bureau of Home Economics, he examined the family budgets of six groups, divided according to income. He investigated 1152 families altogether.*

The food position of the country has been investigated to show the average consumption of the main foodstuffs at different income levels. The standard of food requirement and the standard of health adopted are not the present average but the optimum, i.e. the physiological standard, which though ideal, is attainable in practice with a national food supply sufficient to provide a diet adequate for the health of any member of the community. The main findings may be summarised as follows:-

I. Of an estimated national income of £3750 million, about £1075 million are spent on food. This is equivalent to 9s per head per week.

II. The consumption of bread and potatoes is practically uniform throughout the different income level groups. Consumption of milk, eggs, fruit, vegetables, meat, fish rises with income. Thus, in the poorest group the average consumption of milk, including tinned milk, is equivalent to 1.8 pints per week; in the wealthiest group 5.5 pints. The poorest group consume 1.5 eggs per week; the wealthiest 4.5. The poorest spend 2.4d on fruit, the wealthiest 1s 8d.

III. An examination of the composition of the diets of the different groups shows that the degree of adequacy for health increases as income rises. The average diet for the poorest group, comprising 4½ million people, is, by the standard adopted, deficient in every constituent examined. The second group, comprising 9 million people, is adequate in protein but deficient in all other vitamins and minerals.

Complete adequacy is almost reached in group IV, and in the still wealthier groups the diet has a surplus of all constituents considered ...

John Boyd Orr, *Food, Health and Income* (Macmillan, 1937) pp. 8–9

## SOURCE 13  Infant Mortality Rates

*Infant mortality rates were carefully collated by various investigators in the 1930s. The following table was constructed by C.E. Macnally, and is reproduced in his book,* Public Ill Health.

| | Infant mortality rates per 1000 live births | | | | | | |
| | 1928 | 1929 | 1930 | 1931 | 1932 | 1933 | 1928–33 |
|---|---|---|---|---|---|---|---|
| Wigan | 93 | 129 | 107 | 103 | 91 | 110 | 105.5 |
| St Helens | 98 | 114 | 80 | 88 | 89 | 116 | 97.5 |
| Brighton | 50 | 54 | 51 | 54 | 41 | 47 | 49.5 |
| Oxford | 38 | 64 | 41 | 44 | 61 | 32 | 46.7 |

J. Stevenson and C. Cook, *The Slump: Society and Politics during the Depression* (Jonathan Cape, 1977) p. 285

## QUESTIONS ON SOURCES 9–13

1. What was the scale of improvement in living conditions in London as reflected in Source 9? (C)

2. How adequate was the Needs Standard applied by H.F. Tout to provide a tolerable standard of living (Source 10)? (S)

3. Would you regard the cases of poverty cited in Source 10 as fairly typical? How useful are they as an indicator of the incidence of poverty in Britain in the 1930s? (E)

4. What, according to Tout, were the main causes of poverty? If his diagnosis was correct, what would be the most economical way of relieving it (Source 10)? (S)

5. Compare the research techniques employed by Tout and Rowntree (Sources 10, 11). Whose would you regard as the more reliable? (E)

6. Are there significant differences in the criteria adopted by Tout and Rowntree as to what constitutes an adequate weekly income (Sources 10, 11)? (C)

7.  How many people in Britain, according to Boyd Orr, suffered from serious deficiencies in diet (Source 12)? Do you regard these figures as a reasonable inference from the research he had conducted? **(E)**

8.  Account for the differences in infant mortality rates indicated in Source 13. Would there be comparable differences today? **(S)**

---

# 2B  Income, Wealth, Prices and Wages

## SOURCE 14

### (a) Distribution of Incomes Assessed to Super Tax or Surtax, Great Britain and Northern Ireland, 1924–5 and 1933–4

*This table is taken from* A Survey of the Social Structure of England and Wales, *first carried out in 1927 by A.M. Carr-Saunders and D. Caradog Jones and repeated in 1933–4.*

| Income class exceeding £ | not exceeding £ | Number of persons assessed to Super Tax 1924–5 | Surtax 1933–4 | Total of income assessed £m 1924–5 | 1933–4 |
|---|---|---|---|---|---|
| 2 000 | 5 000 | 63 275 | 61 849 | 192 | 184 |
| 5 000 | 10 000 | 16 940 | 13 715 | 116 | 93 |
| 10 000 | 20 000 | 6 263 | 4 390 | 85 | 59 |
| 20 000 | 30 000 | 1 520 | 841 | 36 | 20 |
| 30 000 | 40 000 | 557 | 339 | 19 | 12 |
| 40 000 | 50 000 | 301 | 149 | 13 | 7 |
| 50 000 | 75 000 | 307 | 165 | 18 | 10 |
| 75 000 | 100 000 | 114 | 49 | 10 | 4 |
| 100 000 | | 138 | 65 | 28 | 11 |
| Total | | 89 415 | 81 562 | 517 | 400 |

From this table we learn that in 1933–4 the number of persons with more than £2000 a year was roughly the same as the population of one moderate sized county borough, whereas the number of those with over £10 000 a year was about that of the population of a small market town. Their swift journeyings about the country and excursions to the Riviera, the chronicle and picture of their doings, all combine to magnify their numerical importance. They appear to constitute an army. It is, however, a stage army – a few battalions appearing again and again in new and striking postures. Disproportionate as is the share of the National Income which falls to them, there is no vast source of wealth whence, if it were shared out, we could all achieve even a modest competence.

The rich, as has been said, are like the Alps, which tower in their magnificence above the plain; but if they were razed and the material which constitutes them spread evenly over the surface of the land, there would be a rise of but a few inches in the general level.

## (b) Distribution of Capital according to Amount Owned and Number of Owners, England and Wales, 1911–13 and 1924–30

| Amount of capital | 1911–13 | | 1924–30 | |
|---|---|---|---|---|
| | Per cent of total capital owned | Per cent of all persons owning capital | Per cent of total capital owned | Per cent of all persons owning capital |
| £100 or less | 11.1 | 88.3 | 6.4 | 78.6 |
| £100–£1000 | 9.9 | 8.7 | 10.4 | 15.5 |
| £1000–£5000 | 15.3 | 2.1 | 17.0 | 4.2 |
| £5000–£10 000 | 9.5 | 0.4 | 10.0 | 0.8 |
| £10 000–£25 000 | 18.5 | 0.1 | 18.6 | 0.2 |
| over £100 000 | 21.8 | 0.03 | 23.2 | 0.04 |

A.M. Carr-Saunders and D. Caradog Jones, *A Survey of the Social Structure of England and Wales* (Clarendon Press, 2nd edn., 1937) pp. 97, 111

# SOURCE 15  Wages, Prices and Real Earnings, 1930–8

*For the purpose of this table 1930 is taken as the base year and all changes are measured in relation to that year. The changes are measured in percentage points, i.e. in 1931 the figure of 98.2 per cent for weekly wage rates represents a fall of 1.8 per cent on the 1930 wage rate. Changes in real wage earnings are measured by taking changes in money wage rates and changes in prices into account.*

| Year | Weekly wage rates | Retail prices | Average annual real wage earnings |
|---|---|---|---|
| 1930 | 100.0 | 100.0 | 100.0 |
| 1931 | 98.2 | 93.4 | 105.1 |
| 1932 | 96.3 | 91.1 | 105.7 |
| 1933 | 95.3 | 88.6 | 107.6 |
| 1934 | 96.4 | 89.2 | 108.1 |
| 1935 | 98.0 | 90.5 | 108.3 |
| 1936 | 100.2 | 93.0 | 107.7 |
| 1937 | 102.8 | 97.5 | 105.4 |
| 1938 | 106.3 | 98.7 | 107.7 |

Aldcroft, *The Inter-War Economy, Britain 1919–39*, pp. 352, 364

# SOURCE 16   Wages and Earnings in Particular Occupations

## (a) Average Earnings for Manual Workers, 1906–35 (£ per annum)

| Skilled | 1906 | 1924 | 1935 |
|---|---|---|---|
| Coalface workers | 112 | 180 | 149 |
| Fitters | 90 | 157 | 212 |
| Engine drivers | 119 | 276 | 258 |
| Compositors | 91 | 209 | 218 |

| Semi-skilled and unskilled | 1906 | 1924 | 1935 |
|---|---|---|---|
| Pottery workers | 77 | 171 | 173 |
| Bus and tram drivers (London) | 107 | 190 | 218 |
| Agricultural labourers | 48 | 82 | 89 |

## (b) Salaries of Clerical Workers, 1911/13–35 (£ per annum)

| | 1911/13 | 1924 | 1935 |
|---|---|---|---|
| Civil service clerical officer | 116 | 284 | 260 |
| Railway clerk | 76 | 221 | 224 |
| Bank clerk | 142 | 280 | 368 |
| Civil service shorthand typist | 79 | 179 | 162 |

J. Burnett, *A Short History of the Cost of Living* (Penguin, 1969) pp. 299–300

---

# QUESTIONS ON SOURCES 14–16

1. Do the figures in Source 14 suggest that any significant changes occurred between 1911 and 1935 in the distribution of income and capital? (S)

2. What can you infer about Britain's class structure from the figures in Source 14? (S)

3. What implications do the authors in Source 14 draw from their figures about the efficacy of penal taxation as a way of raising living standards? (C)

4. Account for the movements in *wage rates* between 1930 and 1938 (Source 15). (S)

5. How do you account for the fact that *average real wage earnings* rose during the worst years of the depression (Source 15)? (S)

6. Apply Seebohm Rowntree's test of an 'income to secure the necessaries of a healthy life' (Source 11) to the wage rates given in Source 16. What conclusions would you draw from this exercise? (S)

7. 'That in 1939 there should still have been a submerged fraction of any size was bad enough but in 1914 the existence of a submerged third had scarcely been revealed. No one could seriously doubt that the working classes on the eve of the Second World War were better fed, better clothed, better housed than their parents had been a generation earlier.' (J. Burnett, *Plenty and Want,* 1968) Comment on this view in light of the preceding evidence. (S)

---

# 2C  Unemployment and its Effects

## SOURCE 17  The Administration of the 'Genuinely Seeking Work' Clause in the Unemployment Insurance Act of 1921

*The umpire's decision reveals the extent of the discretion open to civil servants in the administration of this clause and some of the criteria to be applied to those claiming unemployment benefit.*

In considering whether a person is genuinely seeking work the most important fact to be ascertained is the state of the applicant's mind. If a person genuinely wants to work, that is, really prefers working for wages to living on benefits, it is probable that she is genuinely seeking it. But if a person prefers benefit to wages, or is content to be without work so long as she receives benefit, it may be presumed that she is not genuinely seeking it. Action is guided by desire, and whilst few people genuinely seek what they do not desire, most people genuinely seek what they do desire.

The genuineness of an applicant's desire for work must be considered in the light of all the circumstances available. Her record of employment is most important. If an applicant has been for many years a steady worker, and there has been no change in her circumstances, which relieves her of the necessity of working, the inference that she wants to work is very strong. Her present needs, the amount she can earn when at work as compared with the amount of benefit which she would receive, and the circumstances in which she lost her last employment, are all matters for consideration, though it would not be fair to assume that a person does not desire to work, and is not genuinely seeking work, merely because she can live in reasonable comfort without it or because she is as well off when on benefit as when at work.

As to the present applicants, their record of work, their present needs, the high rate of wages they got when at work as compared with the amount they would receive as benefit, and the circumstances in which they left their last employment, all indicate that they desire work and probably prefer it to idleness.

But though it may be probable that a person who wants work is genuinely seeking work, it is not necessarily so, and an applicant who is genuinely seeking work should be able to show that besides registering for work at an exchange she is making personal efforts on her own behalf to find work and is not content merely to wait until it is thrust on her.

Umpire's decision 1407/26 (14 July, 1926) from A. Deacon, *In Search of the Scrounger* (Bell, 1976) p. 95

## SOURCE 18   The Unemployment Insurance (National Economy) (No. 2) Order, 1931

*This is the Statutory Order on which the means test was based. It was a household test which took into account all the financial circumstances of the applicant, including the incomes of other members of the household.*

(2)  As from and after the 12th Day of November, 1931 where a person who has attained the age of eighteen years proves that he fulfils the following conditions, namely –
(a) that he is normally employed in, and will seek to obtain his livelihood by means of insurable employment; and
(b) that he would but for the operation of the preceding paragraph of the Articles, have been entitled to benefit,
and also proves that his circumstances are such that whilst unemployed he is in need of assistance by way of transitional payments, such payments shall, subject to the provisions of this Order, be made to him out of the Unemployment Fund so long as he continues to fulfil the said conditions.

(3)  Any question arising under the last preceding paragraph, as to whether the circumstances of an applicant for transitional payments are such that, whilst unemployed, he is in need of assistance by way of such payment, shall be remitted to the Council of the county or county borough in which he is resident and shall stand referred to such committee or sub-committee as may be prescribed, and that committee or sub-committee shall determine that question, and, if they determine that he is in such need, shall include in their determination directions as to the amount of any transitional payment to be made to him.

*Statutory Rules and Orders, 1931,* pp. 1412–19

## SOURCE 19   Critics of the Means Test

### (a) George Orwell, *The Road to Wigan Pier*

The most cruel and evil effect of the Means Test is the way in which it breaks up families. Old people, sometimes bedridden, are driven out of their homes by it. An old age pensioner, for instance, if a widower, would usually live with one or other of his children; his weekly ten shillings goes towards the household expenses, and probably he is not badly cared for. Under the Means Test, however, he counts as a 'lodger' and if he stays at home his children's dole will be docked. So, perhaps at seventy or seventy-five years of age he has to turn out into lodgings, handing his pension over to the lodging house keeper and existing on the verge of starvation. I have seen several cases of this myself. It is happening all over England at this moment thanks to the Means Test.

Orwell, *The Road to Wigan Pier* (Penguin, 1962) p. 70

## (b) Ellen Wilkinson, *The Town that was Murdered*

The original idea of the Household Means Test was to prevent the payment of benefit in those cases, greatly exaggerated in the House of Commons at the time, where the household income was so high that the family might reasonably be expected to look after the unemployed member. Immediately it led to far worse and widespread abuse . . . only, as these abuses were against the unemployed instead of against the fund, complaints went unheeded. A son saving to get married compelled to keep step-father and brother; a sister working as a skilled typist made to help father and adult brothers, thus depriving herself of the possibility of saving for old age, or getting the clothes and nourishment needed for her work. Families broken up through children leaving home either to qualify for benefit or to make it possible for parents to receive assistance . . .

Ellen Wilkinson, *The Town that was Murdered* (Gollancz, 1939) p. 202

## (c) Wal Hannington, *The Problem of the Distressed Areas*

January 1937 Special evidence was collected by the National Unemployed Workers' Movement in various parts of the country by means of a questionnaire, headed the Housewives' Minimum. The evidence collected in this questionnaire was in every case verified by the signature either of a doctor, responsible trade union leader or a county councillor. Here are a few examples, taken from many that reveal the appalling conditions of poverty to which many of our people have been reduced, especially in the Distressed Areas.

*Example 4*
Mr W.C. of Jarrow. There are seven in the family – father, mother and five children, whose ages are thirteen, eleven, nine, seven and three. The total income of the family to maintain them all is 40s a week. Whilst they have sufficient cups and saucers and plates to go round, they have only three forks, and five spoons, so some have to wait whilst the others finish their food. There are only three beds, and on each bed there is one blanket and one sheet; there are no pillow cases – the sheet is laid over the bolster in place of a pillow covering. When the bed clothing needs washing it has to be washed in the morning and dried for the same night. When the housewife applied for a grant from the UAB [Unemployment Assistance Board] to get bed clothing she was told that she ought to be able to buy it out of the 40s income and no assistance was given . . .

It can truly be said that the unemployed, particularly in the Distressed Areas, are fighting with their backs to the wall, literally fighting to live, because they know that any further worsening of their condition means another terrible blow against the health and lives of themselves and their children.

But the lowering in their standards is already taking place in another form, namely the steady rise in the cost of living, so that the small amount of purchasing power which they already have is reduced, and less can be bought. Capitalism, which has taken huge profits and wealth from the sweat and toil of these people in the basic industries of this country is now crucifying them, while the Government outdoes the Pharisee by smiting the victim and passing on . . .

Wal Hannington, *The Problem of the Distressed Areas* (Gollancz, 1937) pp. 65–8

# SOURCE 20    E. Wight Bakke, *The Unemployed Man*

*E. Wight Bakke was an American research student from Yale University who spent six weeks in Greenwich in 1931 investigating the attitudes of the unemployed. His findings were based on 161 separate interviews.*

EFFECTS OF UNEMPLOYMENT INSURANCE    There are several effects of Unemployment Insurance which may be restated here. There is evidence that the scheme has alleviated the worst physical effects of unemployment. It has kept the diet from falling to unhealthful levels; it has kept workers from falling into arrears on their rent; it has made it unnecessary to dispose of home furnishings to the extent which would have been necessary without it; it has to some extent made it possible for men and women to keep up their associations with their fellows longer; it has kept unrest at a minimum, the failure of political agitation of Communist factions to flourish among those secure in the knowledge that the State is assisting them to help themselves. It has not relieved, however, and cannot by its very nature relieve, the mental and moral fatigue and discouragement which result from having no job. It cannot supply the loss of status and the sense of self-respect which vanish with the job.

. . .

FINAL WORD    Having examined, as carefully as my limited time and abilities would permit, the actual condition of life and the attitudes growing out of them which have a bearing on the question whether or not unemployment insurance has had a detrimental effect on the willingness and ability of workers to support themselves, I feel that it is only fair to make another statement which has grown out of this experience.

The fear concerning the effect of unemployment insurance on the malingering tendencies of human nature seems to me to miss the whole purpose and achievement of social insurance. I cannot speak for the men who laboured to bring this system into being. I cannot plumb their minds for their purposes. I can, however, speak with some conviction concerning certain results of unemployment insurance which may have a larger part in formulating further plans than any original purposes. The idea of central importance in unemployment insurance is the actual security and sense of security which it has brought into the lives of millions of workers. I have tried to show that those latter results give no cause for alarm, but even if they did, the case would be for reform, and not for abolition of the system.

E. Wight Bakke, *The Unemployed Man* (Nisbet & Co., 1933) pp. 251, 268

# SOURCE 21    *The Times,* 22 February, 1938

To the Editor of *The Times*

. . . Both in the depressed regions (not now so depressed as they were) and in prosperous London there is a growing number of young men between 19 and 30 who, under the easy terms of unconditional allowance from the Unemployment Assistance Board, are no longer trying to live independent lives. They have all refused offers of training by the Ministry of Labour, yet make no other effort at recovery on their own account. They have settled down and usually married . . . They often eke out the 25s to 35s a week which they draw from the Unemployment Assistance Board by a few undisclosed pickings in the market, the docks or the gambling industry. The fact is that under our existing policies there is nothing to disturb their complacent acceptance of this debilitating way of life: and their example is infectious. Relief scales and rules which have been expanded and eased for the sake of the decent unemployed, have proved to be too easy going and tempting for the venal minority . . . What is now required for these thousands of parasitic young men is some new type of compulsory work centres, both residential and non-residential.

LONDON          RONALD C. DAVISON

IDLE AND CONTENT

. . . Though it can be represented that in the distressed areas there have been predisposing causes to lethargy in a generation that grew up in a workless place, the excuse has no validity elsewhere. In a considerable number of the chronically or constantly unemployed young men there is a slackness of moral fibre and of will as well as of muscle. Mr R.C. Davison does not in his letter exaggerate the facts when he speaks of these young men no longer trying to live independent lives, but as having settled down to a permanent reliance on the Unemployment Assistance Board's allowances and casual supplements from odd jobs now and then . . .

*The Times,* 22 February, 1938

# SOURCE 22  Report of the Pilgrim Trust on the Plight of the Long-Term Unemployed

*In 1936 the Pilgrim Trust, a non-profit-making organisation largely financed by Americans, commissioned an investigation into the effects of unemployment. A high-powered committee was set up and it was agreed to interview a representative sample of 1000 workers taken from six different towns: Deptford, Leicester, Rhondda Urban District, Crook (Co. Durham), Liverpool and Blackburn. In all 880 were visited, 760 men and 120 women. The results of the investigation were published under the title* Men Without Work *in 1938.*

| | Length of unemployment by place | | | | | |
| | Men only | Effective record | | | | |
| | 1–2 years | 2–3 years | 3–4 years | 4–5 years | Over 5 years | Total |
| --- | --- | --- | --- | --- | --- | --- |
| Deptford | 20 | 19 | 3 | 7 | 2 | 51 |
| % | 39 | 37 | 6 | 14 | 4 | 100 |
| Leicester | 17 | 16 | 15 | 11 | 26 | 85 |
| % | 20 | 19 | 18 | 13 | 30 | 100 |
| Liverpool | 51 | 51 | 40 | 49 | 56 | 247 |
| % | 21 | 21 | 16 | 19 | 23 | 100 |

*Continued overleaf*

*Length of unemployment by place*
*Men only        Effective record*

|  | 1–2 years | 2–3 years | 3–4 years | 4–5 years | Over 5 years | Total |
|---|---|---|---|---|---|---|
| Blackburn | 12 | 9 | 13 | 15 | 51 | 100 |
| % | 12 | 9 | 13 | 15 | 51 | 100 |
| Crook | 9 | 9 | 7 | 6 | 77 | 108 |
| % | 8 | 8 | 7 | 6 | 71 | 100 |
| Rhondda | 25 | 38 | 25 | 41 | 100 | 229 |
| % | 11 | 16 | 11 | 18 | 44 | 100 |

. . .

*Three case studies:*
'I was one of a gang', said a lad from Lancashire, 'as we called it; there were
twenty or more of us. We used to stay in bed late in the morning so as not to need
breakfast. I used to have a cup of tea, and then we would all go down to the
Library and read the papers. Then we went home for a bite of lunch and then we
met up again at a billiard hall where you could watch the play for nothing. Then
back for tea, and to watch the billiards again. In the evening we all met to go to
the pictures. That was how we spent the dole money. In the end I thought I'd go
mad if I went on like that. So I broke away and joined one of these PT classes. But
I found it made me so hungry that I couldn't go on with it. If I hadn't had the
chance of coming to this place' (Wincham Hall, a College in Cheshire where
educational courses for unemployed men are run) 'I don't know what would
have happened to me then. I felt like going under, I can tell you.'

Sometimes life is less elaborately organised and gives a yet stronger impression
of pointlessness: 'You see that corner?' said a young man of 20 in the Rhondda,
'Well, when I'm on my own, my time is spent between here and that corner.'

'I loved the mills', she said, 'I loved the company and the people and everything about them. I'd do anything in the world if I could get back to them. I'd not
mind working even if things were very much worse than they were before.'
(Blackburn weaver)

The Pilgrim Trust, *Men Without Work* (CUP, 1938) pp. 422, 149–51

# SOURCE 23   George Orwell, *The Road to Wigan Pier*

*George Orwell, whose real name was Eric Blair, was educated at Eton. He served in the
Burma Police from 1922 to 1927, and then spent some time experiencing life at the lower end
of the social scale in London and Paris. He began to make a precarious living as an author
and in 1936 was commissioned by Victor Gollancz, a left-wing publisher, to investigate
and write about the condition of the unemployed in the North of England. Orwell visited
Lancashire and Yorkshire for two months, February and March, in 1936, spending three
weeks in Wigan. He made careful notes on all he saw, and there is no reason to doubt the
accuracy of his observations. He did, however, choose to stay in the cheapest lodging house he
could find in Wigan, and most of his contacts were with members of the National Union of
Unemployed Workers, rather than with ordinary trade unionists or Labour party members.*

When you see the unemployment figures quoted at two millions, it is fatally easy to take this as meaning that two million people are out of work and the rest of the population is comparatively comfortable. I admit that till recently I was in the habit of doing so myself. I used to calculate that if you put the registered unemployed at round about two millions and threw in the destitute and those who for one reason and another were not registered, you might take the number of underfed people in England (for *everyone* on the dole or thereabouts is underfed) as being, at the very most, five millions.

This is an enormous under-estimate, because, in the first place, the only people shown on the unemployment figures are those actually drawing the dole – that is, in general, heads of families. An unemployed man's dependants do not figure on the list unless they too are drawing a separate allowance. A Labour Exchange officer told me that to get at the real number of people *living on* (not drawing) the dole, you have got to multiply the official figures by something over three. This alone brings the number of unemployed to round about six millions. But in addition there are great numbers of people who are in work but who, from a financial point of view, might equally well be unemployed, because they are not drawing anything that can be described as a living wage.* Allow for these and their dependants, throw in as before the old-age pensioners, the destitute and the other nondescripts, and you get an *underfed* population of well over ten millions. Sir John Orr puts it at twenty millions.

Take the figures for Wigan, which is typical enough of the industrial and mining districts. The number of insured workers is round about 36 000 (26 000 men and 10 000 women). Of these, the number unemployed at the beginning of 1936 was about 10 000. But this was in winter when the mines are working full time; in summer it would probably be 12 000. Multiply by three, as above, and you get 30 000 or 36 000. The total population of Wigan is a little under 87 000; so that at any moment more than one person in three out of the whole population – not merely the registered workers – is either drawing or living on the dole . . .

*In this passage Orwell describes 'an extraordinary custom called "scrambling for coal", which is well worth seeing . . .'*

We stayed there till the train was empty. In a couple of hours the people had picked the dirt over to the last grain. They slung their sacks over shoulder or bicycle, and started on the two-mile trudge back to Wigan. Most of the families had gathered about half a hundredweight of coal or cannel [a kind of shale that would burn] so that between them they must have stolen five or ten tons every day in Wigan, at any rate in winter, and at more collieries than one. It is of course extremely dangerous. No one was hurt the afternoon I was there, but a man had had both his legs cut off a few weeks earlier, and another man lost several fingers

*For instance, a recent census of the Lancashire cotton mills revealed the fact that over 40 000 *full time* employees receive less than thirty shillings a week each. In Preston, to take only one town, the number receiving *over* thirty shillings a week was 640 and the number receiving *under* thirty shillings was 3113.

a week later. Technically it is stealing but, as everybody knows, if the coal were not stolen it would simply be wasted. Now and again, for form's sake, the colliery companies prosecute somebody for coal-picking, and in that morning's issue of the local paper there was a paragraph saying that two men had been fined ten shillings. But no notice is taken of the prosecutions – in fact, one of the men named in the paper was there that afternoon – and the coal-pickers subscribe among themselves to pay the fines. The thing is taken for granted. Everyone knows that the unemployed have to get fuel somehow. So every afternoon several hundred men risk their necks and several hundred women scrabble in the mud for hours – and all for half a hundredweight of inferior fuel, value ninepence.

That scene stays in mind as one of the pictures of Lancashire: the dumpy, shawled women, with their sacking aprons and heavy black clogs, kneeling in the cindery mud and bitter wind, searching eagerly for tiny chips of coal. They are glad enough to do it. In winter they are desperate for fuel; it is more important almost than food. Meanwhile all round so far as the eye can see, are the slag-heaps and hoisting gear of collieries, and not one of those collieries can sell all the coal it is capable of producing . . .

*Orwell also knew another side of working-class life which he describes here.*

In a working-class home – I am not thinking at the moment of the unemployed, but of comparatively prosperous homes – you breathe a warm, decent, deeply human atmosphere which it is not easy to find elsewhere. I should say that a manual worker, if he is in steady work and drawing good wages – an 'if' which gets bigger and bigger – has a better chance of being happy than an 'educated' man. His home life seems to fall more naturally into a sane and comely shape. I have often been struck by the peculiar easy completeness, the perfect symmetry as it were, of a working-class interior at its best. Especially on winter evenings after tea, when the fire glows in the open range and dances mirrored in the steel fender, when Father, in shirtsleeves, sits in the rocking chair at one side of the fire reading the racing finals, and Mother sits on the other with sewing, and the children are happy with a penn'orth of humbugs, and the dog lolls roasting himself on the rag mat – it is a good place to be in, provided that you can be not only in it but sufficiently *of* it to be taken for granted.

This scene is still reduplicated in a majority of English homes, though not in so many as before the war. Its happiness depends mainly upon one question – whether Father is still in work . . .

Orwell, *The Road to Wigan Pier*, pp. 67–8, 92, 104

# SOURCE 24   J.B. Priestley, *English Journey*

*J.B. Priestley was born in Bradford in 1894. He spent his early working life in a wool office in Bradford, and served as an infantry officer on the Western Front in the First World War. He then went to Cambridge and became a successful journalist and author. In 1933 he made a journey through England starting at Southampton, and going as far north as Newcastle. He published his account of this journey and his reflections upon it in 1934.*

*Priestley took pride in his northern roots, and made no secret of his left-wing sympathies. The following passages are taken from his concluding chapter.*

Southampton to Newcastle, Newcastle to Norwich: memories rose like milk coming to the boil. I had seen England. I had seen a lot of Englands. How many? At once, three disengaged themselves from the shifting mass. There was, first, Old England, the country of the cathedrals and minsters and manor houses and inns, of Parson and Squire, guide-book and quaint highways and byways England. We all know this England, which at its best cannot be improved upon in this world . . . It has few luxuries, but nevertheless it is a luxury country. It has long ceased to earn its own living. I am for scrupulously preserving the most enchanting bits of it, such as the cathedrals and the colleges and the Cotswolds, and for letting the rest take its chance. There are people who believe that in some mysterious way we can all return to this Old England; though nothing is said about killing off nine-tenths of our present population, which would have to be the first step. The same people might consider competing in a race at Brooklands with a horse and trap. The chances are about the same . . .

Then, I decided, there is the nineteenth century England, the industrial England of coal, iron, steel, cotton, wool, railways; of thousands of rows of little houses, all alike, sham Gothic churches, square-faced chapels, Town Halls, Mechanics' Institutes, mills, foundries, warehouses, refined watering-places, Pier Pavilions, Family and Commercial Hotels, Literary and Philosophical Societies, back-to-back houses, detached villas with monkey-trees, Grill Rooms, railway stations, slag heaps and 'tips', dock roads, Refreshment Rooms, doss-houses, Unionist or Liberal Clubs, cindery waste ground, mill chimneys, slums, fried-fish shops, public-houses with red blinds, bethels in corrugated iron, good-class drapers' and confectioners' shops, a cynically devastated countryside, sooty dismal little towns, and still sootier grim fortress-like cities. This England makes up the larger part of the Midlands and the North and exists everywhere; but it is not being added to and has no new life poured into it . . .

One thing, I told myself, I was certain of and it was this, that whether the people were better or worse off in this nineteenth century England, it had done more harm than good to the real enduring England. It had found a green and pleasant land and had left a wilderness of dirty bricks. It had blackened fields, poisoned rivers, ravaged the earth, and sown filth and ugliness with a lavish hand. You cannot make omelettes without breaking eggs, and you cannot become rich by selling the world your coal and iron and cotton goods and chemical goods without some dirt and disorder. So much is admitted. But there are far too many eggshells and too few omelettes about this nineteenth century England. What you see looks like a debauchery of cynical greed. As I thought of some of the places I had seen, Wolverhampton and St Helens and Bolton and Gateshead and Jarrow and Shotton, I remembered a book I had just read in which we are told to return as soon as possible to the sturdy Victorian individualism. But for my part I felt like calling back a few of these sturdy individualists simply to rub their noses in the nasty mess they had made . . .

The third England, belonged far more to the age itself than to this particular island. America, I supposed, was its real birthplace. This is the England of arterial and by-pass roads, of filling stations and factories that look like exhibition buildings, of giant cinemas and dance-halls and cafes, bungalows with tiny garages, cocktail bars, Woolworths, motor-coaches, wireless, hiking, factory girls looking like actresses, greyhound racing and dirt tracks, swimming pools and everything given away for cigarette coupons. If the fog had lifted I knew that I should have seen this England all round me at that northern entrance to London, where the smooth wide road passes between miles of semi-detached bungalows, all with their little garages, their wireless sets, their periodicals about film stars, their swimming costumes and tennis rackets and dancing shoes. The fog did not lift for an instant, however; we crawled, stopped, crawled again; and I had ample time to consider this newest England from my richly confused memory of it. Care is necessary too, for you can easily approve or disapprove too hastily. It is, of course, essentially democratic. After a social revolution there would, with any luck, be more and not less of it. You need money in this England, but you do not need much money. It is a large-scale, mass production job, with cut prices. You could almost accept Woolworths as its symbol. Its cheapness is both its strength and its weakness. It is its strength because being cheap it is accessible; it nearly achieves the famous equality of opportunity . . .

Unfortunately it is a bit too cheap. That is, it is also cheap in the other sense of the term. Too much of it is simply a trumpery imitation of something not very good even in the original. There is about it a rather depressing monotony . . .

Here then were the three Englands I had seen, the Old, the Nineteenth Century and the New; as I looked back on my journey I saw how these three were variously and most fascinatingly mingled in every part of the country I had visited . . .

Our knowledge begins anywhere but at home. We would understand anything so long as it did not immediately concern us. Aldebaran or Betelgeuse, I told myself, stood a better chance with us than the North of England. That brought me, sharply, back to the England of the dole. This word dole has two meanings. It means a charitable distribution, especially a rather niggardly one. It also means in its archaic use, a man's lot or destiny. We have contrived most artfully to combine the two meanings. As I looked back on it, the England of the dole did not seem to me a pleasant place. We could not be proud of its creation. We could not afford to be complacent about it, though we often are. It is a poor shuffling job, and one of our worst compromises . . .

You have only to spend a morning in the dole country to see that it is all wrong. Nobody is getting any substantial benefit, any reasonable satisfaction out of it. Nothing is encouraged by it except a shambling dull-eyed, poor imitation of life. The Labour Exchanges stink of defeated humanity. The whole thing is unworthy of a great country that has in its time given the world some nobly creative ideas. We ought to be ashamed of ourselves. Anybody who imagines that this is a time for self-congratulation has never poked his nose outside Westminster, the City and Fleet Street, and, I concluded, has not used his eyes and ears much even in Westminster and Fleet Street . . .

J.B. Priestley, *English Journey* (Heinemann, Jubilee edn, 1984) pp. 297–308

# SOURCE 25

### (a) The Eton and Harrow Match at Lords, 9 July, 1937

Topham Picture Library

### (b) 'The Exchange Has Given Him His Money: He Hands It Over to His Wife'

Alfred Smith draws £2 7s 6d a week. 4s a week is extra, which he gets because his two youngest children are ailing. He gives all the money to his wife to pay rent, clothes club, insurance, housekeeping. She gives him back a shilling for cigarettes, newspapers, fares.

*Picture Post*, 21 January, 1939

# QUESTIONS ON SOURCES 17–25

1.  What proof would the umpire in Source 17 require to show that an applicant for unemployment benefit was genuinely seeking work? (C)

2.  On what legislative authority was the means test based (Source 18)? Who were to administer it? (C)

3.  What conditions did an applicant for transitional benefit have to fulfil in order to be eligible (Source 18)? (C)

4.  What is the difference between 'drawing' the dole and 'living on' the dole (Source 23)? (C)

5.  Does the evidence cited in Source 19 suggest that the means test was applied too harshly? (S)

6.  Explain the final sentence in Source 19(c). Is Hannington's indictment of government policy exaggerated? (E)

7.  Compare the attitudes of E. Wight Bakke and Ronald C. Davison to the effects of unemployment benefit (Sources 20, 21). Whose testimony would you regard as the more reliable? (E)

8.  List in order of seriousness the places where the percentage of workers unemployed for over five years was highest (Source 22). Account for the differences between them. (S)

9.  Do the case studies cited in Source 22 lend any support to the views expressed by the editor of *The Times* in Source 21? (S)

10. Do you think that George Orwell exaggerates both the miseries and compensations of working-class life (Source 23)? (S)

11. What were the three Englands Priestley claimed to have discovered in 1933 (Sources 24, 25)? Are the distinctions between them meaningful, and if so, why? (S)

12. How valuable is the photographic evidence in Source 25 as an indication of class divisions in England in the 1930s? (E)

13. Compare Priestley's England of the dole (Source 24) with D.H. Aldcroft's (Source 3). Can they be reconciled? (S)

# SOURCE MATERIAL 3
# Policies for Unemployment

*Sources 26–32 illustrate: A. the thinking of civil servants and ministers with regard to the use of public expenditure to provide employment (Sources 26–8); and B. four different approaches to the problem of unemployment (Sources 29–32).*

## 3A Official Responses to Public Expenditure as a Cure for Unemployment

**SOURCE 26** National Development and State Borrowing: A Note Prepared by the Treasury, July 1930

10. If, in spite of the difficulties surrounding this matter, a great programme of works additional to that now instituted was found a practical proposition and it were decided that the Government should carry them out with its own funds . . . the probable effects of such a Loan upon national credit and general prosperity must be considered. If the investing public . . . accepted these far-reaching additional schemes as useful and desirable and likely to correct the country's difficulties, it might be that despite the enormous weight of Government securities which now burden the gilt-edged market the money could be raised without great disturbance and without any really heavy fall in Government stocks. If, on the other hand, the schemes were distrusted as extravagant and wasteful, if it were believed that this vast extension of direct Government activity would involve interference with private rights and the exercise of oppressive bureaucratic powers, – (and it is difficult to see how any vast programme of works could be set up without such powers being necessarily taken) – it is very unlikely that the money could be obtained save with great difficulty at very high rates and with serious effect of increasing the average rate of interest attracted by long-term loans, a rate which for the general good of the community urgently needs to come down . . . It is a matter for serious reflection whether, if a great Government loan had to be raised in such circumstances . . . many investors would not come to the view that this country was a bad country in which to invest; there might be something in the nature of a flight from the pound with all its serious reactions upon the exchange, upon short-term money rates in this country and upon the prospects of a trade revival. Any increase in the general rate of long-term interest postpones the conversion of the War Debt into cheaper forms. Any increase in short-term money rates increases the Exchequer charge for Treasury Bills and diminishes the sum which is available

for redemption of Government debt and the consequent replenishment of the capital market . . .

11. The Government would only be justified in entering upon such an additional development programme if it could be conclusively proved that (a) the issue of a new Government Development Loan would attract into investment monies at present lying idle; (b) that the above-indicated repercussions would be avoided, and (c) that the disbursement of this capital would be sufficient to start a general revival of trade irrespective of the utility of the works undertaken.

12. There are already abundant openings for investment available in the gilt-edged market, and there is no reason to believe that the offer of a new Government Loan would attract any substantial amount of money which would not otherwise be invested or employed in financing some form of trade activity. On the other hand, the extension of Government development schemes would in all probability tend to accentuate the lop-sided character of our present industrial activity, instead of diffusing prosperity over the industries of the country as a whole. Meanwhile the wholesale expenditure of Government money regardless of economic return, so far from tending to cure the present depression, would be more likely to increase than to diminish the discouragement of the business community.

R. Skidelsky, *Politicians and the Slump,* Appendix 5 (Penguin, 1970) pp. 455–6

## SOURCE 27    Cabinet Proceedings on a Memorandum on Unemployment, 1932

The Cabinet proceedings recorded the opinion that: most of those who had been in office during the last five years were agreed that whatever the attractions of public works policy, its application had been in many cases ill considered and its disadvantages now far outweighed such advantages as it might have possessed. They continued, 'Experience has taught us that they (relief works) do less good in direct provision of employment than harm by depleting the resources of the country which are needed for industrial restoration.'

Stevenson and Cook, *The Slump: Society and Politics during the Depression,* p. 63

## SOURCE 28    *Reports of the Commissioner for Special Areas (England and Wales)*

*Under the Special Areas Act of 1934 two Commissioners were appointed, one for England and Wales, one for Scotland. The Special Areas designated were in southern Scotland, the North-east of England, West Cumberland and South Wales.*

### (a) 1935

para. 46. There is, in my view, no justification for spending money without resultant economic value, merely to provide employment. The amount which would be required to be spent in order to bring about any material reduction in unemployment could wisely be spent with infinitely greater advantage in other directions. The Unemployment Grants Committee in their Final Report covering the period 1920–1932 estimated that a capital expenditure of £1 000 000 provided direct employment for about 2500 men for a year. In addition a considerable amount of indirect employment was provided. As a rough estimate, one may accept the figure of 4000 'man years' of labour, direct or indirect, resulting from an expenditure of £1 000 000. This figure was quoted in the White Paper on the Relief of Unemployment issued in December, 1930, and repeated in the Report of the May Committee (para. 358). Much of the indirect employment is provided outside the area of a particular scheme. It may therefore be estimated that to reduce unemployment by 50 000 in the Special Areas for the period of the Commissioners' appointment would involve an expenditure of the order of £35 000 000. At the end of the period the area would possess a large number of public works, many requiring fairly heavy maintenance charges, but the great majority of the men would again be without employment and little, if any, permanent improvement would have been effected in the industrial position of the area.

. . .

## para. 194. LOCATION OF INDUSTRY

If we are to survive as an industrial nation, we must increase productive efficiency; if our workers hereafter are to enjoy the maximum continuity of employment with improving prospects, economic considerations must in the main determine the location of industry. No decision can be come to without balancing all the factors including the value of the respective merits of old established and new industrial districts. Where there is equilibrium, the decision should be in favour of the old, but it is futile to attempt to establish industries in the Special Areas where the economic facts do not warrant so doing. It would only afford temporary relief, bearing the seeds of future distress, which is avoidable.

However, the Government might with advantage assist industrialists in coming to a decision with regard to the location of industry if it were to set up a central bureau of information to which they could refer for advice and technical data relating to potential industrial districts, not only in the Special Areas but elsewhere. Its influence would tend to establish a better balanced distribution of industrial activity.

*First Report of the Commissioner for the Special Areas (England and Wales), 1935,*
pp. 23, 76

## (b) 1936

para. 28. *State-provided Inducements*
Industry is not seeking the Special Areas, therefore it must be attracted to those districts of the Area which are endowed with suitable economic facilities, and many are available. How can this be effected? My recommendation is that by means of state-provided inducements a determined effort should be made to attract industrialists to the Special Area. The failure of these Areas to attract cannot simply be explained away by lack of opportunity for economic expansion. Fear is the dominant deterrent which holds back industrialists from taking risks

in the Areas; fear that their very distress makes them unsuitable for the development of industrial activity; fear of labour unrest and of further increases in already high rates. However well, or ill-founded these fears may be, they engender a habit of mind which is wholly prejudicial to any favourable consideration of the Special Areas. This mental attitude can be considerably changed if new conditions which challenge attention are set up in the Areas and make industrialists seeking expansion feel that, unless they study them, opportunities may be lost. It is sought by means of state-provided inducements to supply the required incentive.

*Report of the Commissioner for the Special Areas (England and Wales), 1936, p. 10*

## (c) 1938

para. 30. While the Special Areas Acts have made it possible to improve in many directions the conditions in which the people in these areas are living and to bring them new opportunities of employment, the fact remains that the number of unemployed in the Areas is still very large. It is clear to me that there are aspects of the problem which should be considered from a national standpoint. The Unemployment Assistance Board is today disbursing money at the rate of nearly £40 million a year to the unemployed who are not entitled to payments from the unemployment insurance scheme. On the other hand the recent crisis has drawn attention to the fact that a great deal of special work is waiting to be done. Is it not possible to devise schemes whereby new openings can be found for able-bodied unemployed, particularly in the case of young men?

*Report of the Commissioner for Special Areas (England and Wales) for the twelve months ending 30th September, 1938, p. 10*

## 3B   Alternative Policies

## SOURCE 29   *We Can Conquer Unemployment*

*Since his resignation from the premiership in 1922 Lloyd George had been using some of the money in his election fund to finance research into problem areas, one of which was unemployment. In 1928 a Liberal study group, to which both Keynes and Seebohm Rowntree belonged, produced their findings, entitled* Britain's Industrial Future; *Lloyd George and some of his fellow authors distilled its message into a more palatable form in a pamphlet,* We Can Conquer Unemployment, *which was launched on 1 March, 1929. Despite its positive appeal, the Liberal party polled only 23.4 per cent of the vote in the ensuing General Election in May 1929, giving them 59 seats in the House of Commons.*

WORK FOR THE WORKLESS, NOW
We have felt it advisable to refer thus briefly to these numerous directions in which work of national development is called for outside of the six groups upon which attention is here concentrated; and to point out that whilst we consider this policy of national development to be of paramount immediate importance,

it forms only part of a larger whole. Having done this, we return to our main theme, namely, the provision of work for the workless, now.

Adopting a reasoned and balanced view throughout, and stating the details for consideration, we have outlined proposals which we believe will provide a great volume of useful employment over a period of years. In particular, we have shown how by work of necessary development in six chosen spheres alone, work can be directly provided in the following estimated proportions, the figures summarizing the proposals given in detail above.

Estimated additional work for a year in Great Britain for the number of men below, directly provided as a result of our detailed proposals under six specific heads, and apart from indirect results:

|  | *Within the first year from the schemes starting work* | *Within the second year* |
|---|---|---|
| Roads and Bridges | 350 000 | 375 000 |
| Housing | 60 000 | 60 000 |
| Telephone Development | 60 000 | 60 000 |
| Electrical Development | 62 000 | 62 000 |
| Land Drainage | 30 000 | 30 000 |
| London Passenger Transport | 24 000 | 24 000 |

## EMPLOYMENT UNDER OTHER HEADS

This, as we have said, is the additional employment estimated only under these six heads where proposals have been worked out in detail. Other directions in which employment will be directly provided under the policy we put forward will include –

(1) work on arterial drainage on which, on the conditions mentioned, there might be employed, within six months, 50 000 men, this rising within a limited period to a much higher figure;

(2) the re-conditioning of houses;

(3) the improvement of canals;

(4) afforestation;

(5) reclamation;

(6) land settlement;

(7) increased employment upon the land when the cultivator is secure in his position and assured of his market;

(8) work resulting from the re-opening of trade relations with Russia.

## INDIRECT EFFECTS ON EMPLOYMENT

In all this, so far, we have taken no account of the very large increase in employment everywhere resulting directly from the addition to the national purchasing power represented by the wages of those workers directly employed in this way. The income of every one of these will have increased twice or thrice; and this will be reflected at once in a corresponding increase in expenditure on food, clothing, boots, housing, travelling, entertainment, and other amenities. As a

result, a stimulus will be given to the whole of the industry and commerce of the
country, reflected, in turn, in increased employment.

Again, we have included in our figures those employed in industries directly
supplying the materials to be used in our national development schemes, but not
those less directly affected. Thus, while we have included those working on the
roads, we have not included those making the additional vehicles which in consequence will come upon those roads; those building houses, but not those making
the furniture and carpets for those houses; those installing electric generating
plant and cables, but not those manufacturing lamps and fittings which will be
used at the ends of those cables.

After taking all these things into account, we have every confidence that
within three months of a Liberal Government being in power, large numbers of
men at present unemployed could be engaged on useful work of national
development; and that within twelve months the numbers unemployed could be
brought down to normal proportions.

Statistical evidence shows the normal pre-war percentage of unemployment
to have been some 4.7 per cent. Applied to the present insured population, that
represents about 570 000.

We should not, of course, rest satisfied with that, but should resume that
policy which Liberalism was pursuing up to the outbreak of war, designed to
reduce and mitigate still further the burden of normal unemployment.

To summarize: Unemployment is industrial disorganisation. It is brought to
an end by new enterprise, using capital to employ labour. In the present stagna-
tion the Government must supply that initiative which will help us to set going a
great progressive movement.

Kenneth O. Morgan, The Age of Lloyd George, The Liberal Party and<br>
British Politics 1890–1929 (Allen & Unwin, 1971) pp. 217–19

## SOURCE 30   The Mosley Memorandum

*Mosley produced his Memorandum on Unemployment in January 1930; it was considered
by a Cabinet sub-committee, which reported adversely on Mosley's proposals, largely, it
would seem, on grounds of their expense. The full Cabinet rejected the Memorandum
conclusively in May, which led to Mosley's resignation from the Labour government. He
founded his own New Party in March 1931, which then developed into the British Union of
Fascists in 1932. A summary of Mosley's proposals is given here, followed by excerpts from
the resignation speech he made on 28 May, 1930 in their defence.*

Mosley's recommendations were bold and iconoclastic. Unemployment should
be tackled on the same lines that war had been waged. A revolution in the
machinery of government was required to take the initiative in policy-making
out of the hands of the professional civil service. As a short-term measure,
domestic purchasing power should be increased by loan-financed public works
and increased expenditure on retirement pensions. The latter, together with a
rise in the school-leaving age, would reduce the numbers seeking employment.

As a long-term remedy, he proposed a complete reorganisation of the banking system along the lines of the German industrial banks to enable constructive credit expansion for the purposes of rationalisation to be undertaken. The state was to assume direct responsibility for the direction and planning of industry; and foreign trade was to be planned by means of import controls and state bargaining with foreign suppliers.

Donald Winch, *Economics and Policy* (Fontana, 1972) p. 132

*Mosley's speech on 28 May, 1930:*

If we are to build up a home market, it must be agreed that this nation must to some extent be insulated from the electric shocks of present world conditions. You cannot build up a higher civilisation and a standard of life which can absorb the great force of modern production if you are subject to price fluctuations from the rest of the world which dislocate your industry at every turn, and to the sport of competition from virtually slave conditions in other countries.

*Mosley countered the Treasury argument that a big loan for public works might lead to a fall in confidence in the currency:*

Do we believe that such expenditure, or anything approaching to such moderate figures [Mosley envisaged a figure of £200m in all] would involve 'a flight from the pound' especially if it be counteracted by the enormous psychological effect of such great reductions in the unemployment figures and be accompanied by a scientific and explicable long-term programme of economic reconstruction?

. . . Why is it so right and proper and desirable that capital should go overseas to equip factories to compete against us, to build roads and railways in the Argentine or in Timbuctoo, to provide employment for people in those countries while it is supposed to shake the whole basis of our financial strength if anyone dares to suggest the raising of money by the Government of this country to provide employment for the people of this country?

*Mosley concluded:*

You have in this country resources, skilled craftsmen among the workers, design and technique among the technicians, unknown and unequalled in any other country in the world. What a fantastic assumption it is that a nation that within the lifetime of everyone has put forth efforts of energy and vigour unequalled in the history of the world should succumb before an economic situation such as the present. If the situation is to be overcome, if the great powers of this country are to be rallied and mobilised for a great national effort, then the Government and Parliament must give a lead. I beg the Government tonight to give the vital forces of this country the chance that they await. I beg Parliament to give that lead.

Skidelsky, *Politicians and the Slump,* pp. 200–5

# SOURCE 31   J.M. Keynes, *The General Theory of Employment Interest and Money*

*Keynes's epoch-making book was first published in 1936. It had no immediate impact on government policy, but in the next ten years it prompted over 300 articles in professional journals, and revolutionised attitudes to the role of government in the handling of unemployment. The book is far too complex to be summarised, but the two following excerpts convey its basic message.*

It is curious how common sense, wriggling for an escape from absurd conclusions, has been apt to reach a preference for *wholly* 'wasteful' forms of loan expenditure rather than for *partly* wasteful forms, which because they are not wholly wasteful, tend to be judged on strict 'business' principles. For example, unemployment relief financed by loans is more readily accepted than the financing of improvements at a charge below the current rate of interest; whilst the form of digging holes in the ground known as gold-mining, which not only adds nothing whatever to the real wealth of the world but involves the disutility of labour, is the most acceptable of all solutions.

If the Treasury were to fill old bottles with banknotes, bury them at suitable depths in disused coal-mines which are then filled up to the surface with town rubbish, and leave it to private enterprise on well-tried principles of *laissez-faire* to dig the notes up again (the right to do so being obtained, of course, by tendering for leases of the note-bearing territory), there need be no more unemployment and, with the help of the repercussions, the real income of the community, and its capital wealth also, would probably become a good deal greater than it actually is. It would, indeed, be more sensible to build houses and the like; but if there are political and practical difficulties in the way of this, the above would be better than nothing.

. . .

In some other respects the foregoing theory is moderately conservative in its implications. For whilst it indicates the vital importance of establishing certain central controls in matters which are now left in the main to individual initiative, there are wide fields of activity which are unaffected. The State will have to exercise a guiding influence on the propensity to consume partly through its scheme of taxation, partly by fixing the rate of interest, and partly, perhaps, in other ways. Furthermore, it seems unlikely that the influence of banking policy on the rate of interest will be sufficient by itself to determine an optimum rate of investment. I conceive, therefore, that a somewhat comprehensive socialisation of investment will prove the only means of securing an approximation to full employment; though this need not exclude all manner of compromises and of devices by which public authority will co-operate with private initiative. But beyond this no obvious case is made out for a system of State Socialism which would embrace most of the economic life of the community. It is not the ownership of the instruments of production which it is important for the State to assume. If the State is able to determine the aggregate amount of resources devoted to augmenting the instruments and the basic rate of reward to those who own them, it will have accomplished all that is necessary. Moreover, the necessary measures of socialisation can be introduced gradually and without a break in the general tradition of society.

J.M. Keynes, *The General Theory of Employment Interest and Money*
(Macmillan, 1936) pp. 129, 377–8

# SOURCE 32 Harold Macmillan, *The Middle Way*

*Macmillan's book was published in 1938. In its diagnosis it owed much of its thinking to Keynes, but Macmillan went a good deal further than Keynes in the interventionist role he envisaged for the state. At the heart of his proposals was to be an Economic Council which would coordinate government policies in the areas of industrial organisation, finance and foreign trade. In each of these areas new institutions would have to be set up to regulate economic activity.*

## INDUSTRIAL RECONSTRUCTION

### SUMMARY

In an attempt to define the changes that seem to me to be essential, I have outlined a policy which borrows both from Capitalist and from Socialist schools of thought. I have envisaged an economic structure in which provision is made for different forms of ownership, management and control of industries and services at different stages of development. The whole structure of the policy is derived from a recognition of the process of growth and development through which industries and services pass.

It is a threefold policy which might be defined briefly as an appreciation (1) that the new industries, in the early stages of their development and during the periods of their rapid expansion, are best left to the vigorous initiative of private enterprise and uncontrolled development; (2) that in the later stages, when they have become more or less fully developed, and when their productive capacity begins to threaten to outstrip market demand, they require to achieve integration and to adopt a new form of corporate organisation making self-discipline and self-government possible under the statutory provision of an Industrial Reorganisation (Enabling) Act; and (3) that certain industries and services which are of key importance to the vigorous economic life of the community, and which have reached a stage of development when their conduct requires to be governed by much wider social considerations than the profit-making incentive alone will provide, should be brought under either some suitable form of public ownership and management or, in certain cases, a form of statutory control or supervision which may not involve public ownership.

In addition to the proposals that are applicable to these three rough categories of industries and services, I shall propose machinery for the co-ordination of policy within and between them, and for a general co-ordination of financial, industrial and social policy.

. . .

### FINANCE

Obviously the time has come when the Central Bank should become, openly and in fact, the public utility institution which it has already virtually become in practice. It should cease to be directed by a Board drawn almost exclusively from banking and financial institutions. The Governor and members of the Board of the Bank of England should be appointed by the Government, and should be selected with a view to the widest possible representation of specialist economic knowledge, drawn from the fields of industry, commerce, banking and economic science. It might be expected that, with a board of character so widely representative of the different branches of economic activity, there would emerge a direction of financial operations which would bring the idle factors of production into fuller employment.

. . .

## FOREIGN TRADE

All this does not mean that we would be seeking to set limits to our foreign trade. On the contrary, we would be seeking to expand it to the maximum in our profitable lines of trade and in those markets where, as a result perhaps of agreements with countries on a comparable standard of life, we might enjoy a measure of preference against the cheaper products of the less advanced competitors.

To perform these functions I suggest that the powers and duties of the Import Duties Advisory Committee might be enlarged. In conjunction with the Department for Overseas Trade it might undertake responsibilities similar to those which I outlined in 1933 for an Import and Export Clearing House. I suggested then that through such an organisation, which would take account of the export problem as well as that of imports, we might evolve a more scientific method of dealing with our foreign trade. With regard to exports its function would be mainly to register business transactions, except in those instances where the exporting industry required financial assistance to enable it to compete in world markets, while still maintaining wages and conditions of labour at the higher standards that would be compulsory in a planned economy. With regard to imports, it might be possible, through such an organisation, to arrange for the bulk purchase of a considerable proportion.

. . .

## CO-ORDINATION

The Economic Council is the keystone of the structure of a planned economy. It must not be imagined, however, that, in the policy that has been proposed, it is to take upon itself responsibility for the guidance of the economic system in all its detailed operations. The whole case I have been attempting to argue is precisely that it is neither necessary nor advisable that it should do so. To put it briefly, it would be concerned about the relation of one aspect of policy to another . . . It would be a co-ordinating authority. It would co-ordinate the recommendations and decisions regarding industrial policy, financial policy, foreign trade policy, and political social policy . . .

My case is that, through the Economic Council and the bodies responsible for financial, foreign trade and industrial policy, the Government will be expected to achieve full employment of the labour and capital resources of the nation. It will be left with no excuses for failing to do so. For, although it will not control the enterprises engaged upon production, it will control the conditions to which these enterprises respond. If full employment does not result; if we are still enduring the paradox of poverty amid potential plenty; then it will clearly be a result of the Government's failure to take full advantage of the powers and the opportunities that lie ready to its hand to bring about the conditions in which productive enterprise would expand to a full capacity of prosperity, limited only by the productive resources of the nation.

Harold Macmillan, *The Middle Way* (Macmillan, 1938) pp. 237–8, 258, 280–1, 300

## QUESTIONS ON SOURCES 26–32

1. Explain the terms 'gilt-edged market', 'War Debt' and 'Treasury Bill' (Source 26). (C)

2. Why does the Treasury Report take such a pessimistic view of the usefulness of a Government Development Programme as a cure for unemployment (Source 26)? Does this have anything to do with the fact that it was written by civil servants? (S)

3. How reliable is Source 27 as an indicator of the views of government ministers on the wisdom of spending on public works? (E)

4. Calculate the expenditure necessary to provide one job for one year on the figures provided by the Unemployment Grants Committee (Source 28). How does this compare with the cost of one year's unemployment benefit? (S)

5. Why, apart from their cost, was the Commissioner for Special Areas doubtful about the usefulness of expenditure on public works in his 1935 Report (Source 28(a))? (C)

6. Do you see any change in emphasis between the 1935 and 1936 Reports of the Commissioner for Special Areas with regard to the location of industry (Sources 28(a), (b))? How would you account for the change? (S)

7. What can you infer about the effectiveness of government policy towards the Special Areas from the comments made in the 1938 Report (Source 28(c))? (S)

8. Could the Liberals have conquered unemployment had they won the 1929 General Election (Source 29)? (S)

9. Why did Mosley's proposals (Source 30) meet with such a lukewarm response? (S)

10. Can you detect any flaw in the reasoning used by Keynes to assert that unemployment could be cured by burying Treasury notes in old coal mines (Source 31)? (S)

11. Keynes has been described as 'the saviour of capitalism'. Does Source 31 support such a view? (S)

12. How far do Macmillan's recommendations in *The Middle Way* (Source 32) mark a departure from conventional Conservative policies, both in the 1930s and today? (S)

# LOCATION OF SOURCES

1    D.H. Aldcroft, *The British Economy between the Wars* (Philip Allan, 1983) p. 6

2    *Ibid.,* p. 43

3    *Ibid.,* pp. 41–4

4    Wal Hannington, *The Problem of the Distressed Areas* (Gollancz, 1937) p. 31

5    B.R. Mitchell and P. Deane, *Abstract of British Historical Statistics* (CUP, 1962) p. 66

6    *Ibid.,* p. 67

7    D.H. Aldcroft, *The Inter-War Economy, Britain 1919–39* (Batsford, 1970) p. 147

8    *Ibid.,* p. 80

9    H. Llewellyn Smith (ed.), *The New Survey of London Life and Labour,* vol. III (P.S. King, 1934) pp. 6–8

10   H.F. Tout, *The Standard of Living in Bristol* (University of Bristol, 1938) pp. 15, 20, 27, 45–6

11   B. Seebohm Rowntree, *Poverty and Progress* (Longman, 1941) pp. v, 28–33, 476

12   John Boyd Orr, *Food, Health and Income* (Macmillan, 1937) pp. 8–9

13   J. Stevenson and C. Cook, *The Slump: Society and Politics during the Depression* (Jonathan Cape, 1977) p. 285

14   A.M. Carr-Saunders and D. Caradog Jones, *A Survey of the Social Structure of England and Wales* (Clarendon Press, 1937) pp. 97, 111

15   Aldcroft, *The Inter-War Economy, Britain 1919–39,* pp. 352, 364

16   J. Burnett, *A Short History of the Cost of Living* (Penguin, 1969) pp. 299–300

17   A. Deacon, *In Search of the Scrounger* (Bell, 1976) p. 95

18   *Statutory Rules and Orders, 1931,* pp. 1412–19

19   (a) George Orwell, *The Road to Wigan Pier* (Penguin, 1962) p. 70
     (b) Ellen Wilkinson, *The Town that was Murdered* (Gollancz, 1939) p. 202
     (c) Wal Hannington, *The Problem of the Distressed Areas* (Gollancz, 1937) pp. 65–8

20   E. Wight Bakke, *The Unemployed Man* (Nisbet & Co., 1933) pp. 251, 268

21   *The Times,* 22 February, 1938

22   The Pilgrim Trust, *Men Without Work* (CUP, 1938) pp. 422, 149–51

23   Orwell, *op. cit.,* pp. 67–8, 92, 104

24   J.B. Priestley, *English Journey* (Heinemann, Jubilee edn, 1984) pp. 297–308

25   (a) Topham Picture Library
     (b) *Picture Post,* 21 January, 1939

26   R. Skidelsky, *Politicians and the Slump,* Appendix 5 (Penguin, 1970) pp. 455–6

27    Stevenson and Cook, *op. cit.,* p. 63

28    *Reports of the Commissioner for Special Areas (England and Wales) 1935,* pp. 23, 76; *1936,* p. 10; *1938,* p. 10

29    K.O. Morgan, *The Age of Lloyd George, The Liberal Party and British Politics 1890–1929* (Allen & Unwin, 1971) pp. 217–19

30    Donald Winch, *Economics and Policy* (Fontana, 1972) p. 132; Skidelsky, *op. cit.,* pp. 200–5

31    J.M. Keynes, *The General Theory of Employment Interest and Money* (Macmillan, 1936) pp. 129, 377–8

32    Harold Macmillan, *The Middle Way* (Macmillan, 1938) pp. 237–8, 258, 280–1, 300

# INDEX

Entries in **bold** indicate quoted sources.